CRIME IN ENGLAND, 1880–1945

This book is an ambitious attempt to map the main changes in the criminal justice system in the Victorian period through to the twentieth century. Chapters include an examination of the growth and experience of imprisonment, policing, and probation services; the recording of crime in official statistics and in public memory; the possibilities of research created by new electronic and online sources; an exploration of time, space and place, on crime; and the growth of internationalisation and science-led approach of crime control methods in this period.

Unusually, the book presents these issues in a way which illustrates the sources of data that informs modern crime history and discusses how criminologists and historians produce theories of crime history. Consequently, there are a series of interesting and lively debates of a thematic nature which will engage historians, criminologists, and research methods specialists, as well as the undergraduates and school students who, like the author, are fascinated by crime history.

Barry Godfrey is Professor of Social Justice at Liverpool University. He has twenty years of experience in researching comparative criminology, particularly international crime history; desistance studies; and longitudinal studies of offending.

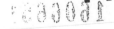

D1141573

3   2893

History of Crime in the UK and Ireland

Series editor: Professor Barry Godfrey

Rarely do we get the opportunity to study criminal history across the British Isles, or across such a long period. *History of Crime in the UK and Ireland* is a series which provides an opportunity to contrast experiences in various geographical regions and determine how these situations changed – with slow evolution or dramatic speed – and with what results. It brings together data, thought, opinion, and new theories from an established group of scholars that draw upon a wide range of existing and new research. Using case studies, examples from contemporary media, biographical life studies, thoughts, and ideas on new historical methods, the authors construct lively debates on crime and the law, policing, prosecution, and punishment. Together, this series of books builds a rich but accessible history of crime and its control in the British Isles.

1 **Crime in England, 1688–1815**
  David J. Cox

2 **Crime in England, 1880–1945**
  Barry Godfrey

CRIME IN ENGLAND, 1880–1945

The rough and the criminal, the policed and the incarcerated

Barry Godfrey

Routledge
Taylor & Francis Group

LONDON AND NEW YORK

First published 2014
by Routledge
2 Park Square, Milton Park, Abingdon, Oxon OX14 4RN

and by Routledge
711 Third Avenue, New York, NY 10017

Routledge is an imprint of the Taylor & Francis Group, an informa business

© 2014 Barry S. Godfrey

The right of Barry S. Godfrey to be identified as author of this work has been asserted in accordance with the Copyright, Designs and Patent Act 1988.

All rights reserved. No part of this book may be reprinted or reproduced or utilized in any form or by any electronic, mechanical, or other means, now known or hereafter invented, including photocopying and recording, or in any information storage or retrieval system, without permission in writing from the publishers.

Trademark notice: Product or corporate names may be trademarks or registered trademarks, and are used only for identification and explanation without intent to infringe.

British Library Cataloguing in Publication Data
A catalogue record for this book is available from the British Library

Library of Congress Cataloging-in-Publication Data
Godfrey, Barry S.
Crime in England 1880–1945 / Barry Godfrey.
   pages cm. – (History of crime in the UK and Ireland)
   Includes bibliographical references.
   1. Crime – Great Britain – History – 19th century.   2. Crime – Great Britain – History – 20th century.   3. Criminal justice, Administration of – Great Britain – History.   4. Police – Great Britain – History.   I. Title.
HV6943.G63   2014
364.10942'09041 – dc23   2013012462

ISBN: 978-1-84392-948-2 (hbk)
ISBN: 978-1-84392-947-5 (pbk)
ISBN: 978-1-3158862-9-9 (ebk)

Typeset in Bembo
by Apex CoVantage, LLC

Printed and bound in Great Britain by
TJ International Ltd, Padstow, Cornwall

For Jane and Alex

CONTENTS

FIGURES

PREFACE AND ACKNOWLEDGEMENTS

This is a good opportunity to take stock. I see this book as an opportunity to revisit some issues that I have tried to examine in the past and to advance some new ideas which may stimulate discussion amongst my colleagues, amongst under- and post-graduates, and in the wider academic community (by which I mean all those people that work in universities, or in libraries, or those who just have a healthy interest in the history of crime). The hope is that this is seen as an ambitious and wide-ranging book. It will take us from case studies of individual prisoners rotting in Her Majesty's Convict Prisons in the 1880s to the middle-class citizen stopped for speeding in the 1930s; it will take us from the lived experiences of normal working-class residents in English and Welsh cities, to cowboys in Arizona, and the forbidding fortress of Alcatraz. We sift through stories, examples, statistics, and theories and the evidence for them, only to have each source of information questioned, critiqued, and interrogated before moving on to the next source. Our journey explores the written documents created by the criminal justice system itself, the fragmentary evidence of crime and victimisation from oral histories, and the new digital media that is just a mouse-click away. Moreover, we follow the dark tourists to the places where crime and particularly punishment are remembered, commemorated, and commoditised for visitors looking for information and entertainment.

The book takes on the big issues. It looks at the sweeping changes to the way crime was understood, controlled, prosecuted, and punished in this period, the effect that crime had on the lives of offenders and victims, and the community in general, and it asks how much crime was there? Why did violence appear to be almost eradicated by World War I? Why were magistrates' courts full of traffic and other regulatory offences by 1940? How do people remember crimes and feelings of risk and insecurity, and can we rely on stories and oral histories? How can we carry out ethical research into the lives of prisoners and criminals? What are the implications for research in having new digital media bring us detailed data on thousands of offenders extremely easily? Will the research undertaken by historians of crime, or family historians, or genealogists, have any impact on the way that we think about crime and criminals? What impact can we have? Why do we remember crimes and sites of punishment in the ways we do? How did the business of policing change between 1880 and 1940? Did the routine duties of bobbies on the beat really alter that much over that period? Were they replaced by the Flying Squad zooming around the streets in panda cars? What about secret and covert policing – how and why did that come about? How was information about crimes committed, and the offenders that may have committed them, circulated around the country? Did the surveillance bureaucracies developed by habitual offender legislation in the 1870s stand the test of time? How were people punished in this period? Why did so many prisons close, and what kinds of noncustodial sentences were introduced? How was eugenics replaced by psychology as a major theory of criminality? How and to what end did scientific criminology come about? This is quite a list, and quite a journey which lies ahead of us.

Over my own intellectual journey I have accumulated many debts, which I cheerfully acknowledge. First I would like to thank the students I have taught at the Universities of Keele and Liverpool for their questions and thoughts, and I would like to thank everyone that I have worked with for the last twenty years. In particular I have benefited by discussing ideas with my co-authors and co-researchers David Cox, Steve Farrall, Helen Johnston, Hamish Maxwell-Stewart, Paul Lawrence, John Locker, Chris Williams, Pam Cox, Heather Shore, Jo Turner, David Taylor, Louise Jackson, and Robin Robinson. My work, and this book, has benefitted from these collaborations and also from the philosophy of that group of historians and criminologists who have managed to convey the complexity of crime historical research with a deft lightness of touch: Peter King, Clive Emsley, Graeme Dunstall, and Bob Shoemaker. As befits my straddling of history and criminology in the last decades I would like to thank sociologists and criminologists that have supported my work through their own intellectual contribution, commentaries on my work, conversation about issues we have a common interest in, or through their own warm friendship: Sandra Walklate, Anne Worrall, Richard Sparks, Pat Carlen, Susanne Karstedt, Ruth Jamieson, Ian Taylor, Ronnie Lippens, Dave Gadd, Ian Loader, John Pratt, and Mark Finnane.

My PhD students have been a delight. In addition to providing company at conferences around the world, they have kept me cheerful at work and have stretched my limited knowledge of the topics they have chosen to study to the limit. In addition to those who have subsequently worked with me, I would also like to thank Bronwyn Morrison, Maryse Tennant, Kate Bates, Kerry Chamberlain, Guy Woolnough, Adam Snow, Adam Calverley, Pam McGuiness, Aidan O'Sullivan, Lucy Williams, and Craig Stafford.

My greatest debt is to Jane and our daughter Alex. They have provided love and emotional support as well as practical help (especially my daughter who is turning out to be an excellent proofreader as well as a dedicated critic). Last I have to mention my friends from the Black Lion, Nige, Andy, and Mike, who have been no help whatsoever and who owe me a pint of Old Dog just for mentioning them.

1

THE CONVICT'S STORY

Just before midnight a group of men skulking in the shadows of Sheffield's Cambridge Street pounced on a hapless victim. One man kept him in an armlock whilst three others robbed him, thereafter pushing him to the ground and kicking him repeatedly. This incident of 'garrotting' reported in 1871 fitted the public imagination of how the city streets contained danger and threat to respectable passers-by. Whilst the courts sentenced three men for this assault, one of the accused, Patrick Madden, was released because he could not be identified by the victim. Madden was a well-known fixture of Cambridge Street. Later he was identified and singled out as a ringleader of a group of 'Irish Toughs', pursued and cornered by the police during a 'Cambridge-Street riot' at Christmas in 1871. It was not surprising that they had recognised him because the teenager was well known to the courts, having had three convictions for violence and for theft by his seventeenth birthday. The police probably had an added incentive to apprehend Madden because two years earlier he had kicked a police officer so hard that the man was disabled for life. When they took him away, four officers escorted him in the back of the police van – for their own protection, or to mete out some informal punishment of their own perhaps. For his part in the riot he received a year's prison sentence, but this would be a relatively short visit to prison for a man who would ultimately serve nearly a quarter of his life in prison. What sort of man was Patrick Madden?

Patrick's story

Born in Ireland, he had immigrated to Sheffield as a youth accompanied by his brother, no doubt looking for work and for a better future. Today he would be considered a man of average height and of slim build, but at 5 feet 8 inches and at more than 10 stone he would have been considered a tall and muscular figure when he plied for work as a plasterer in the 1880s. Men and women were physically much

LIVERPOOL JOHN MOORES UNIVERSITY
LEARNING SERVICES

slighter in those days and certainly shorter in stature. That is why Madden was described as a 'brute of a man' by the newspapers, and his brutishness was confirmed not only by his height but also by his physical appearance, which betrayed a rough background. Notes on his prison record written in 1879 gave his notable physical characteristics:

> Left eye injured as result of accident with a stick which left him partially blinded, scar on crown of head, scar on top of head, scar on right eyebrow and left cheek, scar on right jaw and on nose. Scar on left wrist, scar on left forearm and on little finger and buttocks, scar on hip. Scar top arm and elbow, cut across top of thumb, scar on ribs, scar on side of thigh, and below knee, cuts to back.
>
> (*Prison Licence of Convict F.704 Patrick Madden,*
> *National Archives PCOM 3*)

Unlike many other convicts, he lacked significant (one might even call them communicative) tattoos. One blue mark between thumb and forefinger denoted that the convict had already served time in a juvenile reformatory; blue dots on the knuckles seem to have referred to the number of previous bouts of penal servitude in convict prison; and a 'D' meant either dishonourable discharge from military service or some kind of military discipline (a flogging perhaps). These last marks were made by the authorities, of course, rather than by the convict. But many convicts had homemade tattoos to remind them of past loves, family, places they had been (or served on military duty), and so on. For the prison authorities, these all provided a means of identifying those who tried to hide within aliases, as is discussed later in the book. Clearly Madden liked to drink, for his offending was often connected with drunkenness, and he seems to have made friends (and accomplices) easily in his neighbourhood. Perhaps friendship was mixed with fear and admiration for his fighting prowess, because his allies must have witnessed many of the fights he initiated that then ended up in court, and many other altercations that were never reported or prosecuted. He must have been an unpredictable and unreliable fellow to hang around with, given his unprovoked assaults on people he hardly knew. One Sheffield cabman felt Madden's fists in July 1874 when he disputed the fare he was being charged – in that the cabbie expected some payment at all. With no love lost between Madden and the police, he attempted to strangle the arresting officer when he was being escorted to the police station to be charged. Three years later a publican should have thought better of refusing to serve Madden when the pub was closed. The brutal assault – many repeated blows to the man's head – was interrupted by the publican's wife who put herself between the two men. This was a mistake. Madden never respected the concept of chivalry, and indeed seemed to have developed an unhealthy hostility towards women by this date. Still spitting blood as she gave evidence in court, the woman described how Madden had struck her in the face and strangled her till she was unconscious. The bitter taste in her mouth and the distaste of the authorities for Madden's repeated offending meant that he was heading for a lengthy spell in prison. It came in the summer of 1879 when he found himself before the judges at the Quarter Sessions at Wakefield. Convicted of assault, theft, and robbery with violence, he was sentenced to ten years' Penal Servitude, followed by a further five years' supervision by the police upon his release from incarceration. Thus began his cavalcade through a number of notorious convict prisons – Wakefield, Pentonville, Wormwood Scrubs, Portland, and Millbank – before being released on conditional licence in 1887.

Madden the convict

Prison conditions were harsh, but Madden was tough, and he seems to have coped fairly well with the prison regime and the informal community of prisoners that could make things difficult for prisoners who could not fit in and hold their own. He received punishment for talking to other prisoners during exercise periods or during religious services in the prison chapel, and occasionally he was punished for thieving from fellow inmates or for fighting with other prisoners. He was not – not by a long chalk – a troublesome prisoner. Many were much worse, and many other prisoners racked up a large number of prison offences over the course of their sentences whilst Madden only committed a handful of regulatory breaches. One breach, however, reveals an interesting side to his character. The short entry in the prison records for 13 March 1885 reveals that Madden had a prohibited article hidden in a leaf of his Bible when on parade:

> My dear C_ G_ This is to fulfil my promise. My name is P. Madden. I am a plasterer by trade 30 years of age. I was transported for taking a parcel of books from a man under the impression that they were my own. If you can wait for me I will endeavour to make you quite happy for the rest of your life – If you leave Portland write to me. I would not answer your letter but when my time is up I would come to you to the furthest end of the world. Dear C_ G_ do not shew this to anyone I be very severely punished. If you do not write to me I shall know you have forgotten me. If you knew what a true heart I have you would wait for me, Adieu X.

The letter is stamped 'Convict Department Bermuda' on the back and was written on a colonial issue Bible.[1] Following one's heart in prison could be a very dangerous route, and affairs and liaisons between two male inmates resulted in convicts serving longer periods inside prison walls. Madden risked much in revealing his desires in this way, but he had no wish to remain in prison any longer than he needed to. Indeed, he petitioned the Secretary of State to reduce his sentence from ten years to seven years on the grounds that 'he was intoxicated when the offence was committed, which was not intentional'. Petitioning was a routine right that prisoners held dear. Just as routinely, the petition was dismissed. It would have been extraordinary for Madden to successfully petition for release or reduction of sentence. Petitioners with far better claims for leniency never had any joy from the authorities. However, like the vast majority of convicts, he was released well before his sentence expired.

The final two years and three months of his sentence would be served 'on licence' or, more colloquially, on a 'Ticket of Leave'. So long as he reported regularly to the local police station and committed no further offences, Patrick would retain his liberty. Perhaps not surprisingly given his history he did not manage to see his licence period out. He lasted six months. 'Assault by Ticket of Leave Man' screamed the local newspaper when, again, Madden vented his fury on an innocent woman. Smarting after being turned out of his lodgings when his landlady found out he was an ex-prisoner, he might have drowned his sorrows on his own had he not bumped into her in the streets. Refusal to join him for a drink resulted in a punch to the face and a trip to the local magistrates' court, but his licence was not withdrawn. His next assault was also unprovoked, but was more serious. In March 1890 'A Savage Irishman at Mexbro' rounded on a man in the street. He knew not his victim, nor did he care that he kicked out two of the man's teeth when he was on the ground. All he cared about was that the man did not call the police, and if he did, he would find him and kill him. The threat was ineffective, and so was the short prison sentence. Once more out on the streets, Madden carried out a 'Serious Assault at Swinton'. Looking for drink after a musical evening in the town, and looking for a man who owed him money, he found trouble in the Corner Inn. Failing to find the man he searched for, he found the man's wife instead. She was kicked until she lost her senses, but Madden's offer to pay six pennies for the damage he had caused was frowned on by the magistrates who judged the case. Even so, and although this seems odd to our sensibilities today, the fairly routine imposition of a fine for this act of violence was thought a sufficient punishment; a similar crime took place in the same town a few months later – he assaulted a man and threatened to kill his wife if she interfered, and, again, received a fine. Residents of South Yorkshire must have been sick of Madden, and only when he stole a horse did they find relief (for fifteen months) when he was sent back to prison.

Apparently the animosity between him and the police lasted for decades, and in 1895 he threatened police with a poker, kicked and punched officers when arrested, and served another two months. A year later, he was arrested for loitering in a darkened alley and warned the arresting officer, 'If I ever see you drunk and asleep on a doorstop, I shall murder you, you _____'. Never one to issue an idle threat, a poker was found in his pocket, ready for use. However, that was Madden's last offence, and his last prison sentence.

Notching up just fifty years of life, over which time he had committed more than thirty offences, had numerous fights, had threatened many people, and had suffered loneliness and misery in some of Her Majesty's toughest prisons, he died in Sheffield and was buried in the city shortly afterwards. We do not know whether his brother attended the funeral. This letter Patrick sent to his brother William from prison on 4 April 1887: 'I very much regret not being able to see you when I am discharged. I thank you very sincerely for what you have done . . . I shall be discharged on 27 May 1887 if I am a good boy. Adieu dear brother.' The letter, now kept in Madden's licence file in the National Archives (PCOM 3) was returned unopened. We also do not know whether any of his friends attended the short funeral service; newspapers seldom reported the final doings of men like Patrick, but it seems to have been a sad and lonely end to a tumultuous and sometimes vicious half-century of one man's life.

Patrick, and all the Patricks

Patrick Madden, and indeed all the others like him who caused mayhem across England and Wales, left written footprints. Every interaction with each of the institutions of the criminal justice system – the police, the courts, the prisons – left a paper trail which allows us to trace Patrick's movements over time and space. That is how we know so much of Patrick's chaotic and violent escapades throughout most of his life, from his eye colour and weight to his sexual preferences. In fact, as we will see later in this book, modern research methods and available digital resources now allow researchers to trace a huge number of nineteenth- and twentieth-century offenders. The detail on each person is so good, that, if we ever had time to combine every individual's story, we might have an almost complete understanding of the causes of crime in this period and of how each criminal justice institution affected the offender's life. However, at present, we have a number of interesting individual case studies, fascinating ones actually, and the statistics of crime which can tell us how the bigger picture changed over time. The next two chapters suggest some ways of understanding and using oral histories, memories, and statistics to show how these very different kinds of historical sources can be combined to provide not only a bigger picture but also a sharper, better, and clearer picture of what drove people into offending and of how society and the media reacted to the problem of crime, as well as to examine how and why as modern researchers we remember and study the history of crime today.

Serious versus everyday offending

Who, however, should draw our gaze? Is it the serious offenders – the relatively few burglars and murderers who caused such misery for their victims and who suffered the most severe sanctions of the criminal justice system – on whom we should focus? Certainly they drew the attention of the media, particularly when women were involved as either victims or as perpetrators of the deadly deed themselves.

In Liverpool's labouring district of Garston, Ellen Neill was beaten to death in her own house in Vulcan Street. The day before the murder, her husband had demanded that she bring more money into the house, and if she did not, then he would 'swing for her'. Neighbours, hearing desperate screams from the house next door, broke down the door to find that Ellen was on the floor, her head being repeatedly smashed against the kitchen flagstones. Her husband, James, then stripped his wife of her clothes, dragged her to the fire, and raked red-hot coals over her body whilst screaming that he would roast her naked body. The *Liverpool Mercury* reported that she had only briefly and intermittently regained consciousness, and soon succumbed to her injuries, after which her husband was charged with wilful murder at Liverpool Assize Court. Mrs Nicholson suffered a similar fate to Ellen's a few weeks later in Aston, Birmingham. Her husband struck her with a small axe around the head until she died of her wounds then propped her up in her favourite rocking chair (*Sheffield and Rotherham Independent*, 24 September 1888). Arrested, charged, and convicted, he was hanged in Warwick in January 1889. The eighteen-year-old youth who stabbed, cut about, and almost decapitated a smaller child in Wales in September 1888 escaped the gallows. Thomas Lott was found to be of unsound mind and therefore unfit to stand trial by the jury at Swansea Assizes. Insanity, brutality, and horrific murder connect the crimes, all of these committed in the same month. For contemporary commentators another set of horrific crimes taking place in London could be used to link together these disparate events – the spectre of Jack the Ripper stalked newspaper columns as much as he did Whitechapel:

> the callousness of the culprit, the determination of his conduct, and his subsequent indifference rivals the terrible incidents of Whitechapel life which have recently been brought before the public. It is true that the victim was not disembowelled, but a punctured wound in the stomach shows that some attempt to perpetrate this peculiarity of the London tragedies.
>
> (*Western Mail, 23 October 1888*)

The Whitechapel murders were also linked closely, in the newspapers anyway, to other murders in various parts of England: 'The affair caused quite a panic in the district, the resemblance to the Whitechapel tragedies encouraging the idea that the maniac who has been at work in London has travelled to the north of England to pursue his fiendish vocation' (*Daily News*, 24 September 1888). Jack himself may not have ventured to the north, but the doctor who examined his London victims and Criminal Investigation Department (CID) officer Inspector Roots did, just to satisfy themselves that the Ripper's geographical ambition had not increased – it hadn't (*Daily News*, 26 September 1888). Neither had he ventured to the Midlands, though people were keen to invoke his name. The murderous husband of Ellen Nicholson in Aston had boasted to a friend that he would 'make a Whitechapel job of her' (*The York Herald*, 29 September 1888). Loose words such as these probably helped him on his way to the gallows, for the mere mention of Whitechapel could influence the judgement of juries as well as of the public and journalists.

The editor of the *Pall Mall* seemed to have a better grip on how these things worked:

> The murder and mutilation of a woman near Gateshead yesterday morning will revive, in the provinces, the horror which was beginning to die out in London . . . and already the people in the neighbourhood have begun, it seems, to be haunted by the idea that the murderous maniac of Whitechapel may have found his way to the north of England. The idea is natural but improbable. What is far more likely is that the murder is not a repetition but a reflex of the Whitechapel ones. It is one of the inevitable results of publicity to spread an epidemic.
>
> ('*The Political Moral of the Murders*', The Pall Mall Gazette,
> *24 September 1888*)

The series of murders of prostitutes by person or persons unknown reached a ridiculously high profile in both the United Kingdom and abroad. Knowledge dripped into the public consciousness through tidbits of information released each day in the newspapers, and whilst Jack remained at large, readers could be engaged, scared, entertained, and curious about his identity and where he would strike next. The story seemed to seep into the public consciousness, into dreams, and into everyday concerns, as with an interview with someone who was once a small boy from Shropshire: 'I remember that when Jack the Ripper was in London, he was doing all the murders . . . Father used to sometimes do night work, and this particular time Mother was afraid so she got a lot of furniture and pushed it against the doors so that he wouldn't be able to get in'.[2] It is unlikely that, even if Jack had carried on offending after the three-month spree in 1888 that saw at least five women murdered, he would have left the dark streets of Whitechapel to have a murderous 'holiday' in Shropshire – even so, the woman was clearly scared. The sensationalism of the Ripper murders was part and parcel of the growing power and entertainment focus of the press towards the end of the century, as well as being related to contemporary anxieties about immigration, poverty and homelessness, prostitution, and the general sociopolitical climate in East London.

Murders and murderers were notorious but not numerous. Even though the misery they caused was deep and distressful, cases of murder were comparatively rare. Between 1870 and 1914 the number of murders each year varied only between 372 and 458, that is, approximately 400 a year on average. That equates to a murder rate of one in 50,000 people per year for England and Wales. As with the situation today, the richer and older you were, the more genteel the area you lived in, the less likely you were to be a victim of serious violence. Murders by strangers, again, as today, were very rare. So these figures in themselves only tell us a little bit of the story, and we can see later how we can fully understand and contextualise these feelings of risk and insecurity in the Victorian and Edwardian period. Let us put aside murder and burglary for the moment and think about 'volume crime'. Clearly, any questions about 'how much crime' and 'how serious' was crime in this period are going to have to construct a perspective that takes in the extraordinary but serious offences along with more everyday crimes; it will have to consider press reportage and the view from the streets, changes in legislation, and the operation of the law through its agents, the police, and the courts.

It seems that for most people, between 1880 and 1940, by far the greatest chance they had of being a victim of, a witness of, or a participant in crime was being involved in one of the thousands of public order and drunkenness offences prosecuted before the First World War or a traffic offence prosecuted in the interwar period. The offences dealt with at summary level (by magistrates at the lower courts) totalled more than half a million in 1870 and nearly three-quarters of a million by the start of World War I. Admittedly, these summary offences covered a huge and diverse set of offending behaviour, from vagrancy to opening a shop after hours, from stealing wild birds' eggs to living on immoral earnings (from prostitution), and so on. Nevertheless, that is approximately one offence for every forty people living in England and Wales. Of course, similar to wealth or good looks, criminality was not equally distributed. Indeed, most legislation passed in the nineteenth century was aimed against two groups of people, a small, hard core of serious offenders and the wider group of habitual minor offenders who committed minor common assaults or who regularly became drunk and disorderly in public (there were more than 130,000 prosecutions for drunkenness alone in 1870 and more than 200,000 by 1914). Were Britain's streets full of fighting drunks?

The rough

In 1875 *The Graphic, an Illustrated Weekly Newspaper* included 'The British Rough' in its series 'Heads of the People'. The word *rough* has a long history, being used in the fifteenth century (and probably before then) to denote an uneven, or un-smoothed, object (e.g., rough ground, rough surface, etc.) or discordant sound (rough music). Shakespeare used it to describe rudeness, or incivility in Lear in 1530 (*Lear* II, ii), and it is likely that both uses of the word ran alongside each other, and still do. However, although the term was often used to describe unruly behaviour, it was not until the 1830s and 1840s that *rough* could be used as a noun. For example, in 1837, in 'Life and Letters', Barham was happy to note that there were 'lots of new policemen to control the rogues and roughs' (II, 39, 1837). The *Oxford English Dictionary* (www.oed.com) confirms the common definition of *Rough*, by the mid-nineteenth century, as 'a man or lad inclined to commit acts of violence or disorders in public – a rowdy'. The use of the word to describe the imperfect imitation of a better, smoother, more refined, or cultured object could now be applied to violent, uncivilized, deficient, and otherwise imperfect men. The drawing of the unshaven, unkempt, wild-eyed man in *The Graphic* could not have disappointed the Victorian public in its depiction of a common stereotype. Historical research has tended to focus primarily on the prolific offenders in society, and the steps taken to combat them. Similarly, criminologists who have referred to the theoretical origins of their subject also reference studies of the criminal classes or the habitual offender in the main. In that respect, academic research has mirrored the preoccupations of the public throughout the last few centuries. Indeed, it would be possible to construct a changing history of notorious criminals up to the present day and, in that way, offer a perspective on changing popular sensibilities and fears. However, this book does not focus solely on the notorious criminal, or even necessarily the habitual criminal, but also on those who inhabited the world between the 'respectable poor' and the 'criminal class' – those who were infrequent offenders but who were frequently drunk and disorderly and those who were not violent robbers but who were often involved in street fighting. It looks to the unruly, the disreputable, the disrespectful, the stand-up drunk, and the fighting working-class dwellers of many towns and cities throughout Victorian England. In other words, it also turns to those who occupied the hinterland rather than the heartland of criminality in the public imagination.

These imaginary spaces are not always easy to describe, and some historians have written about the world that existed *between* the respectable working class and the 'criminal underworld' without explicitly acknowledging or naming this conceptual space, indeed some have chosen to only implicitly address the subject. Chesney, writing in the 1970s, for example, in his study of the 'London Underworld', included 'thieves, cheats, bullies, beggars, touts and tarts', but he excluded upper-class embezzlers and countryside poachers. It therefore excluded those guilty of criminal acts, but included those unskilled workers and street traders whose very manner of living, he suggested, seemed a challenge to ordered society and the tissues of laws, moralities, and taboos holding it together. It would seem that Chesney was keen to flavour the London underworld with colourful working-class characters, without identifying them as part of the criminal class he believed existed, and wished to describe (also see D. Thomas 1998).

It is not surprising that Chesney ran into difficulties, for contemporary Victorian and Edwardian social commentators often positioned the world of the rough on the border between the criminal class and the respectable poor, whilst others saw the poor and the criminal as an undifferentiated grouping (see debates in Lawrence [2000] as well as Garland [1987] and Stedman Jones [2013]). Is it really possible to separate out the criminals and the labouring poor from each other? Of course it is not. The economic situation of many lower working-class workers, such as navvies and costermongers, ensured that they lived in poor housing stock, sometimes with neighbours who relied on theft to provide an income – so that the lower strata of the working population were caught up in illegality without being 'core members' of the underworld. One clearly cannot draw a demarcation line between workers and offenders. Many occasional offenders maintained full-time, part-time, or seasonal employment. Moreover, research studies have found that full-time employment does not preclude crime, and employee theft or appropriation was rife in the docks, factories, and many other nineteenth-century workplaces (Godfrey and Cox 2013). Although this comparison can be stretched too far, many of the workers described by, say, Mayhew in 1851, seem similar to the people Dick Hobbs found 'grafting' away in the unfashionable parts of London in the late twentieth century. The street traders, casual labour, and petty criminals, who are at the margins of respectable society and whose entrepreneurial spirit aids survival in a demanding economic climate, do not seem much different from the street dwellers found by Mayhew. They are at least similarly vulnerable to and victimized by economic conditions and are subject to considerable police attention (Hobbs 1988). Many who toiled in low occupations, may have occasionally dabbled in criminal activity, and enjoyed leisure pursuits which attracted police attention, but did not seem to fit into the Victorian conception of habitual offenders. So, is this book dedicated to examining and ultimately overturning a popular myth? Let us remember that the 'myths' of who commits crime, and why, maintain to this day, and are sustained in governmental and public debates about benefit-scroungers, shirkers, (see the *Independent*, 9 December 2012), hard core repeat offenders (BBC News, 9 July 2004) and the 'feral youths' (*Guardian*, 5 September 2011). The common-sense views about crime that we can read about in the tabloids and the phone-ins on local radio seem to be connected to, indeed rely upon, opinions of criminality derived from the late nineteenth and early twentieth centuries, a time when a great many philosophies and scientific theories vied with popular imaginings to create a startling and exciting world of possibilities and dangers.

The imaginary world of the late victorian period

During this period, the intellectual firmament whirled with ideas about the possibilities, threats and hopes held for the new century: spiritualism and fairies (the hoax photographs of the Cottingley fairies in 1917 and Conan Doyle's *The Coming of the Fairies*, 1921), unrestrained science (H.G. Well's *The Island of Dr Moreau*, 1896), some anticipated the Second Coming whilst others posited the death of God (Nietzsche's *Thus Spoke Zarathustra* [1883] gained currency in this period), the uncontrollable poor and the descent of mankind, and exploration into space, the sea, and the human mind (Jules Verne's *20,000 Leagues Under the Sea*, 1870; Freud's *The Interpretation of Dreams*, 1899). Later, around the Second World War, others such as George Orwell (in his impressive prediction of a future dystopia *1984* and H.G. Wells with his more optimistic view of dictatorship in *The Shape of Things to Come*, 1933) would question the new world order, how common people would fare under totalitarian regimes, and the new techniques of surveillance being developed by the state (and by social scientists). However, by that stage many writers, opinion formers, moral entrepreneurs and proto-social scientists, had already asked themselves two fundamental questions of humanity – 'What does it mean to be human, and what does the future hold for humanity?' Those philosophical queries were often expressed in public within and through well-worn rhetorical debates (about the future of British Empire or the condition of the cities, for example). However, the debates about the condition of man, which hitherto had been informed by theology, were increasingly suffused by (questionable) scientific data. As is well known, the character of that debate turned away from religion as its focal point and towards the perfectibility or degeneration of mankind, the social categorisation of mankind into desirable and undesirable, the subsequent decline and fall of the British Empire, and, consequently, the end of civilization. As is well known, the proposed solutions for society's problems included improved social welfare provision, increased supervision and punishment for the immoral poor, and eugenics.

To those who had traditionally seen the problematic populations as a mob or as rabble to be controlled and watched, the increased surveillance of the unrespectable working classes, the punitive Habitual Offenders acts, and the harsher prison sentences initiated in the 1860s and 1870s were thought necessary to at least contain a problem they believed was insoluble. Alternatively, for those who expressed the belief that humanity could be improved and perfected by rehabilitating or eradicating the undesirable elements of the population, social policy initiatives – slum clearance, penal reform, increased educational provision – appeared to offer a better solution to society's problems, as did eugenics. As Major Leonard Darwin asked in 1928, 'What sort of men does society *want*?' Because 'the criminal' was considered so obviously the least desirable type of human, much of the degeneration/progression debate focused on the criminal – usually habitual – offender, and how they hindered the upward progress of the nation. As Pick (1990: 20) said, 'theories of progress always seem to involve the implication of potential inversions, recalcitrant forces, subversive "others", necessary to be excluded from the polity.' Lombroso and his followers provided a pseudoscientific context for these debates, but more than that, they provided what were essentially manuals for recognising habitual offenders. The problem here, as historians have noted, is that habitual offenders formed only a small proportion of those prosecuted for crimes, and an even smaller proportion of the working classes. The 'Roughs' hanging around the streets may have been the nearest that many gentlemen and women got to the bona fide dangerous career criminals that they read about in their daily newspapers. Even if the dishevelled and distressed person sheltering in a pub doorway had not committed a series of offences, they at least *looked* like they might have done. From the Victorian and Edwardian street 'Roughs' to the respectable motorists caught speeding in the 1920s and 1930s, this book seeks to explain contemporary discourses on crime and connect and interact with several wider debates, including the conceptions of violence in late modernity, the demise or growth of civility, and the social memory and the mythologies of the decades on either side of the First World War; last, it reflects on cultural values and attitudes towards crime and violence across the 'Western' world both bringing forward and reflecting back to some larger questions of governance, risk, and exclusion. The following chapter explains how we can go about this.

2

WHAT SHALL WE DO?

This book provides a comprehensive study of the main institutions of the criminal justice system and explains how they worked, how they had an impact on people who broke the law, and how and why we remember and research crime in the way that we do. However, we cannot do everything and we have to be a little selective. There are hundreds of other more specialised books which can be read by people wanting to explore just one of the issues which we discuss here – but which could easily involve a lifetime of research. In order to do something interesting and informative for the length of this book, I have selected a number of important topics and tried to examine them in a systematic and logical manner (sometimes) and sometimes by touching on the same subject in different chapters – prolific repeat offenders in society, violent crime, the lives of convicts, why horrifying places are also fascinating places to visit – to capture different perspectives. But the book starts at the most logical point in Chapter 2 and looks at the foundational building blocks of information that mid-nineteenth-century policy makers used as the backbone of their beliefs about the amount of crime in the United Kingdom – the annually published judicial statistics.

Measuring and capturing crime with statistics

As Chapter 3 outlines, statistics were introduced in the mid-nineteenth century and continued to be relied on until a crisis about the validity of collection methods caused a crisis in confidence in statistics at the end of the century. Statistics are still the starting point for many modern researchers of crime, if they only then go on to critique and dismiss them. If we can examine how statistics were relied on by nineteenth- and twentieth-century social policy theorists we might grow to have a better appreciation of their strengths and weaknesses. However, we might not be able to finally answer the quantitative questions: How much crime was there? Which was most violent – the city or the countryside? and Which groups committed the most crime? Those questions rely on data which are much more subjective than they would at first appear. We can, however, reveal criminal justice statistics which are much more straightforward – how many people were in prison or in juvenile reformatories? What were the major offences prosecuted in this period? How many people were sentenced to prison, probation, fines, or some other punishment? When did the prisons fill up? Investigating these statistical enquiries in this chapter will allow us to answer more complex questions in the following chapter.

What makes crime figures go up and down?

We might think that the amount of crime that people committed governed the crime statistics. If more people broke the law, then surely the figures would rise as well? Chapter 4 reexamines two issues that the statistics seem to robustly describe. Why did violence and drunkenness appear to 'disappear' around the turn of the century? When did traffic offending come to play such a major part of policing? This chapter outlines how statistics can be used to approach some of these knotty issues and makes a case for statistics being brought back in from the cold – arguing that we should again return to the statistics (warts and all) as the first point in any historical enquiry about crime; only if statistics are the first point and not the whole point, however. We will have to return to questions about the decline in violence, the way that police and prosecution decisions altered the number of crimes dealt with by the courts, the part played by regulators and officials in prosecuting crimes, the impact of traffic offending on public perceptions of policing, and so on, right the way throughout this book. Moreover, any serious study of crime must delve deeper into the structure of feelings – what people think and feel about crime and what it 'means' to them. This kind of qualitative data escapes the purely statistical analysis, and Chapter 4 explores the methodologies and means of analysis we can use to explore memories, feelings, and stories about crime and victimisation.

What do we feel about crime?

Chapter 5, then, explores how symbolic myths and popular narratives shaped common opinion on prosecuted crimes and interacted with stories of crime and violence that never reached the courts, but which dwelt on in the minds of witnesses, victims, perpetrators and those who discussed notorious violence within their communities. It takes as its focus the large number of oral history interviews that reside in various archives and libraries throughout the United Kingdom. The interviews themselves are not unproblematic to analyse, and the chapter discusses the problems of social memory, as well as some of the other analytical complexities in using this kind of evidence.

Honouring the dead

Having been shown as so useful in both charting changing social and cultural sensibilities towards crime and violence in this period, and challenging the statistics collected by the government, we must pay more attention to transcribed oral histories. Because the stories that we find in oral histories were related by real people who may or who may well not have appreciated that their words were going to be pored over by researchers and students many decades after they themselves have died, in Chapter 6 we need to think about how we ensure that we do not breach any moral or legal standards in using their words. Or do we? Are there applicable moral frameworks and legal codes that can be applied to the words of the dead? This chapter examines the issue from all sides and suggest some ways forward.

The new worldwide digital archive

Analysis of oral history interviews is now a fairly well accepted historical methodology, even if it is not as well established as documentary analysis. Crime historians such as Gatrell and Hadden (1972) have explained how court-generated documents such as Quarter Sessions indictments, criminal registers, and so on can be used to investigate crime levels. However, because of the revolution in electronic resources, both the range of documentary evidence available and the range of people who are using websites and electronic databases to research their own criminal ancestors have expanded dramatically. Chapter 7 provides detail on a range of available sources and shows how some historians have started to employ them in their work (using detailed examples of cutting-edge micro- and life-history research).

Academic knowledge and dark tourism?

As will have become clear by now, we have a tremendous amount of historical material at our disposal – crime stories, statistics, documents about private institutional processes (from the police, the courts and so on), and we have the means to put them all together to reveal the course of a single offender's life from cradle to grave. It must be time to discuss some of the 'fallout' from the use of new media and digital resources – the ethical usage of personal information which has now become so freely available and the implications of huge amounts of crime data being available for such speedy analysis. Chapter 8 begins with a debate around electronic 'dark tourism' (the website tourism of prison and convict history and how information about crime, prisoners, and punishment is presented online). The chapter then goes on to discuss whether crime history is purely of use to the prurient (as critiques of dark tourism may suggest) or to the genealogist and family historian. Does crime history claim to have any impact on contemporary debates on law and order going on in modern criminological research, or in the media, or even in Parliament? If it claims to, does it? If it wants to, can it? How would crime historians go about this?

Space, place, and crime

Perhaps our exploration of hyperspace and Internet phenomena needs to be tempered with a more down-to-earth investigation of how time and real physical space need to be combined to make crime history more understandable. Chapter 9 begins with a number of particular crimes that all took place on 26 October 1881. On that day, the gunfight at the OK Corral in Tombstone took place, as did the arrest of a drunken gold miner in a failing boom town in New Zealand, and in Crewe, a shopkeeper was prosecuted for opening his premises on a Sunday. What part did geography and the physical/social development of a town or city affect the type of crimes that were prosecuted; and how can we compare crime 'situations' across time and place? The following chapters concentrate on the socio-development of England, and the growth of a criminal justice system – and the extent to which we can describe the interactions between the police, the courts, and the prisons, as a recognisable 'system'.

New technologies of police power

Sherlock Holmes captured the public imagination from the 1880s, and he begins our investigations in Chapter 10. He epitomised everything that the public desired by way of a policing Nietzschean superman who could, despite his flaws, accurately and startlingly deduce the culprit and could spring into action with a loaded revolver when needs be. However, outside of the pages of the *Strand Magazine*, detective services developed slowly in the late Victorian period. 'Normal policing' in Victorian Britain involved a system of beat police officers occasionally relying on detective colleagues stepping in to investigate serious crimes. The well-tried methods of detectives rounding up the usual suspects, or strangers who did not quite fit in, persisted at least until the First World War (Emsley 1991). Nineteenth-century constables emphasised physical presence as a crime deterrent and physical force as a tool of policing. The police had a wide range of discretionary powers at their fingertips. Understanding the reasons that lie behind decisions that officers made on the streets and gaining knowledge of established police practices and daily routines are essential. So too, however, is the need to understand how these practices were undermined and challenged by the new technologies of the twentieth century: forensics and mobile policing. Forensic science was basic and variable in quality until at least the second half of the twentieth century (arguably until computers were routinely used in the 1970s and 1980s). Nevertheless, the application of rigorous and systematic methods of detection (if not forensic investigation) came more and more to characterise policing practices before World War II. The increasing professionalization of policing (the introduction of grades of constables, pensions, better training, unionisation) and the higher standard of police recruits encouraged new forms of policing. Technological advances (motorised policing and better radio communications) were brought in to combat new challenges – criminals with cars, for example. Traffic divisions were formed, and indeed the specialisation of policing continued, so that CID offices became established in major towns and cities. The Special Branch was formed in response to perceived dangers from Irish terrorists and from subversive communist and fascist operatives and agitators in the 1920s and 1930s. The character of policing appeared to have altered considerably since the poor police officer plodded along lonely streets in Victorian England, but had things changed quite that much? The last sections of this chapter explain how media portrayals of policing up to and after the Second World War overemphasised and promoted emerging styles of policing, when, in reality, the routine duties of police officers were little changed from a century earlier. It was not 'at the sharp end' that policing had changed most. It was in the back-office processes of bureaucratisation that the major changes had been made.

Capturing criminals on paper

Chapter 11 describes how criminal justice institutions became linked together by bureaucracy and by the increasing need to share information. Habitual Offender legislation passed from the 1870s to the Preventative Detention legislation of the early twentieth century necessitated the interconnection of penal and police authorities across the country. The Home Office and Scotland Yard established centralised systems of information sharing in order to track released prisoners, until, very quickly, they became vast organisations that were only disbanded on the eve of World War II. Information was sought by police experts and policy makers from academics, scientists, and medical and psychological experts working in England. Continental Europe seemed to provide inspirational models for enhanced evidence-led penal and policing systems, until the influence of U.S. penology came to the fore. Organisations such as Interpol were formed to combat cross-national crime, but, as this chapter explains, it was the flow of ideas about crime and ways of controlling criminals that crossed borders much more easily than the criminals themselves.

Punishing times

Similar to the new technologies of policing, new ideas from abroad about sentencing and penology seemed exciting and appeared to offer possibilities to criminal justice practitioners, but they were slow to be embedded. Back in England, however, significant changes in the way offences and offenders were dealt with were taking place in ways which would have long-lasting impacts far into the twentieth century. For example, this period witnessed huge and important changes in the processing of crime, from apprehension of the defendant to their final release from gaol or police/probation supervision. In 1880, four-fifths of all cases were brought to court by victims of crime, and the victims (or their agents) prosecuted their case before the magistrates. By the start of the First World War four-fifths of all cases in magistrate courts were prosecuted by the police (a situation which only changed in 1985 with the introduction of the Crown Prosecution Service). The courts were professionalised, and victims (and, to some extent, the crowd that came to witness cases) disappeared (having a powerful symbolic presence only). The higher courts also professionalised, relying more on expert testimony and the advice of probation officers (introduced from 1908 to replace the amateur Police Court Missionaries). The courts were more greatly disposed to probation for the young and the first-time offender, and, as well as describing the nationalisation of the prison service, Chapter 12 explains how the increase in probation affected the number of prisoners in the penal estate. The chapter also explains how changing penal theories and psychological theories of criminality would alter how prisoners were treated from 1880 to 1945. It also, for the first time, shows how the number of prisoners in Britain has risen and fallen spectacularly over a run of more than 100 years, as the prison system underwent first expansion, then, after World War I, significant contraction.

Conclusion

So, we have quite a list of things to look at, with each single issue appearing to be connected to a number of other contextualising issues, and all of them complex. This book does not answer all our questions about crime or criminality, and sometimes it only teases us by raising questions for researchers to look at for themselves. Nevertheless, it offers suggestions for how we can go about examining and exploring historical sources in a way which produces answers we are looking for and which, inevitably, will sometimes produce unexpected answers. I hope it will also entertain and enthuse readers sufficiently to find out for themselves more about a fascinating area of historical enquiry for one of the most important periods of history.

3

STATISTICS AND THE 'CAPTURING' OF CRIME ON PAPER

First of all, an apology:

> The chief defect in the old Police Tables, which were compiled from the annual returns made by 191 separate and independent police forces, has been due to the absence of sufficient instructions to secure their preparation on a uniform basis. So far as we have ascertained the figures have been prepared by the police with great care and some degree of accuracy, but on many points they have been left without guidance, and have proceeded some on one principal and others on another. However great the care bestowed on the individual returns, if they are prepared by many persons working on different rules, the results of their compilations must necessarily be unsatisfactory. It would often have been better that they should all be wrong, provided they made the same mistake, than that some should be right and others wrong.
>
> (*Introduction to the 1893 Judicial Statistics 1895: 20*)

Better that they were all wrong? How on earth had the gold standard for statisticians – the annually published judicial statistics, on nearly their fiftieth birthday, gone so badly wrong that the commissioners of the inquiry into judicial statistics could condemn them in such strong terms?

Judicial statistics, 1805–1892

In 1810 clerks of court were instructed to make annual returns relating to committals for trial, the number of executions, and some other information, for serious offences only (Radzinowicz 1948: 147). This picture of crime and punishment, described by a subsequent committee in 1819 as 'unparalleled in the history of criminal law' (Radzinowicz 1948: 544), was used to fuel debates surrounding the utility of capital punishment. Even in their first incantations, criminal statistics would be seized on by social commentators to argue their case. These figures for England and Wales reached back for the previous 5 years, so we now have more than 200 years of criminal statistics to ponder, although these early-nineteenth-century figures were fairly unsophisticated compared to the later attempts to record crime statistically. It was not only social statistics for England and Wales that interested the government.

In 1828, the Colonial Office received returns of the number of prisoners (amongst other institutional data on finances, trade, population, and so on) in each of the British colonies from 1824 onwards. In the colonies that hosted large convict institutions, there were large collections of unpublished data kept on the behaviour of convicts whilst in the system and whilst released on a conditional pardoning system, including the number of their subsequent reconvictions. As part of that general survey of the convict population, Van Diemen's Land (which later became Tasmania) and New South Wales collected data on the number of offences committed in their colonies. In 1836 it had been the plan that these, alongside all colonial statistics, would be published annually, but the costs were felt to be prohibitive and they remain largely unexamined in the National Archives in London.

Around the same time in the 1820s and 1830s, Adolphe Quetelet in Belgium and Andre-Michel Guerry in France pioneered statistical enquiry. Their figures were useful in both questioning existing explanations for crime and in offering a prospective analytical tool for estimating crime levels in coming years (Wetzell 2000: 21). Perhaps their greatest contribution was their belief that crime could be recorded, that it had a predictable quality based on a proper consideration of different contextual factors – in other words, crime didn't just appear, or erupt in society, nor was it an act of the gods – it had a cause, it reacted to societal conditions, and it was determined by the age/sex of offenders. It could be measured. Then it could be contained, and even eradicated perhaps. The work of Quetelet and Guerry became a model for similar enterprises in Sweden, Austria, some German states, and the United States (although uniform crime reports were only published there nearly 100 years later). It also encouraged the British to refine their statistical methods up to and beyond the mid-century, aided by methodological discussions between statisticians from various countries and jurisdictions at international conferences.

The first significant change in the 1830s was the organisation of the statistics into six categories. The criminal registrar, Samuel Redgrave, life member of the Statistical Society and author of *Some Account of the Powers, Authorities, and Duties of Her Majesty's Principal Secretary of State for the Home Department* (1852), established the six statistical offence categories. These were *offences against the person, offences against property involving violence, offences against property not involving violence, malicious offences against property, offences against currency*, and *miscellaneous offences*. Within the 'good order' category are the offences that one would expect – drunkenness (simple and disorderly), vagrancy, and public mischief. However, also included in this category by the statistical compilers were the offences of aggressive drunkenness; riot; threatening, insulting and abusive language; resisting or assaulting a police officer, and escaping from lawful custody – offences which might be expected to fit more

LIVERPOOL JOHN MOORES UNIVERSITY
LEARNING SERVICES

easily within the 'offences against the person' bracket. Nevertheless, the categorisation was virtually unchanged for decades (although names and definitions of the offences within those categories shifted considerably).

From 1856 annual statistics of committals, summary cases, and persons convicted and imprisoned were compiled locally by borough and county police officers and by various clerks to the Assize and Quarter Sessions courts, were recorded centrally, and were published annually. These statistics are all available online now at http://www.parliament.uk/business/publications/parliamentary-archives/archives-electronic/parliamentary-papers/. As the science of statistical collection developed, and as the governmental appetite grew for more and detailed data on the workings of the criminal justice system, the annually published statistics grew in size, sophistication, and stature. Their importance as indicators of societal progress and their importance as a foundation for the development of social and economic theory and policy were lionised (Lloyd-Baker 1860, Sellin 1951: 490). The near-100 pages of statistical tables provided in the main sections of police and constabulary, criminal proceedings, and prison statistics gave a mass of information on the number of arrests, the types of people arrested and charged by the police, details of how the courts dealt with offenders, and the punishments imposed, and a huge amount of other information (or what we would now call process – statistics on the workings of the criminal justice system). Widely welcomed for their rigour and apparent peerless accuracy about the state of crime they were almost as significant a device as were the railway system, the London underground, or other more-well-known Victorian inventions. However, confidence in this pillar of social enquiry and governance was to crumble away very dramatically in the 1890s.

The main problem identified by the 1892 Home Office Departmental Committee and their inquiry into the criminal statistics was in the collection strategies of the many police forces throughout England and Wales. However, this was not the only problem, and general inconsistency in reporting and accounting for the number of criminal offences, the number of criminals, and the general variability of collection methods seemed to completely undermine the annual statistics up to this point. Historians themselves find it hard to reconcile the pre- and post-1892 statistics. Even then, the post-1892 statistics leading up to World War II are not straightforward to analyse. There is, for example, the challenge posed by the constant redefining of criminal behaviour – acts which, in reality, were very similar whether they were committed in the 1850s or the 1920s could be entered in a number of different categories – and those categories themselves could disappear (drunkenness, for example, which was divided into 'simple drunkenness' and 'aggressive drunkenness') or be merged together. This constant shifting makes it difficult to chart long runs of crime, as does the introduction of new categories (of traffic offences, for example), which siphoned off offences which previously would have been recorded in another category. The major problem was the shortage of staff to collect statistics, and the shortage of resources needed to compile and publish annual statistics during the war years. Statistical registrar Edward Troup's introduction to the 1917 statistics simply said, 'The present volume has been prepared under the conditions arising out of the war, and, as in the preceding three volumes, it has been necessary to omit the usual Introduction and several of the tables'. Indeed, the 1917 statistics were only able to be published after the war had ended. For these reasons, it is difficult to fully account for the number of offences committed during World Wars I and II. Even if crime had fallen in the 1914 to 1918 period, as Emsley (2013) reveals, service personnel were still responsible for a lot of crime that took place abroad (and the repatriation of looted goods by British forces overseas is probably vastly under-recorded).[1] Nevertheless, the post-1892 statistics had a number of advantages over the pre-1892 series. In 1856 there were slightly more than 100 pages of tables, but in 1893, 23 new tables were added, and so was some clarity about the categorisation of offences which were now all clearly listed and defined. Second, they had now come up with a way of producing per capita figures for crime which is very useful, and also each year's report started with an 'Introduction' which outlined significant rises or falls in offending, with some speculation for the change, and, occasionally, an analysis of a particular offence. These enable us to gauge contemporary concerns, or at least understand the conceptual frameworks being employed by those whose job it was to explain crime trends. Moreover, if the statistics were being collected on a more rigorous and professional basis, it is possible that they indicated an accurate amount of prosecuted crime. Attempting to try to calculate the 'real' amount of crime would be a different matter. A large number of historians and criminologists have tried to explain the 'dark figure' of unprosecuted offending – there was a vast amount of behaviour, much of which could be classed as criminal if treated as such by victims and/or the police, which was never officially dealt with, and so never found its way into the annual statistics (see Godfrey, Lawrence, and Williams [2007] for a summary of these debates). Nevertheless, the changing amount of prosecuted crime as revealed by the 250 pages of statistical information (by 1914) might tell us something, possibly something quite significant, even if it's not 'how much crime was there' (see Chapter 4). We have to retain a critical perspective when reviewing this evidence, although we might struggle to be quite as dismissive as Lord Byng, Metropolitan Police commissioner in the late 1920s, was. When he noticed his secretary shuffling papers he asked, '"What have you got there?" he said. "More garbage?" (Garbage was his usual expression for official files.)' Being handed the paperwork, which was the 1928 annual report, he noted there was 'an awful lot of it' and, after skimming it, signed it (Howgrave-Graham 1947: 13). Well, anyway, let us first examine trends in prosecuted crime as revealed by the published statistics for the 1880–1940 period.

What do the judicial statistics tell us?

First there are the, and as far as I am aware these statistics are completely unchallenged, figures about the staffing levels of criminal justice institutions (the numbers of police are shown in Figure 3.1, for example). They also show the numbers of people apprehended by the police in every borough and county and the numbers of prisoners in local gaols, reformatories, convict prisons, and other places of

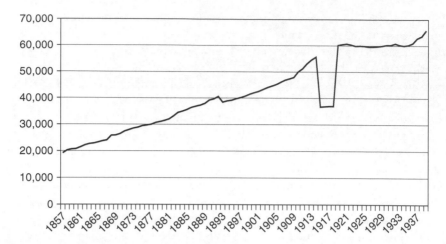

FIGURE 3.1 Numbers of police officers employed in England and Wales, 1857–1939 (figures from annually published judicial statistics)

incarceration; they tell us what sentences were imposed for different offences, the numbers of people dealt with by the different levels of judiciary, and the numbers of suicides, debtors, bankrupts, and general defaulters; they tell us the costs of the whole police, judicial, and prison system; and they do this for every year since 1856. They are a simply tremendous resource of statistical knowledge, of which this chapter can only touch the surface. Nevertheless, it is not the statistics listed previously which have attracted the attention of large numbers of historians and criminologists.

Figure 3.1 is a wonderful example of how statistical analysis can illustrate a point very simply and elegantly. During World War I, large numbers of police officers left the force to join up with the military forces, and the establishment found it difficult to find replacement recruits (even if it had the resources to do so). Can anyone doubt that, having seen the preceding figures? However, the statistics that were most pored over were those concerning the number of offences prosecuted year on year. Figure 3.2 shows the disjuncture between pre- and post-1892 statistics. It also shows the sharp rise in crimes prosecuted in the 1930s. That does not get us very far, however, because these figures contain details of serious indictable offences judged in the Quarter Sessions and Assize courts and the summary offences dealt with in local magistrates' courts.

Figure 3.3 shows that the minor offences dwarfed the number of indictable offences. The shift from pre- and post-1892 collection methods is evident in the sharp rise in apparent prosecutions between 1890 and 1895, which, in reality, has more to do with the way that police statistics were collected, than in a real rise in offending. What is more reliable perhaps is the similar doubling of prosecution of crime between 1895 and 1938. Prosecution rates seem to be pretty flat in the first decades of the twentieth century, but then rise in the late 1920s and 1930s to reach approximately 70,000 prosecutions by the start of World War II.

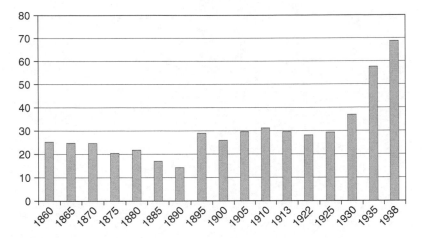

FIGURE 3.2   Total number of prosecutions, 1856–1940 (in thousands; figures from annually published judicial statistics)

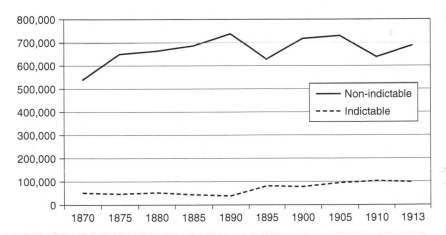

FIGURE 3.3   Indictable and non-indictable crime, 1870–1913 (figures from annually published judicial statistics)

Although this gives us some measure of how much crime in total was being prosecuted, it does not tell us much about the amount of serious or nonserious crime being dealt with, and even the statistics in Figure 3.3 only give us a very schematic picture based on which courts were busiest – the Quarter Sessions and Assize courts dealing with indictable crimes, or the magistrates courts working their way through the thousands of summary offences. However, we can further disaggregate these prosecution trends by examining the six categorisations of offending that the criminal statistics recorded. First let us look at the most serious offences – offences against the person which involved violence, possibly a great deal of violence or even murder.

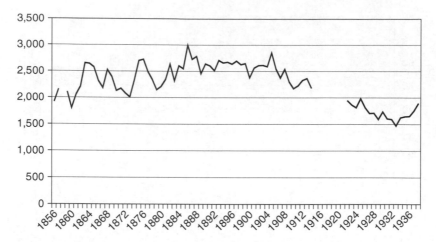

FIGURE 3.4 Category 1: offences against the person (figures from annually published judicial statistics)

There appeared to be a gratifying drop in serious offending until the very end of our period. From the highest number of prosecuted offences in the mid-1880s to the lowest number in 1930, there were about 2,000 serious attacks and assaults on victims per year across the whole period. Even the sharp upwards 'flip' in the statistics approaching World War II looks like a simple variation in the figures. By contrast the amount of 'serious offences against property involving violence' is heading in the opposite direction. Figure 3.5 shows that, with the understandable 'blip' during World War I, there was an alarming trend upwards. Perhaps the economic depression in the early 1930s caused an upsurge in property offending. As Figure 3.5

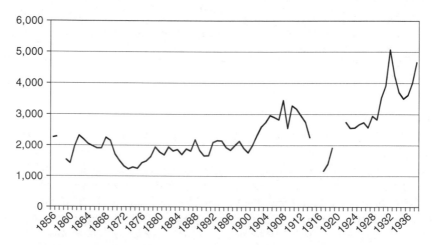

FIGURE 3.5 Category 2: offences against property involving violence (figures from annually published judicial statistics)

shows, similar to the statistics of violent crime, property offences involving violence are also around 2,000 a year until the start of the twentieth century. Again excepting that the figures for the World War I period are not reliable due to wartime shortages and the mobilisation of thousands of men in and out of the country, we have two peaks in property offending (with violence). The period preceding World War I, which was politically and economically turbulent, produces equally turbulent rises and falls in prosecutions. As can be seen in the graph (Figure 3.5), this is small beer compared to the sharp peaks and troughs of the 1930s.

We might expect the same trends to be evident in the statistics of property of-fending that did not include violence (e.g., the petty larcenies, thefts, acts of false pretences, and frauds which could be dealt with at either the higher or the lower courts). It appears, however, that these types of offences were on a profound down-ward trend from the start of our period to the end (Figure 3.6). Although they start at a much higher level than the prosecution figures for more serious property offences (at more than 10,000 a year until the 1880s), they then fell to around the same number of prosecuted offences as serious property crimes by the 1930s (the figures at the start the end of the war are dramatically different).

The final three categories of crime (Figures 3.7, 3.8, and Figure 3.9) contain a very diverse set of offences, from criminal damage to property, gambling, cruelty to animals, keeping shops or public houses open after legal hours, and so on. If we take the categories out of order, then we can see that the forgery and cur-rency offences (Figure 3.7) appear to follow a similar trend to minor property crime (Figure 3.6). This is unsurprising because these two categories both contained of-fences of dishonesty – most probably the kinds of offenders who made up these categories left their lodgings without paying (false pretences), passed off false promis-sory notes (fraud), and stole groceries or small objects on their travels (simple larceny).

FIGURE 3.6 Category 3: offences against property not involving violence (figures from annually published judicial statistics)

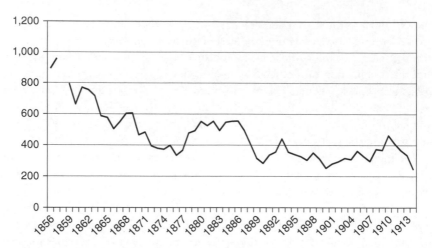

FIGURE 3.7 Category 5: forgery and currency offences (figures from annually published judicial statistics)

The volatility in prosecution numbers for Category 5 (forgery, currency offences, coining) and Category 4 (setting fires, arson, putting smashed glass on the highway) are perhaps inevitable because they are very small and contain a vastly diverse set of individual offences. Category 6 is really just the 'box' for crimes which do not fit into any other category, despite there being some apparently discernible trends. Figure 3.8 shows malicious offences against property rising until World War I, then falling to much lower levels afterwards, and Figure 3.9 shows a similar pattern; these trends are unlikely to say anything meaningful about the direction in which crime rates were moving.

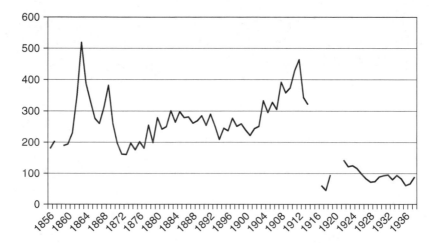

FIGURE 3.8 Category 4: malicious offences against property (figures from annually published judicial statistics)

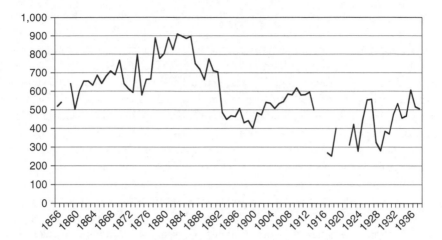

FIGURE 3.9   Category 6: miscellaneous offences (game laws, perjury, riots; figures from annually published judicial statistics)

Well, this is all a bit confusing isn't it? If we look at Figure 3.4 it looks as though the streets of England and Wales were bestrewn with murdered corpses. Yet, if we consider one of the offences contained in Category 1 (murder), there were only about 300 to 400 murders a year on average between 1880 and 1940. Murder and other serious offences were all dominated by burglary statistics, as Figure 3.10 shows, and therefore, Category 1 (offences against the person) is similarly distorted.

There are other conundrums to consider. For example, there is a huge up-surge in Category 2 'property offending involving violence' in the 1930s, but

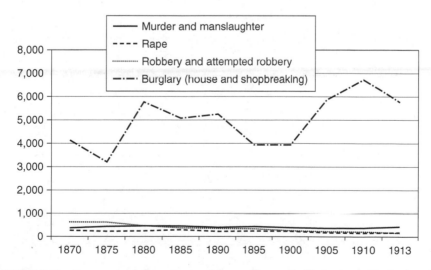

FIGURE 3.10   Prosecutions for serious violent offences in Category 1, England and Wales, 1870–1914 (figures from annually published judicial statistics)

Category 3 'property offences not involving violence' are down in that period? If we associate the rise in Category 2 with the economic depression – and that would seem a reasonable common-sense assumption (more poverty equals more property crime) – why does that not hold up for the property offences not involving violence? The other categories are not that much better. Let us discount Categories 4, 5 and 6; they all deal with offences which do not altogether have much in common with each other – and even if they were added together, the offences in these final three categories do not amount to more than 3,000 offences per year at their highest (and 550 at their lowest). Broken into individual offences, they would only amount to a few tens of cases each year for each of the constituent offences. So, even the supposedly refined statistics, presented within categories, can only provide us with a misleading picture of how much crime there is in any particular year or period. Would it be better to look at the trends for offences that fit into one of the first three categories of crime? Offences of minor violence and drunkenness numbered hundreds or even thousands each year on their own account. Would an analysis of these kinds of volume crime help us to form a more sophisticated view of 'what' and 'how much' was being prosecuted each year?

Prosecutions for drunkenness and assaults mirrored trends until the 1870s when they diverged noticeably (see Figure 3.11). Assaults declined steadily until World War II whilst prosecutions for drunkenness climbed steadily to reach just less than 200,000 prosecutions in 1883. There was then some variability in the numbers until they peaked at 230,000 in 1902. The fall in prosecutions was steep after World War I, and in 1931 the figures of drunkenness and assault were once again within touching distance of each other. These look to be a more rigorous and reliable set of statistics than some of the category statistics previously discussed. They would strongly support a view that England and Wales had witnessed the conquest of violence and,

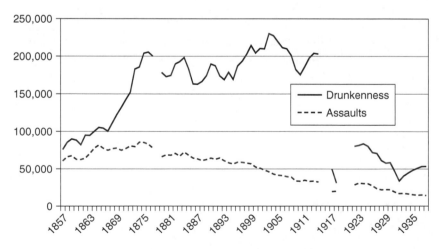

FIGURE 3.11   Prosecutions for drunkenness and assaults, England and Wales, 1856–1938 (figures from annually published judicial statistics)

a little later and much more suddenly, had also seen drunkenness defeated too. Not a bad result, if it was true.

Conclusion

Had the English and Welsh managed to pull off a miracle that eluded other countries? The official statistics suggest so – assaults declined, and drunkenness rose to the 1880s and 1890s, then fell dramatically after World War I and never regained anywhere near the level it had been a few decades earlier. In the following two chapters we explore whether the statistics of prosecuted violence and disorder tell us the whole story. We have already established that, even after 1892, there are some real problems in interpreting and understanding what the annually published official statistics are telling us. We have seen contradictory trends in property crime, and we have seen statistical evidence of a steady fall in violence (without, of course, any other evidence as yet to explain why that would be), and a dramatic (one might say amazing) fall in drunkenness. Yet this is the only evidence we have so far considered. We do not want to dismiss it out of hand, for clearly there is a huge amount of data to be considered from a very large number of statistical tables – one might call it a blizzard of information – but we also have to acknowledge that the statistics have been filtered through a lot of criminal justice institutions which may have reasons to 'finesse' or 'skew' the statistics for their own purposes. Are these figures reliable? Are these figures purporting to show more than just the numbers of cases going through the courts? At this point we still have some nagging questions about validity and meaning that, perhaps, the following chapter can begin to answer.

4

FROM POLICEMAN STATE
TO REGULATORY CONTROL

The previous chapter suggested that the judicial statistics may not be a straight-forward guide to levels of crime, given the problems of different data collection methods in the pre- and post-1892 statistics. This chapter may give us other reasons to doubt official statistics and to look around for more reliable sources we can use to chart changes in offending. For the moment though, we have seen that statistics presented in the last chapter demonstrated an apparent decline in violence from the late Victorian period to World War I (see Figure 3.11). Drunkenness (simple, aggravated, and drunk and disorderliness) very appropriately had a more staggered decline from the start of World War I. Whereas violence had been in retreat from 1875, drunkenness only fell from the start of the twentieth century, after a signifi-cant rise in prosecutions for drunkenness from the 1850s. Nevertheless, the amount of violence and disorder at the start of World War I was only a fraction of what it had been twenty years earlier. This was taken as evidence by penal, medical, and criminological experts that only a small residuum of persistent offenders remained to be reformed or to be controlled by the police.

In this chapter, we first examine the theories that have been brought forward to explain the statistical fall in prosecutions for violence and disorder, asking questions such as what would cause such a decline at this time, was it the dominance of the police that deterred offending, or was it some transformation in society's attitudes towards masculinity that brought about greater self-control? Of course, these ques-tions assume, as many historians have done, that the statistics mirror a real fall in of-fending. What if they do not? What other changes in police and prosecution policy and practice could explain the statistics? The chapter looks at the 'English miracle' of low crime rates and the increasing capacity of publicly funded police services to influence crime levels. In particular, we focus on how and why the police emerged as the main prosecuting agency in court during this period and on how that change affected the numbers of prosecutions for violence and drunkenness.

From an examination of the theories that the 'Policeman State' produced lower crime rates, we then move to the rise of the 'Regulatory State' and examine the rise in prosecutions for breeching a raft of new regulatory offences in the twentieth century. Again we look at the part that prosecutors played in driving the statistics of certain offences up and down. What are the connections between the decline in prosecuted disorder and violence and the rise in motoring offences? How and when did traffic offences, infringements of retail law, and breeches of the education acts come to fill the courts with offenders by the 1940s? Which prosecuting agencies drove up the numbers of regulatory offences dealt with by the courts after World War I? In the light of our investigations into these issues, the chapter questions the validity of judicial statistics as indicators of real levels of crime and suggests that they are better viewed as indicators of changes in the policies and practices of various agencies and of individual prosecutors. Last, it asks where we can turn to find more reliable indices of crime and attitudes towards criminality in the 1880–1940 period.

The conquest of violence and disorder, 1880–1940

The numbers of people prosecuted for minor violence (common assaults) showed that rates of assault in England and Wales were approximately 33 offences per 10,000 persons in 1871. By the turn of the century they had halved (16.1 per 10,000 persons), and by 1931 they had fallen to just 5.6 assaults per 10,000 population (see Figure 4.1).

On the face of it, a person's chances of becoming a victim of violent assault had reduced considerably during this sixty-year period. During this period, assaults against the police (see Figure 4.2), which most contemporary and modern commentators associated with disorder but which today we view as offences of

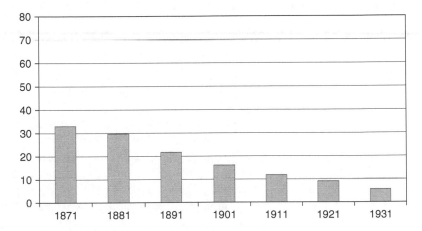

FIGURE 4.1 Prosecutions for assaults, England and Wales, per 10,000 persons, 1871–1931 (figures from annually published judicial statistics)

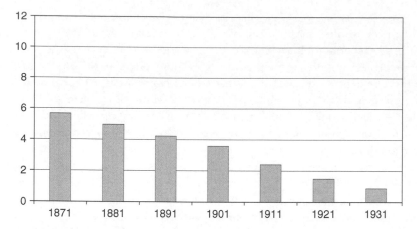

FIGURE 4.2 Prosecutions for assaults on police officers, England and Wales, per 10,000 persons, 1871–1931 (figures from annually published judicial statistics)

violence, also fell (Figure 4.2). The decline was less sharp here, but was still notable. In 1871 there were 5.6 assaults on police officers per 10,000 persons. By 1901 there had been a fall to 3.6 per 10,000 persons, and thereafter, the rate fell more steeply, to fewer than 1 assault per 10,000 persons in 1931.

When it came to disorder, again as we have seen in the last chapter, prosecutions for drunkenness increased in 1881 in England and Wales (see Figure 3.11). Controlling drunkenness also formed the main part of policing in the regional cities. C. Williams (2000) reported that more than half of arrests in Sheffield between 1844 and 1855 were for disorder, chiefly related to drunkenness. There were approximately 75 offences per 10,000 persons in that year, and the rates stayed fairly high until 1901. After World War I, they halved to a rate of approximately 30 prosecutions per 10,000 persons in 1921, and fell to approximately 15 prosecutions per 10,000 persons by 1931 (see Figure 4.3)

Although not violent, but certainly associated with disorderliness, offences of malicious or criminal damage also followed the, by now, predictable decline in prosecutions. The rates for criminal damage halved between 1871 and 1901 (from 10 to 5.3 prosecutions per 10,000 persons). By 1931 they had fallen to 3.1 offences per 10,000 persons (as Figure 4.4 shows).

This profound decline in violence and disorder was lauded as the 'English miracle'. Whereas Continental Europe required an armed police force to keep order, and the United States were roamed by bands of lawless cowboys (at least in the public imagination), the English and Welsh had quietly conquered violence. The police were mainly unarmed, it seems largely supported by society, and together with the courts and the prisons, they appeared to have successfully pacified Britain's streets.

Taking the judicial statistics to be evidence of a real decline in violence and disorder during this period, crime history researchers have tried to explain this change

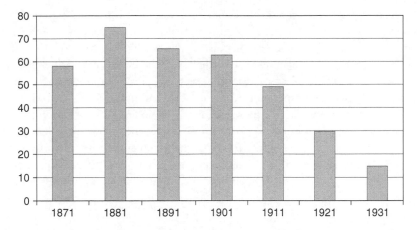

FIGURE 4.3 Prosecutions for drunkenness, England and Wales, per 10,000 persons, 1871–1931 (figures from annually published judicial statistics)

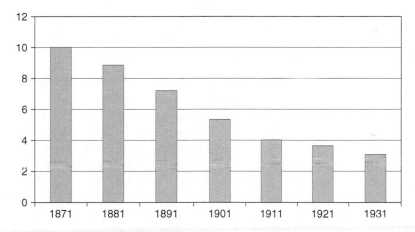

FIGURE 4.4 Prosecutions for criminal damage, England and Wales, 1871–1931 (figures from annually published judicial statistics)

in offending behaviour (Critchley 1967, 1970; Gatrell 1992; Gurr 1981; Johnson and Monkkonen 1996; Sharpe 1989; Taylor 2012). Summarizing their research, they credit both the economic cycle as well as the criminal justice institutions in bringing about the miracle, or more correctly, in providing the socioeconomic conditions whereby people had less need to commit crime and more reason to believe they would be caught and punished if they did. The short-term, bitter downward fluctuations in trade that had beleaguered the 1840s had receded, and there was a general upwards progression in wages and wealth. These conditions allowed the working classes to ride out personal misfortunes without causing the kind of crisis that pushed them into committing crime. By the 1880s those people who, for whatever reason, could not resist the temptation to steal or rob, could expect a more professional and efficient police force to apprehend them (so the theory goes). This seems to be a more credible explanation for the decline in property crime than it is for violence or drunkenness. Nevertheless, Gatrell's (1992) arguments that a policeman state was inculcated during the second half of the nineteenth century, where the agents of control enforced middle-class cultural norms, has been taken by many as an explanation for the statistical fall in violence. Others have gone on to emphasise a more cultural explanation for the decline and suggest that society was in various ways progressively 'civilized' in the nineteenth century (Carter Wood 2004; Eisner 2001; Johnson and Monkkonen 1996; Pratt, 1997, 2002). For Spierenburg (1998) and Wiener (2004), men bore the brunt of civilising processes aimed at curbing their aggression. By the 1880s, respectable men were expected to solve disputes through reasoned argument, or through solicitors, and not by using their fists. Our unfortunate convict, Patrick Madden, (see Chapter 1) would, of course, have failed to live up to new conceptions of masculinity and, like many others, would have been considered to be a 'working-class rough' who could not adhere to the new rules for men. Men such as Madden must have been a dying breed if the statistics can be believed.

Could the statistics be wrong?

Many historians have now outlined the severe limitations of both the national and local series of criminal statistics (Morris 2000; Weaver 1995; C. Williams 2000; and also see Maguire [2002] for a review of debates by criminologists). Even contemporaries were aware of their inaccuracies – however, they did not doubt that they captured the total amount of all criminal offending in their figures, at least until the early 1890s. Is it possible that the statistics hide a dark figure of unprosecuted crimes? Sources such as oral history interviews (which are discussed much more thoroughly in the following chapter) indicate that very many acts of disorder or aggression could have been prosecuted if they had been reported to the police, and had the police decided to take the matter forward, but they never troubled the courts. For example, one oral history interviewee looked back to an episode which could well have ended up in a charge of manslaughter or even murder had a doctor decided differently:

> There was this other girl. I was still at school [between 1900–1913] and she was a schoolgirl too. I don't know, she must have been older than I was and she was telling us. She looked sick and we were asking what was the matter and she said her sister – she was pregnant – and her sister had put a hatpin up her and it caused her terrible pain . . . and she died. She had septicemia and the doctor said he could put the sister in jail but he said that he thought she had suffered enough. He was like that. He was nice, but he couldn't do much about it. The girl was dead.
>
> (EG, Bicentennial Oral History Project,
> NSW State Library, tape 56)

Indeed, study of the oral histories held in various archives throughout Britain suggests that thousands of acts of violence that took place each year between 1880 and 1940 went unprosecuted, and therefore never found their way into the judicial statistics. Thinking back to Patrick Madden again, would it be surprising if the acts which landed him in court were not the only acts of violence, the only threats, the only fights that he committed during his lifetime? It seems very clear that the judicial statistics measure the amount of crime which was prosecuted, whilst leaving the vast amount of behaviour which *could* have been prosecuted as an unknown.

Currently, there have been so many queries raised about the judicial statistics' capacity to be able to record all crime that few criminologists and historians take them at face value. As Hudson stated, 'It is notoriously difficult to interpret criminal statistics because they are affected as much by changing definitions of crime, overlapping jurisdictions of courts, moral panics, and changes in the willingness to bring prosecutions [rather than settle affairs outside court] as a reflection of "crime" itself' (1992: 206). Given that there were reasons to report property crime (in an attempt to get the stolen property returned or, in the 1930s and 1940s, to claim insurance to cover the loss), it may be that violent offences suffer the largest undercount in the judicial statistics. Some are now convinced that the apparent decline in violence and disorder is an artefact only of changing prosecution policies, rather than a real fall in offending. Partly it was the suddenness of the decline that provokes some doubts:

> It has yet to be shown, however, how the forces of civilization could have created such a precipitous drop in prosecutions in the 1880–1920 period (a fall of 87.5% over 40 years). Was there really such an accelerated civilization of society in a period that witnessed considerable bouts of violent industrial and political upheaval, and the bloodiest of world wars? Indeed, although there is much to support the theory that society progressively over the eighteenth- and nineteenth-centuries adopted common 'civilized' values, and that civilization can 'throw-up' episodes of tremendous barbarism, did the public really stop hitting each other so abruptly and to that extent? It is the 'cliff face' decline of violence prosecutions that makes them so suspicious. The national and local statistics are simply not credible as a mirror of a real decline in violence. . . . Nor are the per capita national rates the only problem. In absolute numbers the figures for some towns are unbelievably small. In 1900 there were only thirty-three common assaults proceeded with in Exeter (a busy thriving port); thirteen in Crewe (a growing industrial area) and eight in Durham (a mining town with a reputation for masculine violence). In Shrewsbury (a busy populated regional capital) there were only *three* common assaults in 1910, and those figures are not unrepresentative of the situation in many towns and cities in England.
>
> (*Godfrey 2003a: 352*)

Taking a realistic rather than a 'realist' view, we can agree that, whatever their deficiencies, the judicial statistics tell us how many people were prosecuted and for what offences in any given year between 1856 and 1940 (and well after that date actually). If we could identify and isolate every change in the inclination of victims to report crime, and the police to prosecute it, we might get closer to a real figure for crime in this period (see C. Williams 2000: 78).

If the statistics *are* inaccurate, how can we explain the prosecution trends?

If the statistics did not mirror a real fall in offending, what other theories explain why the figures fell? The following sections explore a number of competing theories which explain prosecution trends for violence and disorder, starting with theories developed by the most sceptical of commentators. A decade or so ago Howard Taylor published some powerful articles alleging that financial pressures in the late nineteenth and early twentieth centuries acted to reduce the murder rate, and indeed the rates of all serious crimes (Taylor 1998a, 1998b; but see Morris 2001). Taking aim at the 'gold standard' of judicial figures – the homicide rates – Taylor (1998a) suggested that, whenever possible, suspicious deaths would be treated as suicide rather than homicide or the deaths were to be attributed to natural causes. Certainly some of the entries in a local policeman's diary in the 1930s suggest a rather cavalier attitude towards investigating sudden deaths:

> Thursday 25th October 1934. Reported that Mrs Mary Swinnerton, aged 65, collapsed and died in Market Square as the result of blood pressure (no inquest necessary) . . .

> Sunday 4th August 1938. Recovery of the body of a woman from the canal under Seller st Bridge. She was 35 years old, reported missing from her home at Wrexham (Inquest, 'found drowned').[1]
>
> (*Diary of Albert Edward Wilcock, PC 39,*
> *Chester City Police Force*)

That kind of approach would have helped to meet any budgetary constraints imposed by national and local government since it would have obviated the need for a lengthy (and therefore costly) police investigation. However, a number of challenges could be made to Taylor's theories of the managerial 'massaging down' of violence statistics. First, homicide is not a volume crime, and the small numbers of murders are not as reliable as the larger volumes – such as assault figures – would be. The very fact that homicide was so serious and was therefore very likely to be reported – which is what made them the gold standard in the first place – meant that murders were less susceptible to any police interference. The route to prosecution for other crimes, such as assault or drunkenness, was much more open to the police ignoring or downplaying the offence. Second, there is little evidence from Home Office records of any budget-setting process which controlled the number of crimes which could be investigated or prosecuted. If this accounting process actually existed, surely there would be some evidence from government committees that would have come to light (even though Home Office files are an under-investigated source of information). After all, a centralised system would need to be embedded locally, and we have no evidence of a stream of communication from the Home Office or even from the local chief constables to local police stations requesting restraint in the scope of their investigations and prosecutions. Quite frankly, 'bobbies' would have needed detailed orders and instructions as to how they would go about this. Third, is it not more likely that there was an invisible mechanism at work, one which relied on police culture to sort out some offences and offenders into the category of 'worth pursuing' and others into 'nonsense cases' that were not worth dealing with?

Did police officers sort out the wheat from the chaff?

Initiating a prosecution could be expensive, and this excluded many people from pursuing justice, and others (female victims of domestic violence, for example) faced similar obstructions to obtaining satisfaction in the courts (Clark 1987; D'Cruze 1998; Emsley 2010: 193–195; Hay and Snyder 1989; Ross 1982; Tomes 1978). Nevertheless, until the 1880s, this was still a victim-led criminal justice system, with individuals taking out summons to compel defendants to face the courts. If the experiences of one north-western industrial town, Crewe, can be taken as a general guide to what was happening across England and Wales, victims initiated approximately eight of every ten prosecutions undertaken in 1880 (Devlin 1960; Lidstone *et al.* 1980; Sigler 1974). However, by the end of World War I, eight out of every ten prosecutions were initiated by the police, not by the victims themselves. How and why had the route to prosecution been so radically altered during this forty-year period?

Victims always had three possible routes to justice. Complainants could obtain a summons from a magistrate and prosecute a case themselves; they could report the matter directly to the police and hope that they would investigate the case and arrest the offender, and thereafter, the victim could continue to prosecute the case themselves. More wealthy complainants could also then secure the services of a solicitor to act on their behalf. Last, and this is clearly what had become the dominant system by 1914, the complainant could act as a witness in his or her own case with a police prosecutor asking the questions, examining witnesses, and presenting the prosecution case. A central aspect of the new Policeman State had been their increasing willingness to act as prosecutors in court from the 1880s. This would have allowed the police to assume a critical role in advancing some cases to court, but letting others fall by the wayside. In this way they could exert the powerful influence over recorded crime that Emsley (2007: 272; 2010: 195) remarked on and Taylor (1999: 580) noted:

> As the police gained a more central place in the prosecution process they were able to screen most reports of crime and largely determine the numbers and range of offenders and offences that were prosecuted – and cap them

within the limits of their resources. They could advise private prosecutors against taking action, or else undertake the prosecution themselves, even acting as unpaid advocates in court, possibly saving the authority the higher costs that would have to be paid out for a private prosecution. In the majority of cases they were able to decide (or at least exert a strong influence over potential prosecutors): (i) whether or not to prosecute; (ii) how serious was the charge preferred, and hence (a) whether the case would be heard cheaply in a police court and (b) the likely cost of punishment; (iii) the amount, if any, of legal expenses incurred; (iv) the number of expensive witnesses called . . . Ultimately resources, both financial and manpower, exerted a decisive influence over prosecutions.

Still doubt remains that police officers altered their behaviour on some cost/ benefit calculation. There does not appear to be much documentary evidence to support Taylor's theories that the police officers on the beat had been told the number of offences they could afford to pursue and screened offences accordingly. However, the mechanisms for ignoring or pursuing crime for other reasons would be the same as they would be in Taylor's hypothesis. Police officers could arrest people (if they saw an offence taking place or found sufficient forensic evidence). Or by using their discretion, they could choose not to arrest someone (because the evidence might not secure a conviction, because they liked or feared the person they could arrest, because they could derive some informal benefit or bribe not to, because they could not be bothered). Really there were an endless number of reasons that could ensure that a person was not arrested. If the offence, say, an assault, was not witnessed by the officer and was only reported to them, they could request the complainant to take out a summons or advise him or her not to (as they may well have done for domestic violence cases, for example, and indeed constabulary occurrence books are full of such cases, see Godfrey and Lawrence 2005:100–101). Again, it was mainly in the police officer's hands to push a case or to inhibit its progress, and thereby lower the number of prosecutions. The police also had the power to arrest people they thought deserved to be taken off the streets or punished. These people were likely to be repeat offenders, or otherwise known to the police; to be abusive or troublesome (or drunk) at the time, or to come from a class or area of town that the police officer involved considered disreputable. The police were clearly tolerant of some kinds of male violence in the home, and did not always leap into action when men indulged in 'fair fights' that were kept within limits (in the backstreets, were not too violent, and did not involving weapons). So, it may be that police-cultural factors such as these did reduce the number of prosecutions for minor violence (Emsley 2010; Taylor 2002; Weaver 1995). However, the same discretion exercised by police officers could also push some types of crime, drunken disorder for example, upwards rather than downwards.

Driving drunkenness

As the previous chapter showed, in England and Wales, public order offences rose particularly between 1890 and World War I as the police attempted to control public space and curb public drunkenness. There were, of course, no individual complainants to pursue drunks, and it was always the case that the police were the main prosecutors of this kind of offence. It was a victimless crime, but the police stepped in to protect a notional community from the excesses of drunken men:

> Chesterfield seems to possess the unenviable distinction of being the most drunken of any town under 25,000 population. At least so I gather from certain tables . . . It is, however, only fair to remember that the borough of Chesterfield occupies a somewhat exceptional position, possessing but a small area and population, and yet forming a market centre for a very wide district. As a matter of fact nearly three-fourths of the convictions for drunkenness are those of outsiders.
> (*The Derbyshire Courier, 6 June 1891*)

On the same day, the good people of Tynemouth explained that their status, as second-most drunken town, was solely due to the number of holidaymakers to South Shields. No doubt wanting to keep the seaside trade but lose the reputation, one person suggested the following:

> I do not mean to say one word in favour of persons taking drink – it would be much better if there were no drink to take – but I think that, if a person, though a little unsteady, was allowed to go home, so long as he was quiet, the number of 'convictions' recorded against Tynemouth might be less than it is.
> (*Essex Standard, West Suffolk Gazette, and*
> *Eastern Counties' Advertiser, 6 June 1891*)

The suspicion must be that it was the people who did not go home quietly, or who were from outside the area, who were first people to go in the police officer's notebook. Many of the modest and unproblematic tipsters from the locality may well have been allowed to weave their way home. The policing of disorder was open to as many discretionary practices as the policing of violence, maybe more so because there was no real victim to take the case to court if the police refused to do so. Changes in legislation between 1914 and 1918 designed to curb drunkenness and to keep the population sober and productive during wartime may well have reduced the opportunities for public drinking. The original restrictions on drinking spirits and heavy beers in the munitions districts in 1915 were seen to have had an immediate impact on public drinking (Rose 1973). The Central Control Board for the Liquor Traffic congratulated itself on reducing drinking by women, and, in fact, they were aided in this by the Women's Foot Patrols (who were volunteers) and

Women's Police (see Jackson 2006). They may have had some justification for the Medical Officer of Health for Liverpool reported to the Board that there was 'much less rough disorder and rowdyism . . . The practice of gangs of men congregating in public houses, which used to be a common feature the whole day through, is much less frequent' (Report of the Medical Officer for Health, Liverpool, to Mr Saunders of the Board, 26 August 1915, quoted in Waites 1987: 165).

Hard drinking and public drunkenness seemed to be less visible after World War I, and, similar to the decline in violence, it is likely that changing concepts of masculinity helped men to take responsibility for their actions and to exercise more self-control. However, although levels of drunkenness probably reflected more sober times and the judicial statistics reflected a real fall in rowdy drunkenness, we should not be in too much of a hurry to attribute this to civilising processes. Anyone strolling down a British High Street on a Friday or Saturday night today will attest to the fact that drunkenness was not eradicated in the 1910s and 1920s.

The motoring underclass

It does appear, however, that the police walked away from drunkenness with a new set of policing priorities in mind from the end of World War I. This was a period when motor cars became emblematic of the new motorised modernity. Around the turn of the century it appears that the police grew as concerned with mobility in public space as much as or even more so than unruly behaviour in public areas (Emsley 1993; Godfrey et al. 2007: 53; Taylor 1999). A sign of wealth in the 1920s, possession of motor cars became more widespread in the 1930s. Annual car production grew from only 25,000 in 1919 to 341,000 in 1938. What tends to be forgotten is that the roads were also populated by bicycles, motorbikes, and motor lorries delivering goods long before World War II – so although associated with the middle class, the motoring public was actually a little more heterogeneous than we might assume.[2] As can be seen in Figure 4.5, there appeared to be a significant change in the focus of police action towards motoring offences – indeed they were forced to address motoring offences because of the tremendous rise in accidents involving cars in the 1930s. In 1934 the highest-ever numbers of road casualties – 7,343 deaths and 231,603 injuries – was recorded. The police prosecution of all kinds of driving behaviour or breach of vehicle regulations (furious or dangerous driving, driving with undue care and attention, speeding, ignoring traffic signs, defective or no lights, and the number plate or road licence not properly displayed) overtake drunkenness prosecutions around the end of World War I and by the beginning of the 1930s occupied a huge amount of police time.

In 1900, six years after the first vehicle appeared on the road, transgressions of the law constituted just four cases in a thousand convicted in magistrates' courts in England and Wales. By 1930, with a little more than 2 million vehicles on the road, they accounted for 43 per cent of all non-indictable offences (Briggs et al. 1996: 207). Indeed, by the 1930s, traffic offences had become the common currency of

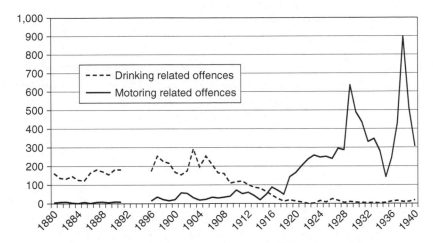

FIGURE 4.5 Prosecutions for drunkenness and motoring related offences, Crewe, 1880–1940 (figures from annually published judicial statistics)

beat policing. The diary of Albert Edward Wilcock (PC 39, Chester City Police Force) had the following consecutive entries on the first page:

> 25th May. Reported accident between a motor car driven by . . .
> 7th June. Reported accident between a motor car driven by . . .
> 19th June. Reported a motor car XM3616 standing unattended without lights . . .
> 21st June. Reported the following [3 names] for insulting behaviour in Bridge St Row (each bound over).
> 2nd July. Reported Richard Harris for causing obstruction with his car . . . (fine 10s).
> 6th July. Reported Harry Redfern for obstructing Werbergh St with car (fine 20s).
> 9th July. Reported Arthur Bourne for obstructing Eastgate St with car (fined 30s).
> 11th July. I arrested Mrs Lily Williams for stealing a box of woodbine cigarettes from shop, 42 Foregate St, Chester at 8pm (fined 40s and 5s costs).

In fact, the very first act of disorder or violence that Constable Wilcock took to court was almost exactly a year after he had started work on the streets of Chester, and even then, it would appear that the defendant was the author of his or her own misfortune, otherwise he or she may well have been cautioned rather than prosecuted:

> I arrested Edward McGrail aged 47 (no fixed address) for being drunk and disorderly in Foregate St and also for assaulting me. He was practically undressed and when I tried to reason with him he used obscene language and

knocked my helmet off, kicked my shins, and bit my arm (he was sentenced 14 days HL for D & D and 1 mth HL for assault).

It is often assumed that motoring was the middle-class crime in this period. However, although many motoring violations were technical offences, insofar as discretion could not easily be applied – speeding, for example – it was probably still the case that working-class drivers were more vulnerable to prosecution:

> Saturday 6th August. A car driven by Vincent Aloysius Walker aged 28 years, skidded and turned completely over and somersaulted over a hedge into a field [both were taken to the Royal Infirmary as they were] injured but at the same time under the influence of drink. They were of very low class and on several occasions I found it necessary to caution Walker for his conduct at the Royal Infirmary. I eventually arrested both and took them to HQ where a charge of 'driving under the influence of drink' was refused by the Police Surgeon. Walker was very aggressive and several times threatened to 'do me in'. I summoned him for [not having insurance and road tax, for which he was fined] and Walker was described as 'a menace on the road'.
>
> (*Diary of Albert Edward Wilcock, PC 39, Chester City Police Force*)

Because the newspaper reports of motoring offences were usually brief, it is hard to determine which strata of society the defendants were drawn from. In all likelihood, however, working-class and younger motorists were probably disproportionately represented, although the number of people prosecuted suggests that the policing of motoring cast so wide a net that middle-class and even upper-class offenders were caught up in it. Indeed, when World War II broke out in 1939, there were hundreds of thousands of motoring cases being brought before the magistrates' courts (Briggs *et al*. 1996: 207).

The new agencies of control

Britain's economic success in the late Victorian and Edwardian period relied on laissez-faire economic policies and liberalising markets, but the market struggled to solve social problems. The liberal sensibilities that emerged in the late nineteenth and early twentieth centuries were fundamentally wedded to the identification and amelioration of diverse social problems (De Groot 1996: 141). The government and local civil societies were implicitly paternalistic and explicitly interventionist, and they turned to directive legislation and social regulation to alleviate poverty and deprivation (see Emsley 1993: 366). A raft of new offences were introduced to support social welfare from promoting universal education and suffrage to preventing cruelty to animals and public drunkenness, to the provision of sewers, and to improving the moral and spiritual welfare of the urban poor (Crossick, 1977; Kidd and Nicholls, 1999). National legislation and local by-laws were enforced not only by the police but also through the actions of market inspectors, nuisance inspectors, rates and truancy inspectors, and other appointees of the town clerk, all working on behalf of the community (or a section of it). For example, Mr Docherty, a basket weaver working at home, was prosecuted for the fifth time for not sending his seven- and eleven-year-old boys to school. The tone of the case can be seen in the newspaper report from 1880: 'Do you know anything about the man's habits – whether he drinks or not?' The witness replied he did not think the man was addicted to drink, but he thought he sometimes took the boys out bird-catching [another regulatory offence] and the daughter thought that the children were beyond the father's control, but this did not wash with the magistrate:

> What your daughter has said about the boys going out every morning and not coming home till night seems to indicate that you were not anxious about whether they went to school or not . . . you have been several times warned, but you still took no trouble to put them to school. Now, although one of the boys is to be taken care of in future [by being removed from the family home to an industrial school], that is no reason why I should not impose some punishment on you, not so much for your own sake as that other people may be deterred from doing the same thing in future, and to show that parties who neglect the education of their children are liable to be punished for it. As you have already been punished for the same offence it would be useless to impose a fine again. The sentence upon you is fourteen days' imprisonment.
>
> (*'PROSECUTION UNDER THE EDUCATION ACT'*,
> *Dundee Courier & Argus, 16 October 1880*)

Not all of these prosecutions were advanced by public bodies. As the nineteenth century ended, a number of private agencies also sought to regulate economic and social activity.

The Society for the Prevention of Cruelty to Animals (later 'Royal') had been formed earlier in the nineteenth century (1824) but established local and regional offices in the 1870s. This society was joined by a plethora of private charitable agencies in the 1880s and 1890s: The Royal Society for the Protection of Birds, the Society for the Prosecution of Offences Against Women and Children, and the very active prosecutorial agency, the National Society for the Prevention of Cruelty to Children (the Liverpool Society for the Prevention of Cruelty to Children was established in 1883, the London Society followed a year later, and the National Society was established in 1889).[3] Almost as soon as the act was passed, the National Society for the Prevention of Cruelty to Children (NSPCC) was keen to prosecute and to have newspapers report their activities.[4] The energy of these bodies massively inflated the rate of 'regulatory' offences being heard by the courts, and they came to form the main business of the courts over the 1880–1940 period as the figures for Crewe demonstrate in Figure 4.6.

In England and Wales, the numbers of people prosecuted for not sending their children to school grew from 21,386 to 76,173 between 1875 and 1885 and

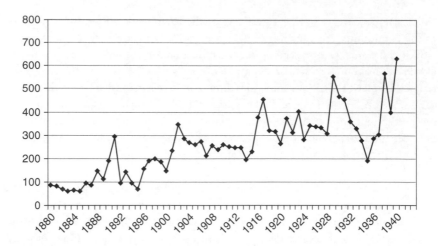

FIGURE 4.6   Regulatory offences, Crewe, 1880–1940 (figures from annually published judicial statistics)

contemporaries estimated that half a million parents were prosecuted in the twenty years following the passage of the 1870 Education Act for failure to send their children to school (Emsley 1993: 360):

> If one adds together the people prosecuted for not sending children to school or to be vaccinated; having a chimney fire or unsanitary drains; riding a bicycle without lights or a bell; selling unsound meat or margarine disguised as butter; or buying scrap metal without proper documents; leaving curtains open during an air-raid; or not paying local authority rates, the numbers are considerable – over eighteen thousand prosecutions just in Crewe.
>
> (*Godfrey, Cox and Farrall 2007: 23*)

Both the capillary growth of regulation through areas of retail, health, welfare, and leisure activity, and the activities of public and private enforcement and prosecution agencies are relatively under-researched. We should also find out more about the people on whom the regulatory gaze fell. Those charged with regulatory offences might not be considered to be '"criminals" in the accepted sense' (Emsley 1993: 360), but they did find themselves in court, paying fines, and going to prison. This was especially true of the normally law-abiding residents who were summonsed to court for nonpayment of rates. For example, between 1880 and 1940 in Crewe there were 6,864 instances of nonpayment of borough rates or income tax, with prosecutions rising steeply in the depression years when people struggled to pay their rates, and local authorities were more anxious to recovered owed money in order to keep their services intact. As with motoring cases, people of all social class were brought to court for their arrears, but, again like motoring, the bulk of the defendants came from the lowest social strata. It was probably the case that those considered 'rough' or were from the wrong side of the tracks that bore the brunt, both of the Policeman State, and the civilising zeal of the new agencies of regulatory control.

Conclusion

It does seem likely that there was a slow, long-term shift in popular attitudes towards violence, that the 1880s were probably less violent than the 1850s, and that the 1900s were less dangerous than the 1880s. It seems likely that there was a gradual, long-term, and uneven decline in violence in society and that the judicial statistics were 'going in the right direction' (Carter Wood 2004; Eisner 2001). The steep, relatively short-term fall in violence from the 1880s to World War I, however, was more attributable to police culture and their management of the prosecution process. Police practices reinforced broader changes in popular attitudes towards violence (especially public violence) and, due to their influence on prosecution statistics, exaggerated the rate of decline of violence in society (and therefore exaggerated the impact of civilising trends).

The judicial statistics have allowed us to examine the changes in policies and practices of those people and agencies that were determined to bring offenders to justice. They take us from the period when victims of assault brought their persecutors to court themselves, to the time when the police became the most dominant prosecutorial agency around World War I, to the inter-war period when a new regulatory grip was taken by a plethora of public and private prosecutorial agencies. The judicial statistics can offer one more useful insight into public policy at this time. Although, as was discussed earlier in this chapter, the case advanced by historians such as Tobias (1972), Sindall (1990), C. Williams (2000), and others is almost unanswerable – the variability of collection methods meant that the figures on crime *were* manifestly unreliable. However, that was not the view of contemporary media and social commentators or the public themselves. They were not concerned about the reliability of the figures (at least until the mid-1890s and probably not much after that if truth be told). Social and public policy between 1880 and 1940 was still largely driven by the belief that violence was declining, that public disorder was falling, and that the war on crime was well advanced:

> Commentators and penal professionals too, took their lead from the published statistics. In 1910, Richard Frith Quinton, Governor of Holloway Prison, looked back over the previous thirty years: 'Both crime and criminals have steadily diminished in numbers to an extent that is hardly realised, and the habitual class no longer produces so large a proportion of reckless desperadoes as it did in former years' (Quinton 1910:7). Robert Anderson, who was Commissioner (Crime) at Scotland Yard (1887–1901) believed that the statistics showed that one more aggressive assault on professional criminals would erase them completely as a social category. The Victorians not only

believed that they were fighting a 'War with Crime' (Barwick-Baker 1889), they were convinced they were winning it. This explanation fits more with our conceptions of an ambitious Victorian state, conquering the world, and establishing a new order of civility at home – a 'Peaceable Kingdom'. It also means that the Victorian legislators were not suffering from false-consciousness about the state of crime, nor were legislators and statisticians 'fixing' the figures in any conscious way.

(*Godfrey, Cox and Farrall 2010: 72*)

Turning away from statistical data, the following chapter explores and promotes sources of qualitative data that are no less problematic; indeed, they may possess a range of novel and idiosyncratic problems that documentary and statistical sources lack. However, they also present the possibility of gaining a more nuanced, reflective, and 'authentic' view of contemporary attitudes towards (prosecuted and unprosecuted) crime and contested relationships within working-class communities than has hitherto been achieved. They are worth persevering with, but only when the particular problems that historians encounter when using them are fully explored and accounted for, as we shall see.

5

TALKING ABOUT CRIME

Raphael Samuel once parodied the 'great chain of being' stretching from the tea room of the Institute of Historical Research in London, where the high priests of history discussed lofty matters, down to the amateur historians (such as the genealogists foraging in county archives for information about their ancestors). The lowest rung of the ladder was reserved, he complained, for oral historians whose critics accused it 'of practising a naive empiricism in which the facts are supposed to speak for themselves' (Samuel 1994). One could say that oral history itself has a hierarchy, a shorter one, which does not stretch so far into the historical stratosphere but runs across a spectrum of professional academic oral historians and local historians conducting a considerable amount of oral historical research within their own communities. For this reason, oral history could be considered the most democratic of historical methods – it does not require a wealth of technical equipment, or a depth of historiographical knowledge, and is immediately accessible to many amateur historians who volunteer their services to the local communities. It is its very popularity, of course, that makes the quality uneven, and which has partly resulted in oral history not receiving the credit it deserves in bringing the history of everyday experiences to large audiences. However, it has popularised 'history', taken it outside of the confines of the academy, and that can be no bad thing.

When Paul Thompson set out what might be termed a manifesto for oral history in 1977, he made a number of claims for the practice. With its ability to uncover hidden stories (of 'the under-classes, the unprivileged, the defeated . . .') it was a practice that corrected or challenged orthodox accounts of social and political changes. It would fill in the blanks. But it would do more than that, according to Paul Thompson. Oral history would engender 'an underlying change in the way in which history is written and learnt, in its questions and its judgements, and in its texture' (Thompson 1977: 66). Since Thompson wrote those comments, the study of oral history or life narratives has developed into a significant, theoretically dense, and diverse subset of historical and social-scientific enquiry (Perkins and Thompson 1998; Thompson, 2000). The practice of oral history is developing a theoretical hinterland and will continue to do so as it further establishes itself within the historical canon (see Misztal 2003: 51–74; Perks and Thomson 1998; Tonkin 1990). Simple questions of authenticity – whether oral history can 'replace' the voices of the excluded so that a full and complete history can be formed or can contradict orthodox histories with the 'real' story – have given way to more sophisticated enquiries (see Humphries' use of oral histories as a means of resisting orthodox histories of youth and schooling [Humphries 1981: 3, 26–7]).

As theories about the use of oral histories have developed and grown, so too has the amount of published and unpublished work. There now exists a considerable number of detailed oral (or those that combine oral and other sources) histories of 'ordinary' lives in the early to mid-twentieth century, with some mention of illegal or quasi-legal activities (Bourke 1994; A. Davies 1992; Roberts 1984; Tebbutt 1995; P. Thompson 1977). A few writers have gone on to use oral history to more deeply investigate criminal activities and the policing of working-class communities. Humphries (1981), for example, selected interviews (mainly) from three collections (the 'Family, Life and Work Experiences before 1918' collection formed by Paul Thompson; the Manchester Oral History Collection; and the Bristol People's Oral History Project, which contains the spoken and written recollections of 200 people born between 1890 and 1925) to discuss social crime and youth gang activities. Both Jerry White and Arthur Harding placed their own personal experiences of growing up in London alongside interviews with peers, and others who lived through that period, to write fascinating histories (the latter one cowritten with Raphael Samuel). These books provide rich material on crime and working class life in the early to mid-twentieth century (Samuel 1991; White 1986).

However, historians do not have a monopoly over oral history as a method of inquiry. The nineteenth-century social investigator Henry Mayhew (1851) interviewed Londoners who eked out a living in street trading and hawking, scavenging and scrounging, singing and dancing, and so on. The fourth volume of his series, titled *Those Who Will Not Work* interviewed those who did not have legal employment and who relied on illegal activities (or on the fringes of the law) for their daily bread (see Bennett 1981). More recently published criminological works have discussed life in the decades before and after the First World War because of their publication date (e.g., Rook 1899/1979; Sutherland 1937) or because the research covers the early life of the interviewee (e.g., Klockars 1974). Where the focus of the research is a sociological study of crime and policing in a particular historical period, oral history has been engaged as a useful tool. For example, Brogden (1991) interviewed twenty-four men who served in the Liverpool City Police Force of the 1920s and 1930s in order to understand the contradictory class position of policemen drawn from the class they were employed to control on the streets. Hood and Joyce (1999) studied three generations of Londoners (born before 1920, between 1940 and 1950, and between 1970 and 1975, respectively) in order to chart changing attitudes towards crime and risk over time. Additionally, what might be called contemporary oral history has been carried out, for example, by Cohen and Taylor (1992) on prisoners, by Loader and Mulcahy (2003) on policing, and by Fergus Mcneill (2005) and Maurice Vanstone (2004) on probation.

The use of transcribed oral histories

Given the success of these studies in increasing knowledge about poor and working communities, there is little need for a lengthy justification for oral history as a historical tool. The method is too well established now to need *yet another* battle fought on its behalf. Nor is it necessary to outline the development of life-history research (see Miller 2000; also see Roberts 2002). The use of *transcribed* histories is another matter. Even amongst oral historians it remains controversial. However, because the bedrock of evidence for this book is drawn from such sources, it is worth reiterating some of the advantages, problems, and complexities in using transcribed interviews and the particular contribution they make to a study of marginal criminality in the late Victorian and early Edwardian period.

In the 1980s the techniques of oral history appeared to offer both to local community groups and to professional librarians/archivists an opportunity to create micro-histories based on place, occupational groupings, or other experiences shared by that group. The proliferation of oral history projects carried out by professional and amateur interviewers has meant that a great number of interview transcripts are now held in county records offices and local libraries (any of which are listed in the Directory of Recorded Sound Resources in the United Kingdom [1989]). Over the same period a similar process was stockpiling many thousands of transcribed interviews in archival repositories and local libraries in Australia,[1] Canada, and the United States. This chapter looks at evidence from some of the large numbers of interview transcripts that are scattered throughout the repositories of England. The semistructured life-history interviews carried out in Nottingham between 1982 and 1984 and archived at Nottingham Central Library were particularly useful, and have been drawn on heavily.[2] Many of the 120 interviewees discussed crime and victimisation. Some had been victims of crime, many have committed crimes (in their youth or as women carrying out home abortions), and two interviewees had served as police officers. Even when not mentioning specific criminal events, many talked of feelings of safety and risk at particular moments or in particular periods of their lives.

This is anathema for some oral historians who believe that transcripts are poor substitutes for sound recordings of interviews. They privilege the authenticity of the interview experience, the subtle body language displayed and viewed, the knowing smiles and hand gesticulations, and so on, which could never be effectively captured in the transcription (nor, actually, on a tape cassette). There are also accusations that transcription is prone to distortion – editing and transforming the meaning of the words, and the interviewee's syntax (see Wallot and Fortier 1998) – and that the information that can be translated into written form is often imperfectly recorded. Since the interviewee and interviewer usually go through the transcript after transcription correcting misspellings and mishearings, and as transcription practices improve, this last point seems less of an issue, and there is little evidence of it in the sources used in this book. Nevertheless, it is true that the transcription does not easily capture the emphases that interviewees lay on certain words or capture in detail the cadence of words, the laughs, or the tears.

Yet the collections continue to grow, and given the antipathy towards transcription,[3] it is worth asking why so many interview tapes have been transcribed and archived, especially because the eventual selection and preservation of documents and sound recordings result from the very discriminating practices of archivists (Wallot and Fourtier 1998). Archivists are obviously expecting their collections to be used, and researchers are beginning to see their potential. In 1971, Rapheal Samuel (1998: 32), talking of the person who originates any oral history collection, said,

> However intelligent and well thought out his work, it is inconceivable that his will be the only selection of texts that could be made. The information which he brushes aside as irrelevant may just be the thing upon which a future researcher will seize – if he is given the chance. Research can never be a once-and-for-all affair, nor is there ever a single use to which the evidence can be put.

There is still (but now more muted) criticism of the secondary analysis of transcripts. Nevertheless, for the historian attempting to 'make sense' of the feelings, stories, and personal accounts of more than a handful of people, and for the late Victorian period, these transcripted oral collections seem invaluable. For whatever reason their archiving takes place, historians should be grateful, if only for the following reasons.

First, and most obviously, oral historians today would struggle to carry out a significant number of interviews with people born in the early twentieth century because most of this age cohort has already died. For example, Brogden (1991) found that of the thirty-eight former police officers he wanted to interview about walking the beat in 1930s Liverpool, eleven had already died or were too ill to be interviewed. I would be surprised if his study of the 1930s Liverpool City Police Force could be conducted today. Most of the interviewees quoted in this chapter were born between 1870 and 1900, which means that some of those who watched television pictures of the Berlin Wall coming down had been born when newspapers carried reports of the Boer War. Many women interviewees would have watched their husbands march off to the Somme and their sons to the Normandy landings. These people were survivors of a series of seismic cultural, social, and political shifts that swept across Europe in this period. By accessing oral history interviews conducted in the 1980s, the reach of oral history and the benefit that this historical method offers is considerably extended.

Second, because of the considerable costs of transcribing interview tapes, and the time involved in conducting oral projects, most of the research based on oral sources has hitherto tended to be both small scale and regional in focus. The use of several hundreds of archived interviews in this study allows wider historical and sociological questions to be asked of a survey population across England. The secondary analysis of sound or visual recordings may give a more sensitive feeling or 'truer' rendition of the interview context. Realistically, however, given the time it takes to access and intellectually process sound recordings, the questions that can be asked of this kind of data are reduced in scale. Answering 'bigger' questions – involving social phenomena that extends across large (national, regional) areas or issues which infrequently appear in interviews (fear of crime in urban areas, for example) – generally requires analysis of large numbers of interviews, and that can be achieved relatively simply through analysis of transcripts.

Last, the range of archived transcripts extends from those that deal with specific issues (memories of a village, a workplace, and so on) to those that are general life histories (i.e., most include questions on school, work and family life, relationships within the community, and memories of crime and policing). When oral history was first being used, the structure of life-history interviews had revolved around memorable events – questions about the Blitz, or the coronation in 1952, and so on. By the 1980s a less structured form of interview, and one that focused more on everyday activities, had largely replaced this approach. Interviewers were more inclined to let people self-structure their stories, which they did more or less chronologically as one might expect. The semistructured approach allowed a greater freedom to the interviewee, and that seems to have encouraged memories of crime and disorder to come to the fore (again for reasons explored later). Moreover, as well as occasionally describing incidences of criminal victimisation, and less frequently of criminal activity, the transcribed oral histories bear a more general reading as everyday narratives of danger, risk, and insecurity. As such they provide a valuable source of information about the incidences and perceived levels of risk in early-twentieth-century society.

However, these narratives are not unproblematic to analyse, and a number of methodological and ethical complexities come into play when oral histories become, effectively, a source for secondary analysis. The following paragraphs discuss those problems and the means of overcoming them, or at least accounting for them. The chapter then goes on to reveal the dominant rhetorical devices that exist in life histories of people living in the late nineteenth and early to mid-twentieth centuries and then concludes by discussing the methodological complexities involved in trying to understand what people thought and 'felt' about crime in that period and how they remember their feelings now.

Methodology and analysis

The first issue to be discussed is one that is general to all oral history interviews – and indeed to all forms of historical evidence. How does the researcher evaluate the 'truth' of what they are presented with? The use of the word *truth* is, of course, a rather disingenuous term for the complex farrago of assumptions, understandings, and perspectives engendered on any one event at any one time by any one person. Words such as *truth* have been erased from the postmodern lexicon and have been replaced with terms such as *discursive narrative*, whereas modernists more shyly replace *truth* with *perspective* or *viewpoint*. Discussions of oral history as a technique for discovering reliable information about the past (see, for example, P. Thompson 1977: 138–164) are part of a wider debate on the validity of historical evidence and indeed the purpose of history (Carr 1961; Elton 2002; Prins 1991). This book asserts that it is possible to recover and reinterpret factual events (although they may not by any means be simply accepted as an accurate account of real events). The information or stories related can be pieced together with care and juxtaposed with other forms of historical evidence to provide an insight into both the life experiences of the individual and the nature of society at particular points in history. However, before describing the tools of analysis that facilitate this approach, it would be prudent to discuss the hurdles faced by any oral historian who claims to find authentic evidence of in their interviewee's accounts. In particular, two challenges are made to its claims to represent reality in any significant regard: the issue of social memory and the dominance of symbolism in narratives.

Social memory and symbolic realities

The first challenge is that individual truths as presented in oral histories or life histories are inevitably swamped, subsumed, or replaced by wider frameworks of social memory. Numerous debates around the theoretical position of oral histories have raised the issue of the relationship between the memories held by an individual and the wider societal structures of social memory that are variously held and employed by disparate groups. It is indisputable that memories and life-stories inevitably both contribute to and draw from more collective experiences (Halbwachs 1925; see also Burke 1989). To quote Fentress and Wickham (1992: 88),

> [Memories] will certainly be selected, out of the potentially infinite set of possible memories, for their relevance to the individuals who remember them, for their contribution to constructing personal identity and relationships. This is true both when individuals recall their own personal experiences, and when they remember episodes from the stock of memories that are collectively held.

So, whereas narratives formed contemporaneously to the historical event they seek to capture survive as artefacts and reappear almost intact in interviews decades after their formation (possibly 'solidified', having been repeated many times), they are refashioned with contemporary articulation, often appropriating modern concepts and linguistic forms to describe and reinterpret a historical event. These narratives are therefore interwoven with memories of the past, present-day concerns, and anticipations of the future.

The second challenge faced by oral historians is that the historical evidence contained in interviews is only obliquely revealed through symbolism and allegory. As some have put it, oral testimony tells us as much about the symbolic categories through which reality is constructed, as it does about the 'facts' of peoples' lives (see, for example, Samuel 1994; Samuel and Thompson 1990; P. Thompson 1977). That is why Portelli (1997: 100) can state that:

> the importance of oral testimony may often lie not in its adherence to facts but rather in its divergence from them, where imagination, symbolism, desire break in. Therefore there are no 'false' oral sources. Once we have checked their factual credibility with all the established criteria of historical philological criticism that apply to every document, the diversity of oral history consists in the fact that 'untrue' statements are still psychologically 'true', and that these previous 'errors' sometimes reveal more than factually accurate accounts.

It is clear that the life story cannot be atomised and dissected to provide evidence for this and that, but that it needs to be treated as a holistic entity, one which is coloured by the emotions of the interviewee and which has a dynamic relationship with real past events, the individual's symbolic understanding of them, their reinterpretation at the point of delivery in the interview process, and within the context of social memory (Hodgkin and Radstone 2003; Paris 2000; Perkins and J. Thompson 1998).[4] The narratives that can be found in discussions of the past challenge the present – the 'broken-down communities' of today, the inability of formal institutions of authority to come to the aid of the citizen, the condition of the country, the behaviour of the young, and so on.

Those who believe that they can reclaim elements of truth from oral histories must realise that separating out 'real' events or 'authentic' memories from stories that have been embellished or altered to suit a modern agenda or viewpoint would be a difficult task. However, by accepting the complexity of life histories it is still possible to reap a rich harvest from oral history research. For example, this book explores how symbolic myths and popular narratives shaped common opinion towards crime, situations that were untrustworthy, places that were to be avoided, suspicious people not to be approached, and so on – a whole panoply of contemporaneous opinion on risk and danger in the early twentieth century. In order to do this, it must be recognised that the key to understanding transcribed life histories is not interrogating them for the truth, but recognising the social aspects of their nature, examining the symbolic construction of reality that is contained within them, and devising appropriate methods of analysis. If there is more than one way of telling a story, there is certainly more than one way of interpreting it, and deciding which may be given precedence is an epistemological and, as discussed later in this chapter, also an ethical issue.

Taking account of context

This book aims to form a perspective on the 'common experience', a phrase that belies the complexity of English society in this (or any) period. The substantial conceptual restructuring of meanings of (particularly working-class) community that have taken place over recent years have complicated both the feelings that 'ordinary' people have about the place and time in which they live and the emotions they express about their past. Transcribed interviews are not timeless sources but are rooted within historical epochs. In this case the subjects of the interviews are asked to remember their experiences of the late nineteenth century (for those who were old enough to do so) up to the mid-twentieth century. That necessarily brings forth information about childhood, growing up, and establishing an adult life in a period that witnessed war, depression, and postwar growth, and these will feature heavily intermixed with personal stories. The second temporal context is provided by the period in which the interviews are conducted. Secondary analysis must take account of the preoccupations of researchers at the time of the original interview. In the 1980s, when the majority of oral histories consulted for this volume were carried out, there was considerable political debate on declining standards of civility, the undermining of 'social superiors' and 'natural authorities' (police officers, teachers, etc.). Crime, youth behaviour, and immigration became linked in some media and public discourses, in a way which often shaped popular conceptions of the place they lived in and the country they had grown up in. The Hyson Green project, which carried out interviews with people living on a high-rise housing estate in Nottingham is dominated by dialogue about crime, vandalism, and race relations.

> I can't mention names, can I? I can't mention names. It's coloured people . . .
> I don't feel safe. I was alright when I first came in because – I'm under the
> doctor and under the hospital at the moment and you're frightened to death
> of all the little things that happen, and they do happen an' all. Once I opened
> my door and I were knocked back and all me rent and everything they took
> off me . . . we had all that kind of thing . . . and you know who's doing it. Can't
> mention names, can you . . . At one time you could get across the road and get
> a bit of shopping in the evening, but you can't do that now now. You've got
> to stop behind doors. You're frightened to death. You don't know when that
> bus stops and they're going to get off, from up town, drunk . . . Sometimes I
> don't sleep. I lie in bed frightened to death . . .
>
> *(Nottingham Oral History Collection,*
> *Hyson Green, tape B32a and B32b)*

> I don't think the police do a good job. They harass the younger children
> on the complex of the flats. All children are harassed by them for things
> we did as kids, that was an everyday thing to do. I' don't say breaking into
> people's houses and stealing things, but climbing up trees and whatever, the
> police are after them . . . I think they have forgotten they were children once
> too . . . The police round here aren't any help to the children . . . I mean, you
> see so many things happening today. Children are being kidnapped and getting
> raped, and it doesn't seem like the police are doing anything.
>
> *(Nottingham Oral History Collection,*
> *Hyson Green, tape B29a and B29b)*

Similar oral history projects conducted by Nottinghamshire libraries, which surveyed more broadly the memories of early-twentieth-century Nottingham residents, were also replete with similar discourses as contemporary concerns evoked particular sets of memories. Clearly memories of past events are coloured by present conditions and, as already acknowledged, by social memory too. But that does not mean that careful oral histories cannot reveal the past, merely that one should recognise that oral histories are made up of symbolic realities which the interviewee employs to carry out emotional or political labour and that they often rely on 'real' incidents to perform this task. For example, people relate stories that are remembered with particular intensity because they were so emotionally affecting. Memories of a particular victimisation – coming home to find one's home has been burgled or a violent or sexual assault – may be so potent that the feelings of that event are preserved. Moreover, they feel a need to preserve the integrity of the memory because it is important to present-day concerns and attitudes, and the memories continue to influence feelings about, for example, prison conditions, street lighting, the importance of locking doors at night, or many other topics.

There are also stories within which criminal events are referred to as part of background information of foregrounded stories. This Shropshire interviewee was relating stories about his Grandmother when he incidentally noted,

> I used to go up and see Grandma – I used to cycle up the end. She died in 1912, Grandma did. I was going up there . . . That was when I was going up there . . . the night she died . . . the night as Alf Turley committed that murder at Cluddley Hill. He cut his wife's throat and cut his own, just about ten minutes after I was cycling up.
>
> (*Interview with resident, Telford, b. 1896,*
> *Tumbridge, tape no 77)*

This kind of contextual detail is also important 'where detail appeared to be embroidered with nostalgia and the benefit of hindsight, that process in itself signified the importance of the event. The illustrative anecdote, for example, could make a valuable contribution, emphasising the way an incident should be understood and interpreted' (Brogden 1991: 166; see also Allen and Montell, 1981: 89). This is also the case when interviewees want to relate community-wide values which may or may not have been at odds with the values of respectable folk at the time, and because they understand that a modern audience would consider what they relate to be disreputable or even criminal.

> Oh yes. We had a woman living next door to us – she had no family – her name was Mrs English. And she was a marvellous woman when she was sober, but she'd get on the drink. He was a builder, working in the building trade . . . Look it was terrible. She wouldn't allow anyone in her house but my mother and the girls used to go in and clean up for her, and there was some filth to clean up too. There was money laying all over the place and drink,

and he'd drink too. And then they'd have a terrific fight. He used to belt her about then. But when they were sober you would not find a nicer couple.

If she had been a man and there had been a world championship, I'm talking about fighting, she'd have been champion . . . She could stand on one leg and kick and throw punches all together, now . . . I've had dozens of fights and I've never had a mark and I fought threes and fours, and in one case a roomful, but I've never been marked and I've always put it down to that, my mother, because without being taught or anything I could ride a punch and see it coming.

Interviewees were quite capable of dividing their communities into the friendly, and those rough families best avoided or treated with caution, with gossip used as a social regulatory force helping to formulate and perpetuate both community norms and to identify socially undesirable members of the community:

I always remember, in the West End were a family called Ryan – they were notorious. They were always in trouble. And it was the same thing when I got in the Army – it wasn't long before I met one of them. But that's the strange thing. You know, when we were in Egypt there were some of these Ryans there and eventually they sent some off, actually home, as undesirables. A thing that would never be thought of, you know, later on. And I never . . . I remember meeting one of them, like – or a couple of them – at that time, but never . . . like, I was never mixed up with them in any way.

(What sort of things were the family supposed to be involved in?)

Well, for instance, what was that theatre past the police station – a corner building – it was a vaudeville show, you know. And one of these was standing out there at night time, waiting as they came out. When they came out they'd knock them on the head and steal their money, something like that kind of thing. See, that was the kind of crime we had in those days (laughs). No there wasn't a great deal of crime.

Interviewees may wish, not to convince the interviewer of their position, but merely to say 'things were different then' – maybe things were better then, despite being at odds with society's views today. For example, one old man being interviewed about his upbringing in the 1920s described being hit by a policeman when he was ten years old because he was hanging about on street corners:

this is when I started rough [began to misbehave]. I went to starting rough with the shit tub men, 10 o'clock horses used to come for shit tubs [the night soil collection], pull someone's line down, tie a washing line to a lamppost and a shit tub on cart, when he went ooooh bang, all shit on everything [laughs] bloody good eh, 'yer bloody villain, you'll get . . . and he got, shovelled it up and phew the bloody stench, but its dissipated now [laughs] you've never seen nowt like it . . . Well you fuckers' he ses, 'I'll kill yer if I get hold on yer'.

(Interview with male Nottingham resident,
b. 1908, Nottingham, tape A8[a-b-c]/1)

He then went on to describe going to the Salvation Army stall to collect bread because his father was fighting in the 1914–1918 war (it is never stated whether his father *was* actually fighting in the war or not). Each of the family went separately so that the family had seven loaves of bread instead of one, and then he would visit every Salvation Army stall in Nottingham with the same story. On the way home he would pinch apples and fish from stalls in the market. His mother valued his efforts, knowing full well where they had come from Presumably times were tough, and any contribution to the family budget would have been very welcome. By now, presumably, he was attracting a reputation locally as someone on the edge of the law, and indeed, he then went on to reinforce this view of himself by relating another story to the interviewer:

Everyone was out on the street, to see the Black Maria you know 'somebody's got nicked' out we come 'God Jesus, them two lads, them two brothers have been in trouble again' . . . we'd nicked the bloody coal, aye we nicked it, well it weren't the first time we'd had it on, we went two, three bleddy times on the trot. I used to get on the coal truck, chuck the bogger [good quality coal that burned well], and my brother used to put it in the bags, too bloody heavy, the wheels on the cart fell off and the police caught us.

(Interview with male Nottingham resident,
b. 1908, Nottingham, tape A8[a-b-c]/1)

These were the last words he said about his childhood criminal exploits, and perhaps he himself had realised that a story about being arrested would not only further challenge his claim to be respectable now, but would also undermine his positioning of himself as a bit of a rogue and a scamp rather than as a criminal or a community nuisance. That is what he may well have been, but, unfortunately we do not have any interview data from neighbours who may have witnessed the scene he describes. That is a shame, because the same incident described by many people (described differently and from different perspectives) can provided a more rounded view even when they contradict each other. Take these two extracts, for example, which both touched on the home life of the Brothers family:

Interviewer: What was the community sort of feeling towards the police?

Jim Brothers: I think it was good. Not only once that they brought my father
                   home drunk and put him to bed . . . Put him into bed and say 'If
                   he gives you any trouble Mrs Brothers, just call us and we'll . . .'
                   He never gave us any more trouble. No, once the police brought
                   him home and put him to bed that would be it. (Bicentennial
                   Oral History Collection, Australian National Library, Canberra,
                   tape 89)

Interviewer: What about in other households were you aware of any parents
                   getting drunk and bashing up the family, wives, children . . .

Kath Berkley: No I don't remember any children being bashed around because
                   people kept themselves, well, they were always good neighbours, if
                   there was sickness or anything like that people would come in, it
                   didn't matter where it was, or there was a death or anything like
                   that, people would come in but I don't remember anyone inter-
                   fering in anybody else's life, the only thing I knew was that Mr
                   Brothers was very firm with his wife. Mum used to say 'Poor little
                   thing . . .'

                                        (*Bicentennial Oral History Collection, Australian
                                              National Library, Canberra, tape 138*)

   Just as the extracts quoted above are contradictory, there are many other narratives in the oral history transcripts which can be read 'against the grain' to reveal a
clearer picture of past events. The following two extracts, for example, describe the
same Sydney dockside area in the 1920s:

> At the Royal Naval House we got to know the police station very well
> because mother was often in there and she used to get escorted home of a
> night time (she was cook at a hotel). She'd call in at the police station and
> always provided with an escort home . . . She'd been accosted on the street,
> walking the streets. But mother was an attractive woman and there was . . .
> she'd be walking home at night time, or hurrying home, because she was
> frightened . . . and there was steps and alleyways and goodness knows what
> where men could lurk.

                                        (*JD, Bicentennial Oral History Project, New South
                                                      Wales State Library, tape 68*)

You could call in at the police station if you were frightened, and they would
escort you home, you see. I remember once I was coming home from work
when I was grown up and I'd finished work at 8 o'clock, and used to walk
home because it was not that far, and the trams were not that frequent. And I
was just walking, you know how you look in the shops on the way home, and
this boy must have been following me, and . . . everytime I'd cross the street
or look in a shop window, he sort of followed me. And Sergeant Farrell, and
he knew me cause he knew my dad see, he said do you know, called me by

name, there's a man following you. And I said no. He said I've been watching him, so I will escort you home, which he did, but you see there was nothing to worry about, cause I didn't know about it and I never heard of anyone being molested or anything.

(E. G., Bicentennial Oral History Project,
New South Wales State Library, tape 90)

The preceding extracts illustrate the contradictory and counterfactual nature that sometimes presents in oral evidence (it was *so safe* that the police provided escorts ...). When these accounts are placed next to many others on the same theme or describing the same time and place, then what may be termed 'normal' historical rules of analysis apply. For example, participants are informed that they can stop an interview at any time; and the researcher can also stop or pause the interview (although this in itself raises issues of power and control in the interview situation). However, because of the sheer density of data on a variety of social phenomena and the coverage across national and international situations, it is possible to layer sources and compare them with other narratives, documents, and sources of data (newspapers, official histories, contemporary diaries, and so on). The common interpretative methods that are routinely applied by historians – the plausibility and authenticity of the evidence (whatever weight one puts on an individuals' narration within/to these social scripts), reference to other evidential forms, and the imaginative construction and understanding of the historical context – are equally applicable to a study of oral evidence (Friedlander 1995; McCormack 2000; Pamphilon 1999).

General themes and rhetorical devices in life histories

The semistructured interviews employed by the majority of oral history researchers generally followed a common chronological format. Interviews about one particular aspect of a person's life, their work, or their school experiences, and so on obviously concentrated most on those areas – it may be that someone examining prison experiences was only interested in the periods of incarceration themselves, and not what led up to them, or what followed after them. However, those interested in more holistic biographies, or who want to situate some event or episode within a wider biographical frame often start at the earliest memory and work through to the present-day experiences of their interviewee. Interviewers therefore often began the interview by asking where and when the interviewee was born, and thereafter interviewees tended to describe, in turn, experiences of school life and childhood, work and career development, housing and neighbourhood, sickness and the death of loved ones, and so on. As stated earlier, even if the interviewees do not always conceptually organise their memories in nice bite-sized chronological bits, few seem averse to that approach when the interviewer leads them down that road. When revealing the chronology of peoples' lives, or the events they remember, it seems to be possible to identify general themes (which are described in the following in no particular order) that occurred repeatedly in the interviews. Whilst it is, of course, a subjective process to construct these themes, and to place the memories revealed during the interview process into one theme or another, the following themes or rhetorical 'boxes' seem to be present in the majority, if not all, of the oral history interviews I have seen – at least in those that go through the whole of their interviewee's life, rather than some small section of it.

Struggle and progress

There is a teleological thrust to most life stories: the post hoc rationalization that events followed on one from the other with form and direction. The multitudinous small, and mostly unacknowledged, decisions and chance events that influence a person's life are too unimportant for people to foreground in their stories, too de-empowering of their ideas of self-agency, and too unwieldy to compress into the seamless narrative that is often projected (see Peneff [1990] on the biographies of self-made men and the making of foundational myths of their lives). That is not to say that the interviewees do not highlight the possible barriers to the smooth progress of their lives to present their lives in a pseudo-heroic light. Stories of adversities overcome, a difficult past successfully negotiated, and so on can be seen in many of the life narratives stored in the oral history collections. For the same reasons as those already outlined, the meanderings of a person's life are delineated as a series of dramatic events. Stories leap from episode to episode (with stories of career advancement, or some other form of intellectual or social development, often presented in a sequential framework subsequently imposed). This is, of course, a marked feature mainly of 'life' histories in which progress can be measured over a number of decades and not specific interviews on discrete periods, say, school or work life.

Nostalgia and loss

This is the downbeat to the upbeat 'progression' theme. Chase and Shaw (1989) see nostalgia as inevitable, and as pernicious, although, because memory therapy with the elderly shows, it can also be therapeutic. Indeed, Chase and Shaw themselves considered nostalgia to be a comforting factor in defiance of a fractured and tempestuous postmodern world (Chase and Shaw 1989: 1–17; see also Lowenthal 1989). Some researchers feel that nostalgia blights the dialogue, and if they could only compensate for the unwelcome false romance with the past, then a 'true' picture could be revealed. In truth, of course, these sepia-toned regrets are integral to the story and reveal more by their presence than would be seen by their removal.[5] Nostalgia is an inevitable by-product of a sense of loss, something that is marked in many oral histories. Asking people to review their lives across a seventy or so year period provides an opportunity for self-evaluation, reflection on the variable progress of their lives, and a chance to speak about deceased friends and lovers (Damousi 2001: 3, see also Damousi 1999).[6] Indeed, sometimes the death of significant actors in a person's life assists the interviewee to apply a chronology to their life story or to divide the life course into clear stages or phases (as life grids are sometimes used to do; see Chapter 7). Whatever the case, because they cover such a time-span, life narratives seldom run their course without mention of death, distress, and mourning.

Change and the decline of civility

Allied to the theme of nostalgia and personal loss, the 'golden age' is a period (delineated differently by different interviewees) that can be juxtaposed against a less-than-satisfactory present. Life stories that mention crime and youth leisure activities are often rich with laments for a period in their life when times were better. As one social theorist commented, 'It predominates as the non-philosophical or sub-philosophical response to the past and the passing of time. It is the unthinking man's way of coming to terms with history' (Dannhauser 1995: 118). In the life histories analysed here, there were linkages made between the physical decline of a neighbourhood and a perceived moral decline:

> there's been a dramatic change in that they're a lot dirtier in comparison to how they used to be years ago . . . its changed that way. The people have changed, I think. When we first came on as kids it was a friendly, really friendly place, you know, all the kids playing together, and toys were safe on the concourse, you know, the playground. Nobody troubled anybody, but nowadays, you wouldn't dare leave a shoe out there, ne'mind toys, 'cos as quick as you'd left it, it'd be gone. I think its changed that way because, like, they've put the problem families in, whereupon years ago it wasn't problem families.
>
> (*Hyson Green tape, Nottingham*)

Most emblematic of the decline in standards were the stories about crime, experienced first- or second-hand, and it was surprising how often these were foregrounded very early in the interview (after beginning the interview by asking where and when he was born, the interviewer asked, 'What were your first recollections of Wrockwardine Wood, eighty-five years ago?'):

> I recollect a great many things. The home-coming from the South African War, also the different things my dad used to tell me about. There is one thing I'd like to mention. The Kinnersley Murder. That was not far away, Kinnersley, a few miles from here [. . .] The row of houses is called murder row now down in Kinnersley.

(What's the story of the Kinnersley murders, Bill?)

> Well, the first I must say the murder was the husband's second wife. They had a child that belonged to the husband but the child seemed to be in the way

and of course, the woman, his wife, didn't like the idea, so what she did, she murdered this girl, cut off her head, wrapped it in brown paper, buried the body in the garden and carried the head across the Kinnersley Moors past Wappenshall and threw it in Apley Pool.

(*Interview with resident, Telford, b. 1886,*
Ironbridge tape, no. 61)[7]

Stories of murder or serious crime were less commonly related than those which discussed almost intangible connections between change, crime, and moral degeneracy. This following extract from a Shropshire resident was typical of a large number that portrayed the past as a golden age:[8]

There was no street lighting in Ketley. None whatsoever . . . darkest Ketley. And then we got some gas lamps but they weren't very much, mind you, I will say this, and I'll emphasise it, you could leave your door open and nobody would walk in, nobody. We had, there was nothing to worry about in those days. Women folk go and visit each other and they'd talk and come back. What's going on today is unbelievable. They were good honest people. It was darkest Ketley too. They were grand old days, really. Its nice to recall some of them, because you could leave your doors open. You needn't bother to go anywhere or worry about anything. We visit each other's homes and there was no . . . well it isn't like it is today. So when I reflect on them, I think, well, they were the good old days.

(*Interview with resident, Telford, b. 1896,*
Ironbridge Tape, no. 77)

They were the good old days to some, and many more also remembered days of difficulty, poverty and disadvantage equally as rosily. Patrick Madden (see Chapter 1) might have done the same, had he been interviewed about the course of his life, for even his chaotic life filled with violence and imprisonment would also, perhaps, have contained episodes of joy, tenderness, drunkenness, and revelry that Patrick might have remembered fondly. That he would privilege some memories over others is not problematic, and indeed, as we have seen in this chapter, it is somewhat inevitable. Therefore, oral histories cannot be said to be false (Portelli 1997), and neither can they be said to be 'true' (oral histories constitute an opinion on the present, and when people relate their past, they are actually talking about how they view their present conditions) if one views them as a complete recollection of real events. However, this does not mean that oral histories do not contain details of real experiences – only that those memories are mediated, interpreted, and expressed within particular individual and collective idioms. People *do* remember things that happened to them, and they remember them in particular ways, and they can relate them to others. Oral history is therefore still about 'history' as much as it about the present. That this needs to be stated so conclusively would perhaps be something of a surprise to those who originally developed oral history as a methodological tool.

Conclusion

For historians of crime, the hundreds and thousands of oral histories (digitally recorded or existing on tape cassettes and those which have subsequently been transcribed) offer a rich contextualising body of information for the pre–World War I to World War II period. Forming one of the few avenues back to popular everyday structures of feeling for those times, oral histories bring forth stories of risk, crime, and victimisation that failed to be captured in official records. More than that, they add perspectives about how ordinary people felt and experienced crime in a vast archive of transcribed interviews that can be explored and examined not only by academics and history professionals, but also by anybody. The following chapter investigates whether the very accessibility of these oral sources is problematic in itself. It explores how researchers can negotiate the complex ethical and legal landscape of 'using' other people's words and life events in historical research.

LIVERPOOL JOHN MOORES UNIVERSITY
LEARNING SERVICES

6

AN ETHICAL CONVERSATION?[1]

Given the possibilities that oral history interviews – whether they exist on tapes, as digital recordings, or as transcripts-offer historical research, in the near future it is likely that researchers of the late Victorian and Edwardian periods will utilise them in their research. We are beginning to unlock their potential as sources, and even the secondary analysis of transcripted data is beginning to be discussed (Boddy *et al.* 2006; Bornat 2002; England and Bacchini 2012; Lyon and Thurgood 2007; Richardson and Godfrey 2003; P. Thompson 2003; Walters 2009; Wiles *et al.* 2006). However, there is some way to go before we can say that we have a mature understanding of how to best use these unique and interesting sources. In this chapter it is the ethical use of these sources that interests us. How can we devise an approved set of practices around these sources, and should we even try? Do dead people have rights? There are defamation laws (1952, 1996 Defamation Acts) which enable people to take legal action in the courts if someone made untrue or harmful statements about them, and indeed The Oral History Society tell us that very prominently in their advice on how to carry out oral history interviews. They remind us that '[a] defamatory statement is one with a tendency to injure the reputation of another person (or organisation, company or business)' but end by stating, with emphasis: '*Statements relating to dead people are not subject to the law of defamation*' *(www.ohs.org.uk)*. Do the words that interviewees have freely given to researchers in interviews have a special privilege which means we cannot interpret their meaning? Does that privilege become redundant when the person originally interviewed dies (Plummer 1983: 143)? If the person carrying out the analysis did not carry out the original interview, but is merely reading a typescript of the interview, can he or she fully understand what the words mean – does the relationship built up between original interviewer and interviewee give them the right to interpret the meanings and emotions that are conveyed? It seems appropriate that we now explore these and other questions within the framework of an (imagined) interview about the conduct and subsequent analysis of oral history interviews:

Interviewer: When you sit down with someone for a few hours and discuss intimate subjects I imagine that there is some kind of relationship created between the interviewer and the interviewee?

There could hardly not be a relationship or feelings of closeness forged when one person tells another the personal details of his or her current and past life: things which may not have been told even to close friends or their own family in some cases (Bornat 2001; Rubin and Rubin 1995: 93–122; Strauss 1987). The relationship is necessarily one that involves a power differential (Heaton 2004; Minichiello *et al.* 1990). It is the interviewee, not the interviewer, who reveals intimate details, and, even if the interviewer takes steps to try to reduce the dependence, it still remains (Oakley 1981). Patai (1991: 139) states that ethical research is probably impossible if that term is taken to mean complete equality between researcher and subject (see Borland 1991: 63–77). In fact, Lieblich (2002) believed that the overwhelming majority of interviews result in a relationship comprising various levels of intensity from short, exploitative 'data grabs' through to long-term friendships. We have to recognise that oral history interviews are only arranged to suit the needs of a particular project. Researchers desire data, and indeed, they want data on the subject that they are researching. It is not surprising that a temptation to connive at strategies that secure that data, even drive people conversationally towards the subject of interest. For example, the following is an extract from the testimony of Heather, an orphan who was resettled in South Australia in 1938 (for the context of the colonial resettlement of thousands of British children, see Bean and Melville 1989; Stokes 1950):

HG: We were told we were coming to new homes, new mothers and fathers, and what would be happening to us. So when we were on the ship everybody used to say to each other 'I wonder what my mother and father are going to be like?' You know, 'I wonder if we are going to have brothers and sisters', and everyday like that. But it never happened. When we got here we were marched down to the gangplank into two buses and taken to the orphanage. And I had hair down to my waist and they cut that and put us all in a DDT bath [DDT was a contact poison which was used to destroy typhus and malaria].

Interviewer: Were you happy or sad to leave England?

HG: Sad. When I was on the ship my name was Heather, and the nun took the name Heather off and put Josephine. I thought at the time, 'they've taken my country, they've taken my name, what else can they take?' I'd lost everything. And they've taken my wonderful place [the Nazareth

> Orphanage back in Plymouth, England] . . . the nuns were like family. They were so caring. I've never ever met people like that in Australia.
>
> Interviewer: Were there any other memories you have on board ship that were a little more pleasant perhaps?

That extract comes from a set of interviews designed to commemorate Australian achievement (housed in South Australian State Archives) and it is not surprising that the interviewer might consciously or unconsciously wish to move the story onto other memories more appropriate to the theme of celebrating Australia.

Another explanation might be that the interviewer was trying not to upset Heather, and maybe just wanted to move the subject on to happier memories?

It is entirely possible that interviewers might avoid upsetting subjects, or quickly leave them when touched on, for the genuine humane reason that they want to protect their interviewees. Without a field diary being kept or an interviewer's contemporary notes being archived alongside the interview transcript, it is difficult to tell if this is the case. When the topic for discussion is crime and victimisation, unsettling events are the meat and drink of the interview however, so avoiding 'awkward' subjects may be impossible. Some people will have pushed some events to the back of their mind, or have 'glossed over' the full implications of the events they now are asked to recall. Remembering in detail (possibly for the first time) their father's rough treatment of their mother, when their brothers were beaten up at school or arrested by the police, or something similar to that may be quite unpleasant, especially if an interviewer dwells on them (as anyone carrying out an interview about crime is likely to do). So despite the efforts of a sympathetic interviewer, taking part in an oral history interview may give rise to 'uncalled for self-knowledge', and this can leave participants feeling anxious or upset (see Miller, 2000; Roberts, 2002). Even when the interview is a positive experience, there is still a danger of harm caused through the researcher's interpretation.

Then it must surely be incumbent on the interviewer to minimise the risks of harm, whether that meant interviewing in a sensitive manner, analysing in a responsible manner, and ensuring that the dissemination of research does not traduce the interviewee's memories, ideas, and beliefs? Some of these issues place individual researchers in a difficult position. Whom can individual researchers turn to for guidance?

General guidance on ethical research for researchers can be found online (British Society of Criminology, http://www.britsoccrim.org/codeofethics.htm, and the UK Data Archive, http://www.data-archive.ac.uk/create-manage/consent-ethics). The British Sociological Association's Statement of Ethical Practice states that researchers have a 'responsibility to ensure that the physical, social, and psychological well-being of research participants is not adversely affected by the research'. They prompt researchers to be aware of the possible consequences of their work and demand that they attempt to anticipate and guard against predicted

harmful consequences for participants in their research (see www.britsoc.co.uk/
media/27107/StatementofEthicalPractice.pdf). Unfortunately, and a little surprisingly, neither The Social History Society nor The Historical Association ('The Voice
for History') provide any information or guidance about ethical historical research.
However, The Oral History Society does provide guidelines (www.ohs.org.uk/
ethics/), although it adopts a rather legalistic approach and is mainly concerned
with a discussion of copyright laws and regulations.

The ethical guidelines thus far described require a researcher to make the
judgement about what constitutes harm to a participant. As Smythe and Murray
(2000: 322) point out, this relies on researchers' making judgements in an 'idiosyncratic manner one that resists any obvious formulation in terms of principles of
minimal risk or uniform procedures for risk-benefit analysis'. Nevertheless, taking
the process chronologically, the guidelines provide a framework for preserving the
rights of interviewees, starting at the outset of the process with the agreement to
go ahead:

> It is unethical, and in many cases illegal, to use interviews without the *in-
> formed consent* of the interviewee, in which the nature of the use or uses is
> clear and explicit. Many of the legal constraints referred to below can be
> very simply avoided if informed consent is obtained; and most of the Ethi-
> cal Guidelines at the end of this document are concerned with the necessity
> and process of obtaining consent. Consent is best negotiated by means of a
> clearance form which should be completed and signed at the time of the
> interview. Retrospective clearance is usually very time-consuming and often
> impossible if informants or interviewers have died or moved away. Where
> informed consent has not been given, interviews cannot be used for many
> purposes and the value of keeping them is much reduced.
>
> (*The Oral History Society, www.ohs.org.uk/ethics*)

The tone of the advice from The Oral History Society is that the interviewer
and interviewee are entering into a kind of contract. The moral responsibility lies
with the interviewer but the interviewee can have recourse to the signed consent
form as a guarantor of their rights. In medical research, and now in a good deal of
social science research, the consent form is a standard routine – often mandated by
a university-based or National Health Service Ethics Committee.

Whilst this appears to be a robust system, if we are interested in the World War I–
World War II period, surely some older people will struggle to understand what this
kind of interview actually involves.

Not only older people, but also no one, could fully envisage what the interview
will touch on or what memories will be dredged up (Josselson 1996: xii). Finch
(1984), for example, sees the very ease with which women give information to
another woman interviewer as making them vulnerable as 'subjects' of research
and as creating a potential for exploitation, often overriding the terms of the 'consent agreement'. Smythe and Murray (2000) agree and warned researchers have to

be aware of this and be aware when the consent agreement may be about to be breached during an interview.

Preserving the spirit of the 'consent agreement' may be a difficult task, surely. Interviewers who may have carried out hundreds of similar interviews might have become so used to the process that they can fail to adequately warn respondents about what they have signed up for.

In response to the concerns about establishing and maintaining consent that has been given at the start of the process, oral history interviewers have moved towards a more 'ethical' form of informed consent, in which consent is ongoing and continuously renegotiated. For example, participants are informed that they can stop an interview at any time, and the researcher can also stop or pause the interview (although this in itself raises issues of power and control in the interview situation). When closing an interview, the interviewer often has details of appropriate helpline or counselling services.[2] It is now normal good practice for participants to be asked at the end of an interview if they still give their consent. This makes much more sense in the context of a narrative interview which may have lasted several hours and covered a lot of memories. Sending the quotations you intend to use directly in a report back to the participants for approval is another way in which a more informed consent can be given.

The interviewee seems well protected during the process, but what happens when the interview is over?

The Oral History Society's Ethical Guidelines (2000) emphasise that interviewers, even before an interview takes place, have a responsibility to 'consider the purpose of the interview and the possible range of future uses to which it might be put'. Similarly, qualitative data to be deposited with Qualidata – the ESRC data archive for qualitative research – is governed by strict procedures on reuse (www.esds.ac.uk/qualidata/about). If anything, the strictures on archiving data have become even stricter over the last decade. At least that is the case for professional researchers. Oral history, it must be remembered, is often carried out by interested lay historians. The tapes or transcripts from their interviews may end up in local history groups, local studies archives, or public libraries. The restrictions on their use may be less rigorous – indeed, they *are* less rigorous – than those insisted on by funding bodies or by professional oral history associations. Repositories such as the UK Data Archive or the Arts and Humanities Data Service allow restrictions to be placed on the reuse of data – it can be restricted by release date, consent by the data collectors can be made mandatory, and so on. Or, you can walk into a local library and simply pick up a set of detailed memories of people's lives off the shelf.

Does the interviewee have any say about who will eventually hear their voice or read their words?

As stated earlier, the original researcher or research team can specify a closure period for the data, restricting access to a length of time, or insisting to be informed when some other researcher wishes to access the data. However, usually the researcher makes the decision, and only rarely will researchers consult with the original interviewee. More usually, they take other protective measures, such as preserving the interviewee's anonymity. The British Sociological Association guidelines state that personal information should be kept confidential, names and pseudonyms used instead; other identifying detail should be removed, and in some cases, they suggest that it may not be appropriate to record 'certain kinds of sensitive information'.[3]

It seems that, rather in the collection or archiving of the data, the greatest potential for harm might be in the analytical phase rather than the interview phase. Smythe and Murray (2000: 321) speculated that '[p]erhaps the most invasive risk for participants in narrative research has to do with the emotional impact of having one's story re-interpreted and filtered through the lenses of social-scientific categories . . . Narrative research can in this way become intrusive and subtly damaging . . .'

It may be that Smythe and Murray have overstated the harm caused to actual participants. Alistair Thompson thought so, commenting that they 'greatly exaggerate their own power to "become intrusive and subtly damaging" to their interviewees, who are unlikely to ever see or wish to read an obscure article in an academic journal' (P. Thompson 2003). However, although there certainly are a lot of obscure journals with a very small and solely academic readership, and that may be a protective factor, it is also the case that research using oral history interview data is most likely to be read by 'lay readers' who just have a general interest in a particular subject. As the Oral History Society states very directly that '[i]nterviewing people serves very little purpose unless the interviews become available for use' (www.ohs.org .uk/ethics.php). Now that online sources and repositories of oral history have made thousands of interviews available at the click of a mouse, it may be that it is even easier to bring peoples' words – and the researcher's interpretation of them – into the homes of the general reader (see Chapter 7).

But don't the interviewees own their own words? Researchers would be outraged if someone took their words or written passages and used them without permission wouldn't they?

Actually, academics have their words and thoughts quoted by other researchers all the time. As long as they are properly credited or referenced, few will resent that; indeed, most historians and criminologists will welcome it! However, quoting ideas and reusing words written in documents may be different from taking a living person's words and telling other people (the readers of academic books) what the interviewee reveals through the things they have said. The researcher may attribute meanings to the words spoken which the interviewee did not consider – and interviewees may disagree with the interpretation given to their own words. Obtaining informed consent from a participant at the start of the interview very rarely involves discussion of ownership of the 'narrative', other than asking for permission to use a participant's words, which is more of a legal requirement than a considered moral evaluation (see Apter 1996).[4]

> Tony Parker seems to have negotiated this delicate situation adroitly when he interviewed many of the marginal, the dispossessed and the disadvantaged during his long research career. He published a number of volumes that detailed the life histories of serious offenders in various prisons in England and abroad. Parker was out to demolish stereotypes of offenders. Prisoners, particularly sex offenders and murderers, are demonised in the media and the public like to think of criminals as 'a breed apart' (misguided as criminological research reveals this attitude to be time and time again). People like Parker, therefore, played an invaluable role, but his attitudes may not be typical of most researchers; and the astute and accomplished work he produced belies a moral complexity to this kind of research.
>
> (*Godfrey 2004: 59–66; see also Parker 1994*)

Spradley (1979) explicitly signed a book contract jointly with one of his life history subjects (James Sewid) to avoid taking over or misrepresenting his subject's words. There is a tension here between protecting the anonymity of the participant (James Sewid, for example, or Arthur Harding in his collaborations with Raphael Samuel, for example) whilst avoiding or reducing exploitation of our research participants. The key issue for a researcher is that transcripts may already be publicly available with the name of the person attached. This means that standard ethical guidelines have been breached, but not by researchers themselves. The other issue is that Samuel and Spradley built up a close relationship (through multiple meetings with them) with a single person. One major advantage of interview transcripts is that they allow a researcher to quickly collect and analyse a number of interviews – sometimes a very considerable number – in order to ask general questions of the data, for example, 'How did people feel about risk of being a victim of crime?' rather than 'How did Arthur Harding experience crime in the East End of London in the 1920s?'

Researchers have to consider whether the steps they have taken are sufficient to protect the rights and integrity of their sources (the interviewees) both in the process and in the subsequent treatment of the data given over in the interview. It would be insufficient to protect the data to the extent that they are unusable – either because they are not in a form that can be analysed or because the results of analysis cannot be disseminated to a wider audience – because this not only is a waste of time and money, but also denies the interviewee the right to have their story told. On the other hand, the researcher has to strive at all times to protect interviewees as they are clearly vulnerable throughout and after the process. This is all a very careful balancing act for the researcher to carry out.

The responsibility for protecting the interests of the interviewee and acting ethically still appears to rest predominantly on the interviewer. Could it also be the case that the interviewers themselves need some protection? The consent agreement, of course, gives them legal protection, and we have established that the vulnerability is mainly on the side of the interviewee not the interviewer, but what about the emotional labour carried out by interviewers during the interview process?

Let us think about how emotion could be transmitted from the interviewee to the interviewer. We do not have an available digital recording of how imprisonment affected one man who had been in and out of prisons from the 1930s, but we do have his words here:

> You lose it – totally lose it. You lose your sense of identity, you lose your confidence. Sense of self-worth, well, you don't have that either. These institutions aren't designed to do that. There's no light at the end of the tunnel. Mutilation – its quite a common thing in prison for various reasons, to get to the hospital, to get sympathy, just because you hate your own damned body. I mean I still don't expose my body in public and yet . . . I mean I don't go to the beach. I was with my girlfriend for a year before she saw me naked [. . .] even now, hasn't smashed away that shit that's been put . . . its an ugly body. To me its still an ugly body. And yes, you mutilate it. Why wouldn't you? Its so fucking ugly [and later, again talking about the longer-term impact of conditions inside the prison] Constant fear, even the fear of eating meals. If you tapped your knife too hard on a plate then you were severely punished; if you ate too fast or ate too slow. Even now I have problems with my dog, with children. If I see a child eating his food really fast then I've got to control myself because what I want to do is just belt him, get the food and just shoving it into his mouth and say, 'Don't be a pig, don't be a pig'.

This extract is from an interview with a man called Nicholas as part of an oral history project in Freemantle Prison recorded by Erica Harvey in 1994.[5] His words arouse strong feelings. As many recognise, incarceration can involve not only the deprivation of liberty, but also the disruption of family life, the restriction of movement, and the restriction of other personal liberties (ownership of property, when and where to eat, sleep, and so on). Criminologists and crime historians may also recognise that prisoners suffer mental anguish that follows them beyond the prison gates on release, but the intensity of his words bring that home in to us in a very visceral way. From that extract, we are unaware of why Nicholas is locked up. Perhaps his crime is a serious or even a truly shocking one, but his words are still likely to arouse at least some feelings of sympathy for him.

Presumably the feelings of sympathy that are engendered can help to form an empathetic relationship between interviewer and interviewee.

When interviews are carried out, sometimes within university buildings, but sometimes within old peoples' homes, or personal residences, the environment can seep into an interviewer's psyche. When the person talking to you is sick, suffering from physical impairment, or is living in a damp house in an impoverished environment, this can clearly affect an interviewer. Morse argued that interviewing the seriously ill and dying is 'the most difficult type of qualitative research' to contemplate doing (Morse 2000: 538), and it is difficult to disagree: 'Most of you, I know, will be able to recall large blocks of quotations and hear the participant's voice in your head many years after conducting a heart-wrenching interview' (Morse 2000: 540–541). Jones made similar points about interviewing Holocaust survivors: 'it would be unlikely if the experience of talking about those memories was entirely without cost for either the interviewee or the interviewer' (Jones 1998: 49). Even before hearing the words they speak, their personal conditions can condition the way that an interview might go. Sit in a damp local authority flat listening to a man in his eighties talking about how scared he is when youths push dog shit through his letterbox. Then see if you are more sympathetic when he relates stories about the fights and minor offences he was involved in when he was a teenager in the 1920s. Sympathy is a natural human emotion, and carrying out a face-to-face interview in that context is the perfect place to nurture and grow an empathetic or sympathetic relationship.

Criminological research often lies at an intersecting nexus of ethical, moral, and sociolegal values that can challenge our preconceptions or strongly held opinions (as researchers or as readers of publications about crime, see Gadd 2012). Oral histories of crime, perhaps, in particular, provoke us to recognise that emotion is being created in the process – for the person hearing the story as well as the person telling it. The responsibility to protect should therefore not be unidirectional. Counsellors, psychologists, and other health experts tend to embrace techniques and practices designed to reduce the emotional wear and tear on their own wellbeing. Qualitative researchers are also likely to be emotionally affected by some of the information revealed to them or by the context of the interview itself. Unfortunately there has only been a small amount written explicitly on the effect the oral history interview can have on the researcher (Arksey and Knight 1999; Jones 1998; Morse 2000). The crime historian who goes in seek of oral evidence of crime and policing practices is likely to encounter other heavily emotive subjects – abortions, the death of a family member, and the crime and domestic violence discussed in the last chapter:

> you see that's why so many went to back-street abortionists, you see they went to . . . two of my friends died through that. One, er . . . oh he were a pig were her husband, er . . . Dolly W.[6] . . . Ooh she looked shocking. I said 'Ooh Dolly, what's the matter with you?' She says 'I'm haemorrhaging . . . I've got to go straight away, see to the kids, I've got to go to hospital'. Well she'd had – they were all boys she had. Ooh he were a pig was Jess W, her husband, he used to beat her up. Anyway they took her to Scafforth Road Hospital, and it were her cousin as it happened, she says, 'You know our Dolly, she's dead'.
> (*Female interviewee, b. 1904, Bradford Central Library, tape A0098/03*)

Simple recognition of the moral and contextual standpoints referenced by interviewees such as Dolly's friends greatly assists researchers to understand the social and individual factors that affected her life and the lives of her friends and neighbours. As Jamieson and Grounds state, '[t]he research relationship must be based on the interviewer's empathic neutrality and respect for the respondent' (2002: 13). They adopted this standpoint in their work on men who had served long terms of imprisonment for paramilitary activities in Northern Ireland. Having empathy does not guarantee a successful interview. Without any empathy at all the analysis may be lacking in insight; on the other hand, to be full of sympathy might threaten the necessary degree of professional detachment required. Empathetic neutrality would seem to be very desirable, but difficult to achieve for interviewers when talking to people sitting in a chair just across the room from them.

Talking about these kinds of issues, the treatment of prisoners, memories of criminal victimisation, and so on could evoke sympathy, or empathy, but couldn't it also engender feelings of dislike or distrust? Given that oral histories of the early twentieth century might touch on unrepentant domestic violence perpetrators, racist criminal justice professionals, offenders who have committed murders or rapes, and so on, do we have to empathise with all of those 'characters' too?

Oral history interviews do not, as a rule, challenge the past behaviour of their interviewees, whether they are former or current offenders, political extremists, or even just regular 'normal' people:

> It is almost impossible to imagine a researcher telling an interviewee that they 'should' not have smoked so many cigarettes in their lives, or 'should' have brought their children up differently, but what about interviews with society's transgressors (criminals, people with addictions, or 'deviant' sexual tastes)? These tend to involve more ambiguous moral and empathetical positions. Whilst researchers have become less inclined to place their own sensibilities at the centre of a moral universe, and more open to a plurality of moral positions, personal sensibilities are likely to remain embedded in the research relationship. It is therefore worth exploring what happens when interview testimonies fundamentally challenge the moral positions personally held and adhered to by the interviewer.
>
> (*Godfrey, 2003c: 60; also see Gadd 2012*)

Researchers have tended to restrict themselves to interviewing people with whom they feel they can build a collaborative relationship. There are few researchers who choose to interview people they know at the outset that they are certain to dislike. Oral history researchers have, of course, studied the disadvantaged, the excluded, and the transgressors in society, who could all be perceived as being victims of their own personal circumstance and/or society as a whole. Blee (1998: 333) lamented that '[h]istorians have paid less attention to the life stories of ordinary people whose political agendas they find unsavoury, dangerous, or deliberately deceptive', but, even when they have, interviewers have managed to achieve a professional rapport with their subjects (Blee: 1998: 338–341; Elwood 1988). This has been made possible by choosing people whose political views and agendas would be considered extreme by any standard. By researching ultra-racists and Nazi sympathisers, for example, Elwood (1998) or Koonz (1986) are unlikely to be accused of becoming implicated in the moral-political worldview of their interviewees. However, what about the researcher of riots and public disorder that interviews a supporter of Oswald Mosley about the Olympia riots in 1936? At that time, Mosley was a popular politician who appeared to talk a lot of sense to a number of people. He was not tainted by his Nazi-esque demagoguery until Hitler's full horror was understood by the general British public. Sympathy for someone duped by Mosley's rhetoric in the 1930s may be understandable. If the interviewer then went on to say that they still supported Mosley's stance on the 1948 race riots, or held anti-immigrant sentiments today, the interviewer might shift his or her moral opinion. Truly an interviewer could dance a merry jig trying to find a moral equilibrium, especially when interviewing offenders whose behaviour society finds hard to accept. Possibly that is why crime historians have interviewed 'morally marginal' and not those whose victim status cannot be established so strongly – prostitutes not rapists, drug users not drug pushers, child offenders not child abusers.

Are researchers who only read or hear the words of offenders and victims of crime second hand as affected – or affected at all – by the emotional charge contained in oral history interviews?

There are no common guidelines that can be applied here. Like an oral historian, what affects one might not affect another. However, it does seem likely, for all the reasons already discussed, that being told something directly in a face-to-face interview is potentially much more challenging and confronting than reading the same information in a transcript. People do not really know how they will feel if an interviewee looks them in the eye and tells them how they killed another person. The transcript reader will already have some idea of what the interview will contain, however, and can prepare him- or herself to read this information. The title of the archived collection might give a clue, or the interview may even be indexed – many transcripted interviews are.

So, perhaps, by using interview transcripts, researchers can simply avoid the emotions that are engendered in the interview process? Reading transcripts surely cannot be compared with looking into the eyes of a distressed interviewee and hearing disturbing memories first hand? When people relate a disturbing episode in their lives, and are clearly upset by reliving the memories, there is a rawness and directness to the experience that affects the interviewer. It would be difficult for a researcher (one presumes) to gaze dispassionately at the visible distress of the person they are talking/listening to – one can walk away from a transcript more easily than an interviewee, after all.

To assume that transcripts have had their emotional power stripped away would be wrong. It would negate the potency of novels, poems, and so on, just because they are printed. Reading the words of a convicted murderer, serious sexual offender, or a paedophile is still likely to produce strong feelings – whatever preparations are made by the reader beforehand. Were the printed words of Nicholas or the memories of Dolly's sad death (both quoted earlier) not emotionally moving? It would be a strange researcher indeed who did not feel something after reading the story of John Thompson's callous and off-hand description of his victimisation of a hitchhiker. He described to a researcher how he strangled his wife after an argument when he was drunk, and was then asked about his second victim: 'Just a young lass I picked up for some reason, I killed her', he stated without further elaboration.[7] However, it is surely the case that the transcript cannot convey the emotional charge that is created during the original interview. We should not, perhaps, be too precious about this, for it is also the case that memories related in an interview cannot carry the full force of being there at the time of the events described.

Possibly the secondary analysis of a transcribed interview will negate intrusive emotion and allow a more 'objective' analysis.

Researchers who too closely identify with their interviewees can lose the professional detachment and questioning stance that is necessary for critical crime history research. Empathetic identification may not be so deep for transcript readers, because they are twice removed from the actual interview process. First, they can only imaginatively visualise the respondent, which might lessen the impact of the distressing story they 'hear' narrated. Second, because researchers of crime between 1880 and 1940 are unlikely to read the interviews of anyone still alive (they would now be, at least, centenarians). In the future, transcript readers may read about people who died decades or even centuries ago. It will be for individual researchers to decide whether a more objective stance necessarily means a better analysis.

With that kind of detachment perhaps we do not need safeguards in the relationship between interviewee and transcript reader.

We should exercise some caution here. For the reader of the transcripted interview, the ethical responsibilities and bonds felt by an empathetic face-to-face interview may be absent, are more distant and more tenuous. It may be that the safeguards need to be even stronger for the secondary analytical processes. After all, archived interviews are in 'the public sphere'; they are easier to access, and the viewers have no real relationship with the people involved in creating the original interview (Silverman 2000). There must be serious concern that the potential for abuse is high, especially because the original agreement or consent is a relationship between the original interviewee and interviewer. Only if archives preserve the spirit as well as the letter of the law in this regard will the original protection remain in place.

In fact, the issue of 'consent' raises a whole range of problems for secondary analysis, doesn't it? How can a transcript reader know whether the interviewee was prepared originally to share their story; and whether they are still willing to do so (providing they are still alive)? If the researcher decides that they were, does this make it ethical to use the story? If they decide that they weren't, what then?

Again using the British Sociology Association (BSA) guidelines as an example of principles guiding social scientists, they state that freely informed consent should be given by a research participant. The researcher has a duty to describe what the research is about, to explain how far participants will be afforded anonymity and confidentiality, and to discuss any other possible uses of the data, if there is a likelihood that data may be shared with other researchers. However, many of the interviews available in archives may have been carried out before rigorous guidelines had been developed by learned bodies. This becomes problematic when we begin to move beyond the actual narrative or the words used to its subsequent interpretation and, hence, the creation of multiple 'stories' – who then owns the narrative or narratives? How do transcript readers know if the interviewee ever wanted to be an author? As Richardson and I argued in 2003, there are no simple answers to these questions, unfortunately. Given the numerous ethical complexities of secondary analysis in this area, it is not surprising that some historians and researchers have become pessimistic, whereas some feel that they are overly constrained by the imposition of 'ethical straitjackets'. The frustration comes with the realisation that, by not bringing this information to the public, it is not only the powerless who are protected but also the racist, the human rights abuser – should not their crimes be revealed? What would the childhood victims of Jimmy Savile say if either the interviews he gave about his life or the oral testimonies of his victims were not given to researchers some twenty or thirty years hence because they had died? Would they want their words to be hidden? There also appears to be a growing concern among academics that ethics committees are creating a 'moral panic' and stifling creative research (Winlow and Hall 2012).

Is there no way out of this situation? Oral histories carried out with living people can take us back to memories of the 1930s and 1940s (and later, of course) but only transcribed interviews offer us a perspective on start of the twentieth century to the 1920s, so it seems essential to our work that we find a way forward.

All is not lost, but putting ethics to one side is not the answer. An ethical approach is not only necessary (and not optional) but also achievable. Although this will not be an easy road to travel for transcript readers, it seems that there are two possible routes. The first is to adhere where appropriate to all of the ethical guidelines that regulate oral history. When those guidelines involve keeping to the rules imposed by archives or libraries of oral history material, they should also be kept to. Because the use of transcripted material is in its infancy, it is unlikely that an acknowledged orthodoxy about ethical usage will emerge in the near future. The methodologies for using transcripted data which are being currently developed may well shape the ethical position, and it is clear that more thought is required within this area. Dealing with transcripted oral material offers rare challenges, but ones that may become more common with the blurring of boundaries between disciplines. There may be a need for a different kind of ethical practice which considers areas such as how we conceive of participants, whether living or dead, and a distinction between codes of ethics and personal morality. The individual researcher will remain at the heart of this process, and so long as historians of crime can balance their need for relevant data with consideration of the original interviewee's well-being – in both the analytical and the dissemination stages of research – there is no problem with using transcripted data as well as carrying out oral interviews with the living.

As the previous chapter has shown, qualitative data, particularly oral history interviews, not only contextualise and illustrate general statistical trends but they also form the main challenge to theories and studies that rest solely on statistical information. Without recourse to transcripted oral histories carried out in the 1980s (for people born nearly a century earlier), analysis of the period from World War I to World War II would be somewhat limited. Indeed, it may be fatally flawed. That would be a shame given that we now have wonderful opportunities to combine oral interviews with new digital data. The use of online digital data and vast, easily searchable electronically retrieved data can bring its own ethical challenges, but it also offers huge benefits to professional crime historians and to family historians. All of those advantages and disadvantages are explored and explained in the next chapter.

7

NEW DIGITAL MEDIA

In Woking Prison 1881, four-times-convicted Eliza Godfrey was informed by letter that her nine-year-old son had died whilst at school in Lambeth. On release from prison, the deaf, widowed, former convict joined her daughter, Sophia, who was working at a brothel in Providence Street. Given some time it would be possible to tell you what her son had died of; if Eliza's ophthalmic problems ever cleared up; whether mother and daughter stayed in the same trade, or moved on, and out of London; and for how long each of them lived. We could even go further. We could discover if and when Eliza's daughter (who preferred to be called 'Sophy') had children of her own, what they did for a living and whether they ever got into trouble with the police, what they died of, what their children went on to do, and so on, until (with a bit of luck) we could reintroduce Eliza and Sophy's descendants living today to the details of their progenitors' difficult lives. Ten years or so ago, uncovering all of this intimate detail might have taken months, even years, but now with the aid of the new digital media, it might take just a day.

We began this book with the life history of Patrick Madden, a convict with a lengthy and interesting criminal record. As Madden careered through life committing assaults, having fights, and getting drunk, he interacted with various criminal justice institutions. He was arrested by local Yorkshire police constables and had to account for his actions before various magistrates and judges (again in West and South Yorkshire), and, of course, he spent time in some local and convict prisons throughout his life (Wakefield, Pentonville, Wormwood Scrubs, Portland, and Mill-bank). As he passed through the chain of justice he, like many thousands of others, left documentary evidence behind him. As Chapter 11 demonstrates, the joined-up paper trail that stretched among the criminal justice institutions was felt to be integral to controlling and watching habitual offenders. The charge books, indictments, court and prison registers, and so on, all help to shed light not only on Madden and his behaviour but also on the workings, attitudes, and organization of criminal justice institutions.

Now, because of the revolution in electronic resources, many of these documents are readily available. There has been a huge extension in both the scale of documentary evidence available and the range of people who are using websites and electronic databases to research their own criminal ancestors. This chapter describes the sort of criminal justice records (both archival and digital) that are available, and illustrates how some historians have started to employ them in their work (using detailed examples of cutting-edge micro- and life-history research). It then discusses some of the 'fallout' from the use of new media which have barely been mentioned in historical research – the ethical usage of personal information which has now become so freely available and the implications of huge amounts of crime data being available for such speedy analysis – and the chapter ends with a debate about electronic 'dark tourism' (the Internet tourism of prison and convict history) and how information about crime, prisoners, and punishment is presented online.

A toolkit for criminal justice research

Let us run through some of the documents that are available to us and in the order that they may have been created, starting with the commission of a crime, through to the final disposal and punishment of a convicted offender.[1]

News of the crime

Most criminal-justice–generated documents have at least the bare bones of the crime being dealt with. This can be a simple listing of the charge (manslaughter, simple larceny, and so on) or a descriptive narrative about the event (the sort of thing found in indictments or Quarter Sessions records, all discussed in the following). However, for the fullest description of the behaviour which has led a defendant into court, historical newspapers are the most useful source (Clarke 2004; Conboy 2004). Trial reports contained detailed information on many crimes (the more serious or noteworthy crimes tended to receive the greatest attention) because these were of great interest to their readers. Researchers are also interested in the way that defendants and victims were described and represented. For example, the trials of Florence Maybrick (1889) and Beatrice Pace (1928), nearly forty years apart, have been used to examine gendered attitudes in sentencing offenders, and have become case studies in press manipulation (Frost 2004; Carter Wood 2008). Visual material such as Punch cartoons (www.punchcartoons.com), the lithographs printed in the *Illustrated London News* and the *Police Gazette*, and cartoons in other contemporary popular journals also (literally) illustrate contemporary attitudes towards crime and offending.

Ploughing through pages and pages of daily or weekly issues of newspapers kept at the British Newspaper Library at Colindale was once the lot of the lonely doctoral researcher – either that or sitting in a local library scrolling through yet another microfilmed newspaper. For researchers, managing to keep their eyes open to search for crime reports amongst the mass of reports of social and sporting events (the thoughts of some vicar in, say, Coventry, who had something important to say in the letters page, or an editorial on the state of cheese prices during World War I, amongst other things) was almost impossible. It certainly wasn't a good use of research time. Now we have a number of digitalised newspapers at our disposal that can be electronically searched with keywords that direct us to specific reports or dates of our choosing (and immediately).

The Gale News Vault (http://gdc.gale.com/products/gale-newsvault/) contains more than seventy local and regional newspapers taken directly from the extensive holdings of the British Library, including the *Sheffield Daily Telegraph*, the *Leeds Intelligence*, the *Evening Telegraph*, the *Yorkshire Gazette*, the *Nottingham Evening Post*, the *Newcastle Guardian and Tyne Mercury*, the *Brighton Patriot and South of England Free Press*, *The Bristol Mercury*, *The Caledonian Mercury*, *The Champion, Daily News*, *The Examiner*, *Freeman's Journal*, *Genedl* (Wales), the *Glasgow Herald*, *The Graphic*, the *Hampshire Telegraph*, *The Hull Packet*, *Jackson's Oxford Journal*, *The Leeds Mercury*, the *Liverpool Mercury*, *Lloyd's Illustrated Newspaper*, *The Manchester Examiner*, the *Northern Echo*, *The Northern Liberator*, *The Northern Star*, the *Western Mail*, *The Blackburn Standard*, the *Dundee Courier*, *The Essex Standard*, the *Isle of Man Times*, the *Lancaster Gazette*, the *Leicester Chronicle*, *The Morning Post*, the *Royal Cornwall Gazette*, the *Sheffield Independent*, *The Standard* (London), *The Wrexham Weekly Advertiser*, and *The York Herald*.

Aside from these regional newspapers, national reports for this period can be found in *The Times Digital Archive, 1785–2006* which, like the newspapers mentioned earlier, can be searched for individual events or names. This is also true of the *Guardian* Archive Online (www.guardian.co.uk/gnm-archive) which houses almost 13 million articles dating from 1791 up to 2003. Access to crime reports is now very easy, and what once took weeks, if not months, can now be done in days. All of these digital newspaper sources are usually available through library or university sites (or with a subscription) and are therefore what we might term 'public'. A source of crime data which is more hidden, and which is certainly less straightforward to analyse, is crime scene photography.

This is a much trickier beast, both ethically and in the simple terms of getting hold of it. Some individual police case files will contain photographs of the crime scene, and so it is possible to come across them – and also newspapers in the 1920s and 1930s were increasingly willing and able to publish photographs of car crash sites, murders and so on (particularly in the United States, but also in the United Kingdom). There are also some books which have reprinted contemporary scenes of violent crime, suspicious deaths, and suicide (the incidents that police were called out to deal with) for the early to mid-twentieth century (see Buckland 2001; Doyle 2005). Perhaps the largest online collection is the forensic photography archive within the Justice and Police Museum in Sydney (www.hht.net.au/museums/justice_and_police_museum). Originally the archive was created by the New South Wales Police between 1912 and 1964. It contains an estimated 130,000 negatives of mugshots, accident scenes, crashes, murders, fires, forgeries and fingerprints, and the movements of suspicious characters around town. As well as the collection, there is a blog for crime scene investigators and archivists to discuss their subject (http://blogs.hht.net.au/justice/). The website does issue a warning for people wishing to view the photographs:

Warning

Images from the Justice & Police Museum forensic crime photography collection may contain images of deceased persons. The Historic Houses Trust has published these images in good faith with no intention to cause distress or embarrassment to anyone.

As researchers we are used to finding and republishing revealing details of crimes, and of the defendants, and sometimes of the victims. Photographs seems to be qualitatively quite different: the murdered bodies covered in blood, or the photographs of visibly very distressed female rape victims, or the sad suicides sitting lifeless beside a razor or with a gun held forlornly in their drooping hands. It seems much more invasive of the victim's privacy at a time when, really, they are *most* deserving of privacy. All of these scenes are available to us as casual visitors to the museum, or when surfing the web. I should also make it clear that the pictures can be horrible, or worse than that, horrific. They have the capacity to affect the viewer to a considerable degree and, although I have provided some references in this chapter, I am also aware of other publications in this area for which references are not provided in this chapter.[2] We will return to the question of ethics later in this chapter because the new digital media raises all kinds of ethical questions which are only now beginning to be thought about.

We should now probably issue another kind of warning. Many of the crime scene photographs are stripped of context. We do not have any other details of the people involved or wider circumstances. We should therefore ask some analytical questions such as who 'owns' the images – the victims, the photographer, the police? Should the names of people in the photographs be revealed or hidden? Should they be abstracted from the police files they were originally placed in or kept integral to them in order to retain context? Are they works of art, as they sometimes appear to be presented? These photographs are of accidents and crimes committed on the other side of the world in Sydney. Should we treat them differently from suicides and accidents in England (which look very similar) or view the images as somehow universal? I suppose that the most pressing question for researchers is what can we learn from the pictures? Nothing that can be quantified, of course, but qualitatively we can see at first hand some of the physical circumstances of the cases – where the body lay, possibly the economic conditions of the victim (if the crime took place in their house), and something of the forensic techniques of the time. These might all be useful, so we should not write this off, but we should also not get carried away with the immediacy of the photographs. We live in a very visual age now, but researchers must remember that documentary sources usually still provide the greatest level of research data. I am going to leave us with one more form of photographic evidence, however, which may be the most useful of all – the mugshot.

Mugshot photography has been around for a long time – from the habitual offenders files (discussed in Chapter 11) to police photographs in the 1920s and 1930s (Doyle 2009).[3] However, a new form of recording the lives of prisoners and ex-offenders has pushed crime photography conventions. The sensitive photographs taken by Luigi Gariglio of male and female prisoners show their resilience and their vulnerability within prison walls (Gariglio 2006), so too do the portraits of ageing 'hard men' and British gangsters found in Mahoney and Anderson (2011). These collections of photographs serve as a reminder that behind the terms *offender* and *convict* there are human beings, something that perhaps researchers and policy makers occasionally forget.

Police sources

At the arrest and charging stage, where the police were most involved, there are not that many surviving records. The charge books are very useful in that they often give information not found elsewhere (this might include the time of arrest, or the things that the person had in their pockets when searched at the police station, or it may even provide details such as their age and religion). Refused charge books are even better, because they tell us a little more about the boundary decisions which took place before an arrested person either advanced through to prosecution by a complainant (or the police) or was released. Together with 'occurrence' books (which revealed something of what officers actually did on their beats), these documents can shed some light on the questions about prosecution and diversion raised in Chapter 4. Other documents, such as investigations into the complaints the public made against police officers, or staff records, or even plans of the physical organisation of police stations, and so on, can all offer benefits to researchers. Access to police records can sometimes be a problem, and closure periods can be extensive (these are usually set by the depositing police force rather than by the archivists). It should be remembered that closure periods are merely guidelines, not set in legislation, and can sometimes be negotiated.[4] Barriers to the documents can sometimes be removed with a letter to the relevant chief constable – one of the benefits of historical research is that serving police officers often consider historical material to be uncontroversial (see the debate about the impact of historical research in the next chapter). I am not convinced that the gatekeepers of police records are correct in this view, but I am happy to take advantage of it – as Chapter 5 showed, it is often incumbent on researchers themselves to make these kinds of decisions.

Documents that link together information from the police and the prisons tend to contain important biometric details – if only to identify that they are talking about the same person. The Habitual Offenders Act of 1869 and the Prevention of Crimes Act 1871 both created a set of bureaucratic records which lurk in archives under a variety of names and catalogue titles: Rochdale's Rogues Gallery of offenders (LA/D/2/11/2/POLICE/1 1887–1929), Burnley's Register of Habitual Criminals (PLBu16/2 1911), Gloucester's Register of Convict

Licence Holders (Q/Y/4/3 1869–1933); Stockport has a Town Thieves Book (1908–1928), and so on. These registers captured information on repeat offenders from 1871 to the 1930s[5], and provide individual-level data including a full offending history, with a physical description of the individual (including an exhaustive list of distinguishing features such as tattoos, scars, or deformities), known aliases and previous offences, police remarks (which gave additional details such as the individual's reporting history), and general remarks (which could include the individual's trade and administrative details of correspondence between police forces concerning the individual). The local copies of these books have more information than that kept by the central information clearing house in London (for example they contain dates when the ex-prisoner reported to the police station as they were required to do, the dates they missed, and their subsequent punishment for their absence, and so on). However, local habitual offender registers are not available in many places, and it may be necessary to consult the national registers (MEPO 6) which are now kept in the National Archives. Also at the National Archives is a full set of the *Police Gazette*.[6] These are voluminous and impressive records. In 1914 the *Gazette* began to be issued on a twice-weekly basis rather than the previous weekly edition, and in 1927 the publication became daily. By 1936 there were also six regular supplements to the Gazette:

> *Supplement A* – issued fortnightly and containing details of 'expert and travelling criminals', including their name and unique Criminal Record Office(C.R.O.) number, personal weaknesses (e.g., addiction to alcohol) and peculiarities (e.g. slowness of speech), criminal history, modus operandi, photograph, and (when available) details of where specimen of handwriting was kept. *Supplement B* – issued weekly and titled 'Convicts on Licence, Persons under Police Supervision and Others whose Apprehensions Are Sought for Failing to Comply with the Requirements of the Prevention of Crimes Act'. It contained the convict's name (and any known) aliases, C.R.O. number, year of birth, height, complexion, hair colour, eye colour, distinguishing marks, occupation, birthplace, previous convictions and details of release, reason for revocation of the licence, name of the police proving identity, and details of police forces that had had previous contact with the missing convict. *Supplement C* – published weekly, this supplement contained details of aliens wanted for crime and alien offences. *Supplement D* – also published weekly, this supplement was a list of absentees/deserters from Her or His Majesty's armed forces. *Supplement E* – this fortnightly supplement (published on alternate fortnights to that of Supplement A) was commenced in 1933 and contained photographs and of active criminals not considered sufficiently important to be included in Supplement A. *Supplement F* – published daily, this supplement gave details of deaths and reconvictions of criminals previously circulated.

The last things to consider are those records that come from the police perspective. From the late nineteenth century it became popular for police officers, prison officers, and other officials to set down on paper their thoughts on their jobs and crime in general (see Lawrence 2003), and there are a number of published memoirs of police officers working at various levels of the hierarchy – in the late nineteenth century (Caminada 1895; Chadwick 1901/1974; Smethurst 1914), and the early to mid-twentieth century (Beveridge 1957; Dell 1997; Gosling 1959; Harrison 1956; Howgrave-Graham 1947; Sillitoe 1955). These works of memory cannot be taken at face value any more than any historical source can (see Chapter 5). They are obviously highly selective and tend to be flashback-style accounts of memorable cases or trials; nevertheless they also reveal much about the organisation, hierarchy, and operations of police forces, which otherwise would remain lost to us.

The courts

Continuing our journey through the criminal justice system, we come to the courts. Because the courts needed to know who was being delivered to them, the names and charges against all offenders were recorded for each appearance at the magistrates' courts, the Quarter Sessions, and Assize courts. For the early part of our period, up to 1892, the easiest way of finding someone tried for indictable offences were the Criminal Registers available on the ancestry website. Although the registers continue past that date they have not (yet) been digitised. Even more details of the defendant were recorded in Quarter Sessions calendars (not just previous offences, but also the age and occupation of the defendant and some contextual information about the offence itself), and for defendants tried at the Central Criminal Court there is a marvellous online repository.

Old Bailey Online (www.oldbaileyonline.org/) has details of 197,000 trials, of which 29,269 relate to the 1880–1913 period (about 15 per cent).[7] With so many cases it is impossible to find a 'typical' case, but the trial of Henrich Fuchs on 19 March 1912 for bigamy gives an idea of the type and amount of information provided on the website:

> Detective WILLIAM ALLEN, L Division. I produce the two marriage certificates, the first being dated June 28, 1891, and the second September 30, 1911. On February 9th I went to Rattray Road, Brixton, where I saw the prisoner and told him I was a police officer and that I should arrest him for bigamously marrying Maud Emily Dettmar in September, 1911, his wife, Rachel Fuchs, being then alive. He said, 'Quite right. I have been expecting it. I won't give you any trouble. I have sent money to my wife in New York on several occasions. I left my wife in New York seven years ago on the 17th of this month. I ought not to have married a second time, but you know what it is. I got the girl into trouble so chanced it and married her. A man I know came from New York and told me my wife in New York was carrying on with a man.'

ABRAHAM BLASKY, tailor. I was present at the marriage of my sister Rachel to the prisoner on June 28, 1891, at the East London Synagogue . . . In 1905 prisoner went to New York alone and she followed him. I followed. The last time I saw them together as man and wife would be in March, 1905, when I left New York. I believe she is still alive.

REUBEN ROSENTHAL, licencee, the 'Britannia' Berwick Street, W. I know prisoner as a customer; I have heard him speak of his wife and family. On a Sunday towards the end of last September he came into the house and said he was going to get married on the following Saturday, September 30. I thought he was joking and said that of course I knew that he was a married man and it was impossible. He said, 'That's right. I have arranged everything.' I met him a week afterwards on Black Fast Day and said, 'Have you got married?' He said, 'No, you know yourself I have not got married because I have got a wife in America'.

MAUD EMILY DETTMAR, 67 Rattray Road, Brixton. On September 30 I went through the form of marriage at the Registry Office with the prisoner as 'Henry Fuchs'; I thought he was single; I had known him a year last August. After the marriage I heard that he was married. I have lived with him up to the time of his arrest. I have one child eight weeks' old by him.

HENRY FUCHS (prisoner, on oath) stated that ever since he had married his first wife she had not given him a day's peace; that he went to America and had sent for her two months afterwards in the hope that she would be better; that he worked as hard as he could for her and his children, but she was not satisfied with New York and wished to return, but he could not afford this . . . on his return to England in 1905 he worked hard and constantly sent money for her and his children's keep; that in 1906 at her request he had sent her money for her ticket home, but had not since heard from her or of her; that in August, 1911, he met Miss Dettmar and having got her into trouble felt bound to marry her.

Miss Dettmar stated that she had not been seduced by prisoner under promise of marriage; that he married her because of her condition and had since been very kind to her.[8]

Henrich received three month's hard labour for his bigamous offence, and if he could have afforded the cost, he may have been better off going through the divorce courts. If he had, he may have turned up in the records of those courts (which can be useful for revealing unprosecuted cases of domestic violence). Indeed, the records of tribunals are worth searching (licensing matters for example, or inquests). There are also business and staff records which can be used to study fraud and workplace appropriation. These are private records, but many businesses have deposited their historical records in the various county records offices. Last, there are the quasi-official records of charities such as National Society for the Prevention of Cruelty to Children which are available to researchers via local records offices and the National Archives (www.nationalarchives.gov.uk/a2a/records.aspx?cat=138–179cru&cid=0#0).

Punishment

Old Bailey Online and other sites also reveal details of punishments, of course, as do data sets such as the British Academy–funded data set which contains details of prosecutions and sentences in the lower courts in Australia, Canada, England, Wales, Scotland, Jersey, New Zealand, and the United States from about 1880 to 1940. Approximately 120,000 cases have been recorded – some contain more details than others (often because of the privacy regulations that operate), and some have had the original details garnered from court records enhanced with data on offenders secured from census data and other sources. The data, which will be available on a dedicated website from 2014, have been entered in both Excel and SPSS and is designed to be of use to researchers interested in crime rates, prosecution rates, prosecution practices, and sentencing practices and in how they changed over time. They are aimed at researchers interested in making comparisons across national and local jurisdictions for roughly the same period (1860–1940) and will complement existing international data sets such as the 'Historical Violence Database' (http://cjrc.osu.edu//) from the Criminal Justice Research Center at The Ohio State University and the Quetelet Project on Belgian criminal statistics (www.fundp.ac.be/en/research/projects/page_view/03299003/).

Prisons, workhouses, and other places of punishment also have publicly available records. For example, the London Metropolitan Archives have the records of Wormwood Scrubs Prison (LMA/4417). The records consist of prison registers of prisoners for 1917 through 1967 which are indexed by name and give details of the weight, height, and physical characteristics of each prisoner on reception to the prison. Similar records exist for prisons in Lincoln, York, Wakefield, and so on, which are kept in county records offices, and some records have been placed online – either on pay-for-view sites (the Dorset, England, Prison Admission and Discharge Registers 1782–1901 and Dorset, England, Calendar of Prisoners 1854–1904 are on Ancestry.com) or on public websites. Choosing a random name from the Victorian Crime and Punishment site (http://vcp.e2bn.org/prisoners/) we can find the following information about East Anglican prisoners, one of whom was Walter Barker:

> **Age:** 29
> **Offence:** Wilfully neglect his child
> **Sentence:** £5 5s 0d or 1 calendar month hard labour
> **Type of trial:** Quarter Sessions
> **Type of offence:** against the person
> **Height:** 5 ft 4 inches
> **Hair colour:** Brown

Identifying marks:
Trade or occupation: Blacksmith
Education: Imp
Number of children: Unknown
Religion: Church of England
Birth town: Cambridge

Walter spent his time in a local prison. Had he been incarcerated in a convict prison he would probably have been released early on conditional licence at some point. PCOM 3 files at the National Archives contain 45,000 licences issued between 1853–1887, 1902–1908, and 1912–1942. They list details of the prisoner's name, sentence, where and when convicted, dates and conditions of the current licence, previous convictions, age, previous occupation, and when and from where the prisoner was released, and most have photographs of the prisoner. The licences give the dates when the prisoner required medical treatment (and what for), the labour they completed inside the prison, and the letters that they wrote to friends and family.[9] When they are pieced together with prisoner autobiographies they form a rich and comprehensive record of prison life (see Dendrickson and Thomas 1954; Henry 1952; Mackenzie 1937; Mountain 1930; Priestley 1985; William Beauchamp Nevill 1903).

A somewhat more fragmented set of records exist for children prosecuted (or taken into care) in this period. By the end of the nineteenth century, England and Wales had a wide range of state and charity-supported (semi)carceral homes for 'delinquent', 'difficult' and destitute children (Cox and Shore 2002; Fishman 2002; Griffiths 1996; Humphries 1981; King and Noel 1993; Pearson 1983; Radzinowicz and Hood 1990; Shore 1999). The records of some of these institutions survive. For example, by the time Thomas Barnardo died in 1905, the charity he founded ran ninety-six homes in which more than 8,500 children were cared for, and their records are kept by Liverpool University. It can be difficult to identify children in the Old Bailey Online and other archived court records. Investigating why these children were sent to court or to reformatories/industrial school is not easy unless you are searching for a particular child (knowing their name and date of conviction). Children were, at least until the early twentieth century, treated essentially as adults – appearing in the same courtrooms and receiving similar punishments to adult offenders. Little wonder that they are undifferentiated in the general records of offenders. A more efficient way to trace juvenile offenders would be to look at HO 349 files kept at the National Archives. These contain miscellaneous records for selected reformatories and industrial schools including admissions books, but also some reports on the individuals after they left the reformatory (letters back to staff at the school, photographs, memoirs, and so on). Borstal after-care records, which are extensive, also follow youths for a considerable period after their release. Obviously the more successful 'graduates' from the schools were more likely to keep in touch, so there is some selection bias at work here. Nevertheless, it is possible to piece together the lives of some children who were 'in care' of one kind or other and to begin to devise research questions that arise from the reconstruction of their lives.

For example, two eight-year-old boys, Peter Barratt and James Bradley, were convicted at Chester Assize Court for killing two-year-old George Burgess, a child they had never seen before the day that they murdered him. The small child was abducted, stripped, beaten, and finally drowned in a brook. Records show that the two accused boys had previously been suspended from Stockport Sunday School. For their crime, as was normally the case with youth, the boys were sentenced to a short period of custody (one month) followed by an order to stay in a reformatory until they were fourteen (nearly five years in their cases). Records of Bradwall Reformatory (Cheshire) kept at the National Archives revealed that Bradley could neither read nor write, that he had no previous convictions, that his parents were hat makers in Stockport, and that he had two siblings. He was discharged on licence in 1866 despite the home secretary opposing his early release because of the severity of the original offence. It appears that he was released on the authority of George Latham, founder and manager of Bradwall Reformatory. The regime at Bradwell was strict, but allowed for privileges to be progressively earned (the progress of each child was recorded) and the institution was praised by HM Inspectors of Reformatory Schools for their success rates. Indeed, Latham and his successors received many letters of thanks from ex-inmates. Home Office statistics from early this century attest to the fact that, in contrast to most reformatories in the country, 60 percent of boys detained at Bradwall reformed.

As the journalist who subsequently investigated this case in 1995, Gitta Sereny, found, Bradley never returned to Stockport and it is likely that he emigrated to either Australia or Canada (*The Independent, 23 April 1995*). Fifty years later, William James Brown, a fellow Bradwall boy also immigrated to Canada. He had come to Bradwell in 1901 and spent three years there. After leaving, he enlisted as a 'band boy' with the Twenty-First Lancers but was discharged a year later. His character was recorded as 'very good' by his regiment, and he picked up a number of temporary jobs (barman, mechanic, chauffer, waiter). In 1910 he found his feet and started work as a photographer's assistant in London. Due to his failing health he left London for Ontario and found employment as a photographer. Commenting on the regular reports and photographs he sent back to Bradwell, they call him 'a fine young man, quite a swell'. Some thirty years after leaving, he and his wife visited the school. Like Bradley, he never reoffended. However, other children failed to continue their good progress in the reformatory, and continued (and indeed accelerated) their criminal careers. For example, Rose Butler was committed by a court to an industrial school in 1914 at the age of ten because she had been sexually assaulted. Discharged on licence in 1920, with a history of violence and unable or unwilling to hold down a domestic service job, she drifted in and out of institutional care for the rest of her adult life. Her case notes in the Children's Society archive showed that she passed through at least eight other institutions, including a Waifs and Strays Auxiliary Home, two Church Army hostels, a Salvation Army home, a detention home, a workhouse, and two infirmaries (Cox 2002: 106). Piecing together the records to make a narrative naturally generates questions: Why did some children reform, and others not? What was the impact of different regimes on the children after release? The post-punishment phase is clearly as important in the lives of offenders as was the period that carried on their criminal career or the periods when punishment was endured.

Post-punishment

As family historians and genealogists will have found, it is something of a blessing if one's ancestor fell into the clutches of the State (asylum, workhouse, etc.), because an institutional record would have been kept. This is doubly true for those who were convicted and imprisoned. However, records of noncustodial punishments such as probation files are not so easy to find. Indeed, it is a matter of luck whether records exist for the area or person you are looking for. Fortunately a few of the early probation officers and police court missionaries produced memoirs. Thomas Holmes (1900, 1908) and Robert Holmes (1915), for example, wrote about the people they had guided after their appearance at magistrates courts. Although they have a particular moralistic tone, especially when describing the lives of the convicted, they can be used together with the odd institutional record (for example, Probation Officer's Notebooks 1923–1926, Chester and Cheshire Records Office CPS 3/1/1) to reveal the management of noncustodial sentences and attitudes towards offenders around World War I. The social and economic conditions that existed between the late 1890s and World War II can also be seen in Prisoners' Aid Society's records. Again, these records are fairly rare. Alongside the biographical details of offenders (age, occupation, marital status) they have comments about the perceived character of prisoners made by the Society's visitors: James Grote (age fifty-six, drunk) *'seem[ed] queer!'*, William Cooper (twenty-four, farrier, four months' gaol for assault) was *'back from Mons – wounded – discharged medically unfit – states that he is fit and made application to go back'*, or Charles Lines (thirty-nine, fruiterer) was *'mental'*.[10] For the 1930s, the descriptions of practical aid that they gave to ex-convicts (boots, glasses, a place to sleep for a day or two, the name of an employer who may offer them a job, and so on) are telling of the poverty of the depression years. It is frustrating therefore that few Prisoners' Aid Society records survive, and that the ones that do have received such little academic attention. If these records had been digitised, they would be much more likely to be used by family and other historians.

What is new about the new digital media?

Clearly it is easier to find a particular person or record (or even the existence of a set of records whose existence was previously unknown) if it has been digitised. There are a number of sites that can help to identify where records of 'criminal ancestors' can be found (see www.blacksheepancestors.com, www.origins.net, www.societyofgenealogists.com, www.geni.com/. . ./do-you-have-a-criminal-in-your-family-tree-354741.html, or www.ancestry.co.uk/[11]), and these sites have greatly boosted the numbers of genealogists who now track down criminal records with ease. Similarly, professional researchers now routinely use online resources in their teaching and in their research activities. The intensifying pressures on research time in academic posts today means that more academics use digital sources in the gaps between teaching, where once before they may have had time to go to the archives themselves. For these reasons we might actually underestimate the pervasiveness of digital sources. For example, whilst researching the life histories of three sets of offenders (minor offenders from Crewe 1880–1940, habitual offenders in the north-west of England, and licenced convicts in England and Wales 1853–1940), a team of academics produced a large number of life grids which outlined the offending careers and family lives of hundreds of people. In the following I have randomly selected an example of each type of offender, and (this time) I have identified whether the data came from an archival or a digital source (digitally derived data has been italicised).

Life story 1: The minor offender

Julia Joyce was born in Ireland in 1858. In 1871 *she is living in Crewe at 30 New Street with her father Michael (thirty-nine), mother Hannah (thirty-six) and siblings: Ann (nine), Thomas (six); Edward (two), and William (nine months)*. Her father leaves Crewe Railway Works in 1886 to set up in business himself. *Two years later, Julia leaves the family home to marry her Manchester sweetheart Joseph and moves into a house with him at Herdman Street*. Joseph is a chemical engineer, and all seems well between the couple. Julia, as is traditional, *returns to Crewe for the birth of their first and only child Norah in 1881*. *Julia's mother dies six years later*, and (for some reason) Joseph leaves the family home in 1887 or 1888. Julia seems to have taken to drink and is convicted for public drunkenness three times in 1890–1891, and more seriously, she is also indicted for receiving some stolen cloth which is brought to her by her daughter Norah. A little while later, Norah is convicted for stealing some eggs and receives a twenty-one-day prison sentence followed by five years in a reformatory. The magistrate commented that Norah was running wild: 'A child of nine sent to gaol. A disgraceful case. It seems that if she goes home with nothing she is not welcome'. Julia cannot be found in the 1901 census but was convicted of threatening behaviour in 1904, and a year later she was committed to Upton Asylum at Chester for being 'of unsound mind'. *She died in 1910*.

Life story 2: The habitual offender

Edward Palmer, also known as 'Ned Kelly' was born in London in 1869. First convicted of stealing a purse, he received a three-month gaol sentence in 1893. Over the next decade he was convicted of warehouse breaking (six months' hard labour, 1896), attempted larceny (nine months' hard labour, 1897), larceny of a watch chain (six months' hard labour, 1898), and larceny of a watch (twenty months' hard labour, 1899). As a result of that last conviction he came under the habitual offender legislation that qualified him for an additional two years' police supervision on release from prison. *In 1901 he was claiming to be a U.S.-born sailor living in Spitalfields,* and in the same year he was convicted of larceny of a watch at Nottingham (two months' hard labour) and breeched the Prevention of Crimes Act at West Ham (three months' hard labour). Later that year, he went to the aid of his brother who had got into a pub fight in London and stabbed a man, who subsequently died. He was originally charged with murder, but the charge was reduced to manslaughter at the Central Criminal Court. *He received a three-year gaol sentence.* During a robbery in 1905 he stabbed a constable and received a five-year gaol stretch and three years' police supervision at North London Quarter Sessions. After serving his time he was released to a Discharged Prisoners' Aid Society who found him work as a miner in Durham (where he had a good character). Nevertheless, he was again convicted for possessing and uttering counterfeit coin at London in 1909. *Back at the Old Bailey he received an eighteen-month gaol sentence.* Later, after release, he found employment as a docker. By now in his mid- to late-fifties, he seems not to have committed any further crimes.

Life story 3: The licenced convict

Amelia Counsel was born in 1839 in Lambeth. Aged twenty-six she was the complainant in a rape case in 1865 (*The Lloyd's Weekly Newspaper,* 14 May 1865). She was living in as an unmarried woman in Kensington workhouse as servant out of employ. She is reported to be a sickly figure. The *Illustrated Police New* (Saturday, 9 February 1867) reported that Amelia and her friend Elizabeth Clements were charged with distraction burglaries whilst pretending to apply for jobs as servants. The same newspaper reported that she was convicted with others of assault the following year and was fined £5–00 at Marlborough Police Court (28 March 1868). In 1870 she was convicted at Middlesex Sessions of stealing a watch (six months' gaol). She was out in time to be recorded in the 1871 census as living at Royal Street, Lambeth, with her professional singer husband Henry, but she was back in gaol later that year. *The Standard* (18 May 1871) reported that she had been part of the garrotting of private detective Henry Field. One of the gang escaped whilst on remand, but eventually all stood trial in Southwark and received a six-month gaol sentence. A similar offence in 1877 gained her another month, and another three months for frequenting the following year, and yet another twelve-month gaol for larceny from the person in 1880. Still living with her husband in 1881, they were now living at 2 Johanna Street, Lambeth, with Henry now working as a cabinetmaker. She became a convict in 1882 when she received five years' penal servitude for theft of boots whilst drunk (she was 'nearly always drunk' according to *Reynolds's Newspaper* [30 July 1882]). The convict licence reveals her life inside various London convict prisons:

> 22.8.82 14 days hospital for Fistula.
> 3.8.82 writes letters to her friend, a respectable married woman in Blackfriars Rd.

16.2.82 writes to husband Henry Brown in Pentonville Prison. Reply in 17.3.83 from Wormwood Scrubs.

13.2.83 visited by sister and male cousin.

29.5.83, 2 months in hospital with Fistula – operated on, and put on light duties.

13.8.83 visited by brother (in law?) and two sisters.

15.11.83 Admonished for threatening to disturb silent time when given needlework by the Matron instead of knitting for her work. She was most violent in her language.

Letters continuing to be sent/received from sister, and husband.

4.2.84 visited by sister, brother in law and nephew

9.5.84 Petitioned to be removed from laundry because a shill (a prison 'nark') was annoying her. This was investigated and 'fault found on both sides'. Amelia was removed from laundry.

16.6.84 visited by brother, sister in law, and child.

24.2.85 Complains that she hasn't yet been removed to a Refuge; replied that that she isn't eligible to go until 3rd March.

8.8.85 At Russell House Refuge she shouts and blasphemes loudly to members of public outside House. Threatens violence to lady Superintendent. Punished with close confinement; 18 days no. 1 diet.

3.12.85 visited by sister and brother.

2.3.86 Herpes, hospital for 2 weeks.

27 Feb. 1886 Licence issued. Released on 3rd March from Fulham. Destination was Christopher Griffiths (Brother in law?) 67 Johnson St, Commercial Rd, East London.

The 1891 census records Amelia as living at 92 Richmond St, Marylebone, with painter husband Henry, both aged 52. However, ten years later she is recorded as a widow, living in Hackney on her own. Two years later, in 1913, she died.

It may be a general rule that the more minor an offender, the less chance there is of their offence being digitally recorded, especially if they come from outside of the big cities. However, had the *Crewe Chronicle* been digitised (as many regional newspapers have), then there would be little variation in the proportions of archival to digital sources used across the three preceding life-story case studies. Between carrying out the research for Life Story 2 (in 2010) and writing this chapter, the Habitual Offender Registers, which provided much of the data for Life Story 2, have now been digitised. When it comes to the licenced convict in Life Story 3, every single piece of information came from an online source, so it would appear that digital online resources are king, or if not king, then certainly the heir to the throne.

Scale, speed, and searchability

Without digital resources, it would still have been possible to construct those case studies presented earlier but impossible to construct *so many* of them (the three projects together constructed more than 2,000 case studies).Very quickly one can assemble knowledge about the lives of offenders when they were inside the system, and what happened to them outside of the system. For example, every ten years in the digitally available censuses (1841–1911) we can see where people lived, what their employment was, whether they were living with family or not, and who those family were – indeed, we can refine our knowledge of when children were born by reference to records of birth, marriage, and deaths (see www.freebmd.org. uk/, and most counties also have their own site; for example, Cheshire's is http:// cheshirebmd.org.uk/). Details of war service can be added into the mix through other sites (see ancestr.com or the Commonwealth War Graves Commission site – www.cwgc.org/). It really is possible to reconstruct the lives of Victorians and Edwardians in a very short time. We can even follow the family line through to their children and, in some cases, their children's children.[12] We can also use digital resources to carry out huge surveys that allow us to supplement micro- or single case studies (we can aggregate hundreds of single case studies in a comparatively short time). The Old Bailey Online (http://oldbaileyonline.tumblr.com/) allows researchers to undertake some limited statistical enquiries, for example, counting the number of crimes over time and so on, enabling us to contextualise some of the individual life stories within a wider context. This site, incidentally, receives more than 2,500 hits a day and is used by a wide range of professional and nonprofessional researchers. Last, as well as the main sources of information, there is plenty of room in cyberspace for the small-scale collection, so we can do some research (or even just casually look at) records which we would never have had access to (because they have been physically deposited abroad or because we simply did not know that they existed). Who amongst us could resist having a quick peek at the following collections on ancestry.com: List of Atlanta Penitentiary inmates, prisoner index, 1880–1922 (with photographs); Dorchester Prison Admission and Discharge Books 1782–1901; and Tennessee Divorce Court Records 1800–1965. Where might our interest in those records lead? We don't yet know – but it could open up a whole new area of interest or knowledge.

What's wrong with the new digital media?

Inevitably there are problems associated with the new digital media as there are with all sources and methodologies. Despite our enthusiasm for the obvious benefits of online sources, we have to retain a critical stance and examine the shortfalls and pitfalls along with the advantages of spending our lives before a computer screen.

There is, of course, most prosaically, that very problem. Researchers of all levels spend a long time working away at our laptops finding the digital nugget that unlocks our work. We spend less and less time in the archives (and this is especially true for students, who can find archival work intimidating and difficult to get into). We run the risk that digital sources become the only sources, and we find our peripheral vision reduced. I suppose it is the difference between a student going directly to the online copy of a book and reading it, and searching for a published copy of it in the library, and thereby en route discovering something next to it on the shelf which offers a different perspective. If I bemoan the loss of academic craft or archival expertise too much I will sound like a handloom weaver awaiting mechanisation, but I reserve the right to feel nostalgic when the libraries are empty and the archives closed.[13]

Commodification and commercialisation

Aside from the not insignificant expense of subscribing to some websites (Ancestry. com has an annual fee) which means that students can only (realistically) access the sites through institutional subscriptions, and some nonprofessional researchers may be put off using them altogether, there is the matter of whether a fee should be charged at all. Old Bailey Online and London Lives were in development for a long time and took a lot of hard work by an experienced team of academics, and approximately £1 million of public funding to develop them. They have revolutionised research by freely providing public documents to the public. Most court records, historical newspapers, and indeed most archival sources are publicly available because we pay for their upkeep through the taxation system. Should the records be privatised and restricted to those that can afford to pay to view them? Should some of the records of the National Archives be digitally available only through the Find My Past site? Have private websites earned the right to market historic records that they have enhanced through the digitisation process? Although users may sigh at the increasing commercialisation of public records, it appears that this is now the only route to more and more records becoming publicly available. Given the state of the economy at present, it seems very unlikely that archives and museums will be funded to increase their digital holdings, and researchers will continue to thank private websites for the chance to carry out their research, whilst muttering under their breath about the cost.

Decontextualised genealogies

Earlier we mentioned the speed at which information about individual offenders can be gathered. Where once researchers or family historians would have spent considerable time researching details of a single person or family, now we can surf records to pick out this or that offender – and if he or she is not suitable – we can simply dip back into the records to find another. Need to illustrate an essay on social crime with something about poaching? Here are several names that pop up in Old Bailey Online. Need to find some offending females in 1890s Liverpool – here are hundreds to choose from in the criminal registers from Ancestry.com. Is there something ethically dubious about industrial-scale searching through people's lives? We have raised the issue of anonymity in Chapter 5, but with reference to the new digital media, it seems both more pressing (because it is just *so* easy to access names and biographies) and irrelevant (for the same reason). If the website has transcribed records there would be an opportunity to remove names and identifiers. However, digitised records are mostly reproduced wholesale – the photos of documents reveal all, as do the digital newspaper crime reports. The issue of anonymity, with regard to these kinds of official records, may be a dead letter. We seem to be able to know everything about anyone we choose. This brings us to another problem. Researchers feel that they know enough about a person and the direction their lives took in order to state with a certain amount of authority the connections between offending and other life events (Godfrey, Cox, and Farrall, 2010, 2007). We should remember, however, that these official documents (useful as they are) can never reveal the whole picture. Humans have complex relationships, impressive imaginations and reasoning abilities, some of which find expression in their actions, making them do some things, and stop doing other things. We will never be in a position to fully understand why human beings did the things that they did, especially when they are at a historical arm's length when different socioeconomic and cultural conditions existed. Historians explicitly or implicitly acknowledge this fact, and we must now remember that digital sources (in bringing together so much data about one person) can give the illusion that we know more about their lives and motivations, than we actually do. At the same time, conversely, we should be optimistic about the new opportunities that digital online sources offer, and we should now go on to use them to construct new hypotheses about crime and offending.

Conclusion

As the opening paragraphs of this chapter make clear, archival sources can greatly inform us about crime and offending. Not all research takes place in cyberspace. Many researchers labour away in libraries and in archives, turning over dusty pages. Looking for that one detail that may have been missed, but which may illuminate so much, is immensely pleasurable. The new digital media have given us options. We can still journey to the archives, but, if we wish, we can also access a vast range of records in the blink of an eye. As the next chapter explains, the digital age may also enhance our chances of disseminating our work back onto the Internet in ways that can affect knowledge about crime – the online digital revolution is not a one-way street – knowledge can flow backwards and forwards along the superhighway.

8
IMPACT

Anyone with enough money can now spend a night in gaol. The cells in Oxford prison are larger, and warmer, and more comfortable now than they were before the gaol was turned into a luxury hotel in 2006 (www.malmaison.com/). The award-winning development renovated what was essentially a late Victorian prison into a four-star hotel.[1] Converting former gaols into hotels is a world-wide phenomena (see, for example, Sweden's largest Victorian prison, Langholmen Prison in Stockholm, built in 1875, www.langholmen.com/en/, or Charles Street Jail/ Suffolk County Jail in Boston, www.libertyhotel.com/), but an overnight stay in them is not cheap. There appears to be an 'incarceration premium' for those who wish to experience . . . well, what do the guests who stay there experience?

> Tired of doing hard time in run-of-the-mill hotels? Well, this time you're going to the slammer in style, at the former gaol now known as Malmaison Oxford. You're not going to be behind bars though: you're going to be sipping the coolest cocktails in the free world at MALBAR. And don't worry about doing porridge. Mal Brasserie serves an eclectic mix of classic dishes with a twist, from freshly caught fish to the famous Mal Burger. So who wants to escape? After all, good behaviour gets you privileges like free wi-fi, drench showers, plasma TVs and even toiletries that are just begging to be nabbed by light-fingered guests. This is one hotel in Oxford where you'll be happy to get a long stretch.
>
> (*www.malmaison.com/locations/oxford/?*
> *gclid=CPSkrMesu7UCFeXLtAodFyoAUg*)

The publicity blurb invokes the terms associated with imprisonment – porridge, escape, a long stretch, good behaviour, light-fingered guests, and so on – but the residents can scarcely experience the same conditions as the people who *had* to spend time within the prison's walls. Inmates such as Hardy Percy Dunne, who was imprisoned at HMP Oxford in 1924 for giving paid lectures about his heroic deeds that had earned him a Victoria Cross in World War I. Unfortunately for Hardy, it was proved in court that he was not a Victoria Cross holder, and as he confessed, 'I am sorry I had to tell lies to make an honest living' (*The Times*, 27 August 1924).[2] About ten years later, Sidney Thorpe, a thirty-year-old carpenter, committed suicide in his cell whilst on remand in HMP Oxford (*The Times*, 16 May 1933). I doubt the guests at the Malmaison *want* to experience the same conditions as Hardy did and certainly not the same as Sidney, but the hotel is very popular, and there must be some quality that guests feel is worth paying for, over and above the comfy bed and 'coolest cocktails in the free world'.

Academics are beginning to discuss the prison hotels and gaol museums that are in the vanguard of the heritage movement (Brown and Barton 2012; Langley-Smith 1998). Across the British Isles, a number of former prisons have been reopened as heritage centres: Kilmainham Prison in Dublin was closed in 1924 and reopened as a museum in 1971, Beaumaris followed shortly afterwards (closed in 1878 and re-opened in 1974), and other places, including Eden Camp Prisoner of War Museum (1949/1987), Bodmin (1916/2004), Ruthin (1976/2004), Oxford (1996/2006), York Castle (1934/2009), and Crumlin Road Belfast (1996/2010). The former Lincoln Castle Gaol is currently being redeveloped as a heritage centre, and with the next tranche of prison closures scheduled to begin in 2014 (www.bbc.co.uk/news/uk-20969898), more gaol museums will surely come into being in the near future.

The websites designed to attract visitors to the prison museums often employ images and narratives about prison life of the 1880s onwards, but concentrate on the more punitive elements of incarceration (and some include anachronistic penal punishments such as the crank, or the rack, which do not belong in the period they are trying to represent): 'Sit in a prison cell, hear the door slam shut and imagine the harsh conditions of Victorian prison regimes. Try on prison uniforms, imagine the horror of being set in the pillory, strapped in a restraint chair or hung in chains. Turn the crank, carry out shot drill or work the treadmill' (http://riponmuseums.co.uk/museums/prison_police_museum). Dartmoor's website (www.dartmoor-prison.co.uk/) has links to sections on the 'manacles and weapons' used by warders, illegal weapons confiscated from inmates, details about famous prisoners, and insignia and uniforms of prison staff. Indeed some seem intent on reimagining the prison as a place of gothic horror rather than rational punishment. The themes that are emphasised are darkness, terror, and violence, rather than the daily tedium of late Victorian and Edwardian prison regimes (and least of all do they describe any form of rehabilitative treatment):

DARE YOU VENTURE WHERE ACCESS IS NORMALLY DE-NIED . . . IN THE MOST HAUNTED BUILDING IN THE UK? CERTAIN AREAS OF THE GALLERIES OF JUSTICE MUSEUM are not normally accessible to the general public however they are to be exclusively opened for their 'Terror Tours' which take place on the last Friday of very [sic] month. This unique event takes the visitor underground into the Sheriff's Dungeon and the sights, smells and sounds of the prison cells, caves and dungeons can be experienced. These tours will instill fear and make the visitor recoil in terror . . . after all this is where poor souls were incarcerated before transportation . . . or death.[3]

(www.galleriesofjustice.org.uk/special-occasions/
terror-tours/ – with original emphases)

Both Rapheal Samuel (1994) and Patrick Wright (1985) have critiqued the role of museums and those charged with preserving historical buildings and artefacts in the repackaging of the past by a heritage 'industry' that panders to dominant national myths. The preservation and re-presentation of the physical remains of institutions and their interpretation by educationalists is an attempt to make complex sociocultural changes understandable to public comprehension. The political and academic orientations of the archivists, exhibition organizers, and museum bodies inevitably collude in this enterprise of turning complex and often contradictory histories into a narrative for consumption. The propensity for museum managers to over-employ distinct and rather narrow visions of traditional values and characteristics in order to map out and normalise historical forms of incarceration and punishment as progressive has meant that the public is confronted with a rather simplistic rendering of crime, policing, and punishment for the late Victorian period until World War II. It seems incumbent on academics as well as museum specialists to join together to refine these representations and to help make sense of the competing notions, interpretations, and explanations for punishment in this historical period in a way which allows for different interpretations – not just a teleological explanation of the historical route to today's criminal justice system.[4]

However, despite carrying out (often publicly funded) high-quality research, and carrying out vigorous and engaging debate in international colloquia, academics are not as engaged in public debates as they could be. Academic discourse, which usually applies a more complex analysis to historical data than is wanted by journalists or needed by museum managers, is not highly visible in modern media discourse (indeed, the relationship between the news and current affairs media is at a very low ebb in Britain at present[5]). Modern media debates on crime and order tend to marginalise academic history because they fail to see its relevance or cajole historical data into forms which appear to support conservative political agendas (this is particularly the case with crime and policing).[6] Academics, in turn, decry the media's popularist and simplistic approach to complex issues, and the 'master and servant' attitude of some journalists (Wilson 2011). The relationship is truly a distant and unhappy one.

Nevertheless, despite the inability of academic discourse to penetrate the mass media to any significant extent, the study of the past is still popular at the undergraduate level, oral history is a widely practised craft carried out by people and groups across the country, and important academic research still continues to inform local and family history. As the following paragraphs show, crime historians are becoming more and more involved in interpreting sites of justice and punishment for the general public (and also for TV viewers). So, academic history is still having some impact on the way we view the history of crime. It is therefore now worth considering whether this has become the main (or only) form of impact that crime historians can have, or whether there is a role for them to play in formulating new criminological theory, or social policy. Indeed, what is the 'impact' of crime history?

Popular crime histories

There are approximately nine million family history researchers in the United Kingdom. The new digital media described in Chapter 7 feeds their enthusiasm and makes it easy for new adherents to start researching their family histories. The ease of finding online data means that it does not take people very long to trace their family history back to the mid-nineteenth century (about as far back as their great-great-grandparents). Almost inevitably this popular pastime has developed a commercial element, with its own websites (for example, www.blacksheepancestors.com, www.origins.net/, www.societyofgenealogists.com/was-your-ancestor-a-criminal/, www.geni.com/. . ./do-you-have-a-criminal-in-your-family-tree-354741.html), popular magazines (there are tens of them on the shelves of High Street newsagents), and radio and TV shows (for example, *Tracing Your Roots* on Radio 4, *Who Do You Think You Are?* on BBC1).[7] Approximately 6 million viewers watched actress Patsy Kensit unravel both her father and grandfather's involvement with the courts (www.bbc.co.uk/whodoyouthinkyouare/past-stories/patsy-kensit.shtml) in 2008. Ancestors who have had brushes with the law feature quite heavily on these shows. Ex-England football star Gary Lineker is just the latest to reveal an ancestor with a prolific offending history (he was a poacher) in 2013.

As discussed in Chapter 7, having a criminal ancestor is a little like hitting the jackpot for family historians. In addition to the increased chance of an official record being available, there is usually an interesting story behind the facts of the criminal case. Crime seems to be inherently fascinating, and having a forefather convicted of, say, poaching, or horse stealing, means that one's ancestor stands out from the crowd. Of course, the excitement might wane if the family member concerned was a convicted bigamist or a sex offender. Family historians may be unprepared for the emotional consequences of that kind of unwanted knowledge (especially because many people still believe that criminality is passed genetically down the family line, see Chapter 11).[8] On finding a 'criminal past', in order to make sense of the discovery, some will turn to sites such as Old Bailey Online in order to find out more about particular crimes, or the specific punishments (this might explain the nearly 1 million annual visitors to the website). They might also, as so many other people, want to watch either factual or fictional representations of Victorian or Edwardian crime and policing. Some have suggested that the fictional Constable George

Dixon (of Dock Green fame) epitomises the golden age of policing in the 1940s and 1950s (McLaughlin 2006; Reiner 2011) in the way that the fictional North Yorkshire police officers do in the BBC series *Heartbeat*. These gentle homages to community policing have been swamped latterly by depictions of the pre–World War I period – the landscape in television's *Ripper Street* or Guy Ritchie's *Sherlock Holmes* films seems more appropriate for depictions of violent crime and disorder (something that seems more suited to the fears we have for modern society in the new age of austerity perhaps?). Unfortunately, however, the considerable interest in televisual representations of crime in this period has not readily translated into an upsurge in academic interest amongst the viewing public. More often it encourages not a trip to the university to sign up for a degree course in criminology, but a visit to some (admittedly more sensational) sites of 'dark tourism'.

Dark tourism

The phrase 'dark tourism' has gained currency in the last fifteen years as a way of describing the heritage industry's opening up of former sites of pain and punishment (including, but not restricted to, the gaol museums discussed earlier; Lennon and Foley 2010).[9] Some places which have come to be associated with this term were opened from the 1960s onwards: Anne Frank's house, 1960; the Slave Depot in Senegal, 1978; Auschwitz, 1997; the Hiroshima Atomic Bomb Dome, 1997; Robben Island, 1999; the Australian Convict penal colonies, 2008; Topographies of Terror (Gestapo Museum, Berlin), 2010; and the Stasimuseum (Museum of the East German Secret Police), 2010. Together they are a range of places, sites, and institutions representing the legacy of massacre and genocide, prisoners of war, civil and political prisons (Logan and Reeves 2009). In many ways these sites are very different, trying to illustrate different kinds of histories with narratives specific to their own distinctive history. What they have in common is that they commemorate a dark past in human affairs as 'a way of claiming that the past has something to offer the present, be it a warning or a model' (Olick 1999: 381). They are also, in many instances, polished commercial operations that 'form a growing part of a burgeoning heritage industry' (Misztal 2003: 157). Dark tourism has been the saviour of many former prison buildings, because they are popular with the public and interest in what went on behind the prison walls is a valuable revenue stream. Of course, there is a very different feel in and around decommissioned gaols in the United Kingdom than there is in Auschwitz or in the Killing Fields of Cambodia. They should perhaps not be mentioned in the same context. The depth of horror and misery that a visitor to a concentration camp feels is incomparable to the feelings we might develop whilst walking along a Victorian prison wing. In measuring 'darkness', therefore, we could place gaol museums on a continuum that stretches along a line from the recent to the distant past, commercial to nonprofit enterprises, mass institutions of pain and punishment to the single example, highly interpreted to naïve, and being a physical site you have to visit to a virtual site, that is, a wholly online experience. When visiting an old gaol or prison (or any site of

Dark Tourism) it is a worthwhile activity to 'map' it along those lines; it would then be interesting to revisit the websites advertising those places to see whether they capture the experience of the visit.

Cyber–dark tourism

Almost all gaol, police, and court museums now have websites to advertise their attractions, but they are still primarily places that you have to physically visit. To fully participate in the convict experience visitors will have to feel the cold dampness of a stone prison wall, feel the claustrophobic conditions of a cramped cell, and lie on an uncomfortable prison mattress and feel every lump and bump of the basic metal bed below. I am not saying that this fully reproduces the experience of being a prisoner – after all, visitors are not locked in a cell twenty-three hours a day for months on end. However, there is something valuable in standing on a Victorian prison landing; or standing in the dock of, say, St George's Hall (Liverpool Assize Court) and feeling how exposed and vulnerable a defendant appearing there must have felt – Florence Maybrick, for example, who was prosecuted there in 1889 (Watson 2004). At the moment there are no virtual environments which attempt to recreate the Victorian or Edwardian prison (although it is possible that one will be developed at some point); however, some heritage sites do have very sophisticated 'online doorways' through which you are led in order to further entice you to visit the actual site itself.

So to some extent we can journey to dark sites of pain and punishment whilst sitting at home in front of the laptop. When we do, the interpretation of what we are seeing becomes even more important. It also becomes much harder, for it is difficult enough for museums to devise interpretive devices which present information to visitors in person at the site, but trying to appeal to the hugely divergent set of online viewers in the short period of time that 'surfers' spend on a website must be impossible. Museums must feel constrained by the divergent needs to both educate and entertain online viewers as they do for visitors to the physical site itself. Museums are, after all, trying to keep their financial heads above water, and an overly didactic website full of academic text may put off some who might otherwise have been tempted to visit. The jarring nature of some website blurb reveals the strain of trying to be authentic to the experience whilst also seeking to gather in the greatest number of 'bums on seats': 'Many families planning a visit to Alcatraz worry about bringing children to a former penitentiary – they often ask us if it is appropriate for them. Our answer is a definite "yes!" There is no reason to hesitate bringing children to the Rock' (http://www.nps .gov/alca/forkids/index.htm). The intention of gaol museum websites is to attract people to go there; they encourage inclusive involvement, which is a good thing. The vast majority of people will never have the opportunity of visiting a prison and therefore going to a gaol museum (even a former one which may have closed years or decades earlier) might encourage some insight into what life is really like for prisoners today.

However, there are a few 'places' which are nearly or wholly websites of Dark Tourism. For example, although there are a few permanent museum exhibitions which portray the horror of the RMS *Titanic*'s demise (in Liverpool, Belfast, and Halifax, Nova Scotia) there are also 132 million websites dedicated to the sinking (and its aftermath). Jack the Ripper has a few 'Murder Trail' guided walks around the Whitechapel area, but also 1 million websites discussing (and re-presenting) the case in cyberspace. Simply put, the closest we can get to the actual site of the sinking of the White Star liner in 1912 is by viewing a website. Some of the millions of websites dedicated to the Titanic or Jack the Ripper are more historically accurate than are others and have obviously been constructed by diligent researchers who have a deep interest in those events. For more general histories of crime, or the interpretation of gaol and court sites, what role is there for academic crime historians?

Historians as tour guides?

Bushranger Ned Kelly was executed in 1880 and reburied in 2012 when his body was found in a mass grave in Pentridge Prison in Melbourne. His body was entombed in concrete to deter souvenir hunters, but still there are fears that the site will become a shrine, a place to remember the person himself, or what he has come to represent – resistance to Anglo-Australian elites? His reputation, which has now become a huge conceptual space for others to celebrate, denigrate, and pour in their own views on crime, colonialism and so on might be considered disproportionate to his actual crimes. His meaning in Australian history has been pored over, interpreted, and reinterpreted by hundreds of academics, politicians, and political activists. His new burial site will now also become a physical site of commemoration, but will provide yet another opportunity for reinterpretation. At the other end of the scale, the city of Chicago, which is so very closely associated with 1930s gangsters, has no 'museum of the Mafia'. Maybe it is an unwanted connection that the city wants to move away from, especially as the city still has the reputation of being 'mob-influenced' (http://mafiatoday.com/tag/chicago-outfit) and possibly that is why it has never employed historians or museum experts to reconstruct a physical site of remembrance (even the place where the 1929 St Valentine's Day Massacre occurred has been built over).[10]

Of course, history is written, interpreted, and 'unwritten' by the winners, and it is no surprise that the British heritage industry, as the Australian and US industries, also promotes some kinds of tourist sites and not others. How do U.K. gaol, police, and court museums go about interpreting and representing their sites? In my view they are very responsible and do a pretty good job of fairly interpreting much of what the public see, albeit with an emphasis on the darker and more punitive elements (as stated earlier). Nevertheless, greater involvement between academics and museum staff would perhaps offer a richer experience for museum visitors and a more authentic portrayal of the institutions concerned. Where this close relationship exists, as they do between convict site managers and academics in

Tasmania for example, the benefits are clear to see (http://www.heritage.tas.gov.au/ convict_sites.html, http://www.portarthur.org.au/).[11] In working with the heritage industry, historians play a public role which extends knowledge about their areas of interest to the public and helps to construct a sociohistorical context which can be used to inform public understandings of crime and offending.

Public crime history?

Crime historians interrogate power (the legitimate and the illegitimate use of force), and therefore, they inhabit an intensely political conceptual realm. As the last three chapters of this book show, the 1880 to 1940 period was a pivotal time for criminal justice in the United Kingdom. Huge political theories swept people into fascist and communist political parties; the country saw unemployment and poverty blight many communities, with the police apparently siding with authority against the poor and unemployed. There were anarchists in Sydney Street, warships moored in the Clyde, and tanks on the streets of Liverpool. The police themselves went on strike in 1919. In academia, the rise of scientific criminology firstly supported dominant theories about habitual offending and inherent criminality – eugenics and criminology became appropriate subjects for university lectures – and later psychology brought forward new institutions meant to reorientate offenders away from crime, especially the youthful offender (e.g., the introduction of the probation service in 1908). In the 1920s and 1930s there was a massive prison closure scheme; the police also came into contact with large numbers of 'respectable' motoring offenders. Juvenile delinquency was redefined and reconceptualised several times in the 1920s and 1930s. The way those movements, trends, and events were interpreted at the time, and how they are thought of now, should play some part in guiding future government policy. If historians believe that they have developed insights which can guide or challenge current political theory and social policy at all (Burke 1980; Dayan 2011; Finnane 2005; Hamilton 1994; Hobsbawm 1997; Zedner 2006), then surely studies of the late Victorian and Edwardian periods would be at the forefront of evidence-led policy making? The period is at a sufficiently arm's-length distance for a perspective to be formed, but recent enough for it to be deemed relevant by policy makers. Yet, historians seem to have little purchase on policy making. Politicians and their advisors seem to not consider historical research useful in formulating policy. Many historians are not interested in fulfilling this role in any case, and those that do find it very difficult. For those reasons it is the humanities and social sciences that have complained most about the government's new 'Impact Agenda' (imposed through the Research Excellence Framework and the Research Councils).

If not on public policy, crime historians at least continue to have an impact on the development of the social sciences, particularly on criminology. Most criminology undergraduate programmes have a historical element. Crime history features in standard undergraduate criminology textbooks (Carrabine et al. 2008; Newburn 2013), and although there have been some pessimistic views about the chronocentric approach of criminologists, and their relative ignorance of cutting-edge historical research (see King 1999; Rock 2005), there are others who feel that the relationship between history and criminology has a solid foundation which can be built upon in the future (Godfrey, Lawrence, and Williams 2007; Lawrence 2012). There might even be a route that way for 'historical criminology' to play a part in developing social policy (Godfrey, Lawrence, and Williams 2007).

Conclusion

In 2010 two eminent criminologists called for a public criminology to complement the public sociology demanded by Gans in 1988 (see also Riesman 1953; Smith 1994; Turner and Turner 1990). What they set out to discuss were 'the predicaments, possibilities and pitfalls of criminological engagement in the public sphere today and [. . .] to explore how criminologists have understood their craft and positioned themselves in relation to the crime control controversies of recent times – whether as experts, advisors, players, activists or prophets' (Loader and Sparks 2010: 2; see Carrabine *et al.* 2008: 452–460; Wilson 2011). What would public crime history look like? I am not so sure that it would look very different from what exists today. We may have a more 'populist' than 'public' crime history, with crime historians being drafted as interpreters for television-based history or to act as advisors for museums, but I suspect that we therefore have a greater reach toward the public than most academics. It is true that we have an awkward and slight relationship with the news and current affairs media (crime historians usually have different political leanings than do newspaper editors, and therefore, we give the 'wrong' answers to media questions, and we stick to complexity in our answers which do not easily fit into a ten-second sound bite or a short interest piece in the national papers). However, we regularly 'speak' to millions of nonprofessional crime and family researchers, and there are not many academics who get that kind of opportunity.

9

TIME, PLACE, AND SPACE

On 1 October 1881, *The Lancaster Gazette and General Advertiser for Lancashire, Westmorland, and Yorkshire* reported that an errand boy called Ernest Bland had been prosecuted for throwing stones at a chestnut tree in an attempt to bring down some conkers. The police officer who prosecuted the case requested that the magistrates impose a lenient penalty as the boy had been polite and civil when approached, and the officer just wanted to make a point that this kind of boisterous behaviour was frowned upon. The magistrates agreed, and after paying the costs of the case, the boy was allowed to leave court in order to spread the word to his friends that the practice would be dealt with more seriously if it were repeated.

Matthew Connolly was convicted at the Old Bailey for stealing a handkerchief and transported on the prison ship *Maria Somes* to Van Diemen's Land as a young man (aged eighteen). After serving his time in the penal colony he was released to make a new life for himself. In the same month and year as Ernest went 'conkering', Matthew found himself before the Hobart magistrates apologising for his drunken behaviour in the streets (Hobart Magistrates Court Registers, 1881). Paying up his five shillings' fine he may have wondered at the turn his life had taken from his birth in London to drinking and carousing under Australian skies as a released convict in the 1880s.

Around the same time as Connolly was sobering up in Hobart, on three separate occasions in the same year, James Burk appeared before the Tombstone Justice Court in Arizona to answer two charges of threatening to kill a man and one of assault with intent to commit murder. His offences justified what the *Weekly Arizona Miner* called Tombstone's 'reputation in cutting and shooting' (12 September 1879). That reputation was projected around the world two years later after the gunfight at the OK Corral when 'Three Men Were Hurled Into Eternity in the Duration of a Moment':

Stormy as were the early days of Tombstone nothing ever occurred equal to the event of yesterday . . . firing became general, over thirty shots being fired. Tom McLowry fell first, but raised and fired again before he died. Bill Clanton fell next, and raised to fire again when Mr. Fly took his revolver from him. Frank McLowry ran a few rods and fell. Morgan Earp was shot through and fell. Doc Holliday was hit in the left hip but kept on firing. Virgil Earp was hit in the third or fourth fire, in the leg which staggered him but he kept up his effective work. Wyatt Earp stood up and fired in rapid succession, as cool as a cucumber . . . The feeling among the best class of our citizens is that the Marshal was entirely justified in his efforts to disarm these men, and that being fired upon they had to defend themselves, which they did most bravely. So long as our peace officers make an effort to preserve the peace and put down highway robbery – which the Earp brothers have done, having engaged in the pursuit and capture, where captures have been made of every gang of stage robbers in the county – they will have the support of all good citizens. If the present lesson is not sufficient to teach the cow-boy element that they cannot come into the streets of Tombstone, in broad daylight, armed with six-shooters and Henry rifles to hunt down their victims, then the citizens will most assuredly take such steps to preserve the peace as will be forever a bar to such raids.

(*Tombstone Daily Epitaph, 27 October 1881*)

The hero in this shootout story, and in many others that followed later, was Wyatt Earp. His family originally hailed from Staffordshire but had long been established in North Carolina.[1] But not all violent offenders brought to justice in U.S. courts had been born there. Despite the locations of their crimes, these offenders (Ernest, Matthew, and James) were actually all born in the British Isles and had either stayed there, had tried their luck in new lands, or had been flung thousands of miles from the place of their birth by the criminal justice system. Should we include these offenders in a book on English crime? Cowboys fighting it out in a 'wild west' town, convicts sweating in an Australian bush – these are tropes that have helped create national stereotypes. So, were they English people carrying out typically U.S. or Australian crimes, or were they new settlers carrying on in the way they would have done back in mother England? Were colonial subjects and settlers who were subject to English common law and prosecuted in a legal system very similar to that used 'at home' (often by judges and legal personnel trained in Britain) at the mercy of British justice? How was the experience of a drunk punished by a New Zealand court in 1907 different from the same man dealt with by a New Zealand court the following year (after the country became a self-determining government)? We can ponder these questions whilst we continue with our main focus on England and Wales because these examples from abroad are useful in drawing our attention to the importance of geography and sense of place both on offending and generally on the lives of criminals.

Research published in work by Anderson and Killingray (1991); Arnot and Usborne (1999); Shore and Cox (2002); Gurr, Grabosky, and Hula (1977); Mellaerts (1997); Monkkonen (2001); Godfrey, Emsley, and Dunstall (2003); Godfrey and Dunstall (2005a, 2005b); and Sibley (1995) have all enriched our view of social conditions across time and across the world. This chapter will add to their work by further exploring how 'space' and 'place' has featured in crime history research (see Jackson 2010). It will then go on to question how the physical and social development of a country, city, or town can affect the type of crimes that were prosecuted and how we can compare crime and punishment across time and place, especially when those situations are often changed rapidly. For example, six murders were committed in Tombstone in 1883, but twenty years later the local court (now in nearby Bisbee) dealt mainly with low-level misdemeanours (and in line with other countries, regulatory offences leapt up in the early twentieth century; see Chapter 4). Between 1881 and World War I, the social and economic base of southern Arizona had changed from silver mining carried out by peripatetic entrepreneurs (single young men, many of whom seemed to like drinking and fighting) to a large-scale copper-mining operation which employed thousands of men (family men with more settled lifestyles) on a permanent basis (Bailey 2002, 2004). Arizona had not been transformed from Sodom and Gomorrah into the Garden of Eden, but there was certainly a wholly different set of social circumstances brought into play with this new kind of economic development, ones which now encouraged stability and for disputes to be resolved peacefully, not with a six-shooter. Similarly in Australia, the colony that Matthew Connolly arrived into was very different by the 1880s, and, of course, it was very different again by the time he died in the 1920s. Britain also changed greatly over that time.

Economic changes in England and Wales 1880–1940

Between 1880 and 1940 Britain experienced huge swings in prosperity and depression. There was a trade depression in the 1870s which then fell dramatically between 1880 and 1887; a slight rally in the market around 1891 was eradicated by another dip in 1896. The pamphlet written by Reverend Andrew Mearns, 'The Bitter Cry of Outcast London' (1883; see Mayne 1993); and Seebohm Rowntree's classic study of York (1901) *Poverty: A Study of Town Life*, helped to draw attention to the plight of the poorest in society at this time. Their situation was only slightly improved by the modest recovery that continued until 1914 (Crouzet 1982: 59–61). It does seem that wage rates were not immediately affected by the Great Depression of the 1870s and 1880s (Levi 1885), and the violent large-scale labour disputes of the 1910–1912 period indicate that it was only at that time that workers were feeling the impact of a general widespread slump in trade (and a fall in the real value of wages).

As Figure 9.1 shows, World War I and its immediate aftermath stretched British economic resources to their limits, and the following slump of the late 1920s and 1930s has been well documented in academic texts and in popular

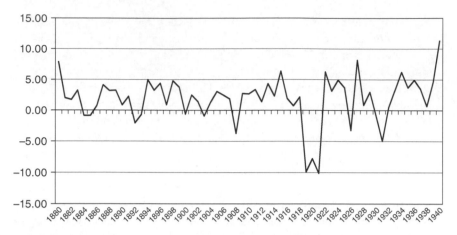

FIGURE 9.1 Rate of growth (percentage), gross domestic product, 1880–1940*

*Figures taken from Hills, Ryland, and Dimsdale (2010).

documentary-style publications. Whilst some cities and regions grew in scale, importance and wealth – notably in the south of England – others underwent severe deprivation, particularly in the north and parts of London in the 1930s. George Orwell's *Down and Out in Paris and London* (1933) and his *Road to Wigan Pier* (1937) are depressing but elegant descriptions of the abject poverty that affected many regions in England and Wales. We have plenty of statistics and contemporary descriptions of the booms and busts of this period (Jeremy 1998), but what if we didn't? Would we be able to reconstruct the state of the economy from the statistical information we have on crime trends?

As can be seen from Figure 9.2, different offences can be plotted against economic performance. Indeed, aggregating all crime together would ride roughshod over the different motivations that lie underneath different forms of offending; for example, the property offender might be driven by having empty pockets, whereas the drunken reveller may go out on a Saturday night because his pockets are full of coins to spend. In addition, as Chapter 3 has shown – so much rests on prosecution policy and practice that it would be almost impossible to gain anything other than an impressionistic view of how economic cycles related to real crime rates, no matter which offences we chose to match against economic rates (although Home Office statisticians did make comments linking unemployment rates to crime rates; see Emsley 2010: 32). Modern studies which have tried to do this have quickly run into stormy waters because it is by no means an uncomplicated task (see Box 1987; Detotto and Otranto 2012; McRae 1997; Radzinowicz 1939, 1971). Statistical charts are, then, but one kind of crime map, and they do not seem to get to the heart of how socioeconomic landscapes and crime fit together. Some more nuanced attempts to map crime 'on the ground' without the help of statistics originally began in the 1880s, as we shall see. By that date, connections between environment and criminality were well established.

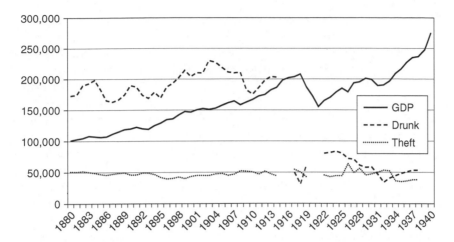

FIGURE 9.2 Annual gross domestic product (£m) and prosecutions for drunkenness and theft, 1880–1940★

★Chained composite measure of gross domestic product. Chained volume measure £mn. Figures taken from Hills, Ryland, and Dimsdale (2010).

Slum life

In the Victorian period Charles Dickens and Henry Mayhew brought back descriptions of London's poorest districts and filled them with characters for the public imagination. The street hawkers, beggars, card sharps, and petty thieves that lived in the heart of the 'rookeries' leapt off the pages of *Oliver Twist* (1839) and *Great Expectations* (1860) and featured predominantly in investigative journalism, such as *London Labour and London Poor* (1851–1861). The garrotting panics of the 1860s cemented the idea that the criminal classes were concentrated in particular impenetrable areas of the cities. Some modern authors have further bolstered the spatial aspect of crime in the mid-Victorian period (Chesney 1972; D. Thomas 1998), whereas others have critiqued their stance (see summaries in Godfrey and Lawrence 2005: 110–125; Godfrey, Lawrence and Williams 2007: 77–101; Taylor 2012).

Commentators in the later Victorian and Edwardian periods carried on the investigative tradition of journeying into the dark hearts of the city in order to bring back knowledge of a hidden troubling world:

> Do you really care very much? I daresay you do. I daresay it is foolish of me to be writing here at all. I should be sitting securely in my Club in St. James's Street, surrounded by familiar things, looking down at Poplar with detached benevolence. That would give me the right perspective. I should see the East End as a statistical problem – houses to the acre, families to the room, the infant mortality rate and the whole complex tale of human suffering set out to three places of decimals.

> *(Marshall 1933: 3)*

> Nowhere in the streets of London may one escape the sight of abject
> poverty, while five minutes' walk from almost any point will bring one to
> a slum . . . the streets were filled with a new and different race of people,
> short of stature and of wretched or beer-sodden appearance.
>
> (*London 1903:6*)

What they found was that a different kind of 'race' of people dwelt in the tum-
ble of poor housing and cramped bedsits: a 'lost people' at the bottom of a
pit from which there was no escape (Marshall 1933: 6, 144). As well as pity,
these slum dwellers deserved to be feared, because the slums seemed to be
factories of crime: 'Mass production is something more than an industrial technique. We mass-produce everything from public opinion to motor-car bodies;
and we mass-produce criminals too . . . overcrowding does not breed only the
stunted and the anaemic. It breeds murder, sexual crimes and other abomina-
tions' (Rhodes 1937: 1–3). The correlation between poverty and criminality
was still so entrenched that centres of poverty were clearly positioned as places
to avoid because the behavioural norms of the inhabitants were so completely
identified with the physical conditions they endured: 'Try to picture, if you can,
streets with pseudonyms such as Blood Alley, Shovel Alley, Frying Pan Alley, and
Bull's Head Yard, remembering that all these places received their nicknames for
reasons sinister enough, whilst their wretched inhabitants were a perfect match
to their localities' (Leeson 1934: 89).

In printed articles in the newspapers, or in pamphlets, and in the popular novels
there was a long tradition of trying to capture this lost race – the People of the
'Abyss' (London 1903). However, Charles Booth's studies in the 1880s and 1890s
offered a new technique for picturing and mapping criminality within two of
Britain's cities (Liverpool and London). Now society could visualise criminal areas
much more easily.

Mapping the vicious and the semi-criminal

Using information from school board visitors about the levels of poverty and types
of occupations amongst the families for which they were responsible, in 1886
Charles Booth began work on a new study of London's poor.[2] His impressive study
Life and Labour of the People in London was published in seventeen volumes some
years later. As part of his research he produced two series of colour-coded maps
which represented varying levels of poverty in different districts across London. The
1889 series was followed a decade later with the *Maps Descriptive of London Poverty
1898–99*. On the maps, the streets coloured dark blue stood for 'very poor, casual,
chronic want', whereas black-coloured streets represented 'the lowest class, vicious,
semi criminal' areas. Although the maps were based on subjective data, they gave an
immediate visual indication as to the places where poverty was deepest, and were
therefore immensely useful as diagnostic tools for social policy.[3] We don't know

whether Booth's maps acted as a guide and template for the slum clearances in the 1890s and 1900s, but they cover the same areas (in London at least).

The Chicago school to the present day

Later, in the 1920s, the Chicago group of social scientists also attempted to make sense of the spatiality of crime, poverty, and disadvantage in the 1920s. Their theories of social disorganization rested upon a schematic mapping of the city in concentric circles (Sutherland 1924;Thrasher 1927).Their mapping exercise was different in conception and execution from Booth's, partly reflecting the different patterns of urban growth in the United States.The Chicago School presented the city as having a central business district surrounded by successive bands of residential and retail development which determined which areas were wealthy and which were slums. Booth's maps are more idiosyncratic and textured, but the central ideas were the same – mapping spatial relationships would allow researchers to understand where crime, poverty, disadvantage, and social exclusion were most likely to occur. This was a lesson latterly taken up with some alacrity by New Labour in the 1990s and 2000s when attempting to identify areas needing regeneration (Sibley 1995) and by the U.K. Conservative-led coalition government who saw crime mapping as an empowering (and populist) device. For example, in 2011 a website was produced for people to look at crime maps for their own town or neighborhood (www.homeoffice.gov.uk/police/street-level-crime-maps/), and in the United States it is possible to map where convicted paedophiles have resettled after release from incarceration. Crime mapping is now routinely used by police forces, and is a growing area of study for social scientists (Chainey and Ratcliffe 2005; Manning 2011; Santos 2012) where it is sometimes termed 'socio-spatial criminology' or 'geo-criminology' (Bottoms 2007;Van and Garson 2001).

Mapping crime for the 1888–1939 period

Going beyond simple attempts to map crime, some have interrogated spatial data to see how historical patterns of crime and exclusion played out in urban spaces in the 1880s to 1930s. Indeed there is a good deal of very interesting work to draw upon, as new geographies of crime become an ever-more important part of crime historical work: Joyce's (2003) study of literary geographies of crime in Victorian London, Houlbrook's (2001) study of illicit homosexual liaisons in London, (2001); Chamberlain's (2012) study of prostitution in interwar Liverpool, Jackson and Bartie's (2011) study of the policing of youth leisure in English and Scottish cities, and Adey, Cox and Godfrey's study of wartime Merseyside, funded by The Leverhulme Trust, which mapped prosecutions for blackout offences against actual bombsites, and so on (also see Howell 2009; Hubbard 1999; Nead 1997; Ogborn 1998). In addition to this research on the spatial organisation of offending and policing, we must remember that studies of punishment also explicitly or implicitly reference place.

Displacement

Punishment has always involved displacement of one kind or other. Capital sentences removed offenders from the world, and transportation removed convicts from their homes, surroundings, and families. When these forms of punishment were replaced by the growth of a prison estate, researchers have looked at the spatial organisation of prisons and have focused on subjects such as the effects of separate confinement (see Chapter 10). This is not surprising because prisons regulated behaviour within their walls by controlling space (Foucault 1991). However, even in the late nineteenth and twentieth centuries, some vestiges of transportation remained. Since around 1847 until at least the 1930s, the Jersey judicial system appears to have operated a system of banishment for (presumably persistent) offenders.[4] The families of convicted offenders subject to this banishment order were often dispatched alongside their sons and daughters to France, to Guernsey, or to southern England, often but not always, according to their perceived ethnic origins. In 1912, in Jersey, Yves Marie, a French teenager, and his Jersey-born codefendant, also aged fourteen, were both convicted of robbery. Yves Marie, at least, had previous convictions – including a charge of burglary the previous year.[5] Both boys were banished along with their parents (Albert's father had already died by this time) for a period of five years. Both Yves and Albert, and their siblings, and perhaps even their parents, would be young enough to return to the island after their punishment had expired. However, at the age of sixty-seven, it seems unlikely that Adelaide (a deportee convicted for assault and for keeping a disorderly house) would have returned to Jersey from her native France, unless, of course, she had important relationships there which could be resumed. She had, in effect, been exiled from Jersey for life.[6] The part that punishment has played on the lives of people such as Adelaide, Yves and Albert is a developing area, and the following section tries to join together the spatial with the biographical in a way which gives a new dimension to current work on micro-histories and whole-life studies (see Chapter 7).

The biographical and the spatial

As discussed earlier, simply comparing crime rates with economic rates (gross domestic product, for example) is not only too complex to be meaningful, it also pathologises crime statistics. The statistics are made up of thousands of offenders committing thousands of different crimes for individual reasons – the line of statistics is not a living person. It doesn't seem possible to understand how different economic or physical/spatial arrangements had an impact on the lives of criminals, without studying individual biographies. We have already seen the utility of that approach in Chapter 7, and we should see if we can adopt the same approach to investigate the impact of 'place' on criminal careers. Aside from its everyday meaning, place, let us remind ourselves, has been understood as the general 'feel' of an environment, as how individuals react and relate to their physical surroundings and the extent to which social institutions have been developed; and as how well-developed are the important, weak social ties that stretch beyond kin to acquaintances, neighbours, and people in the locale. The 'everyday structures of feeling' (cf. Certeau 1984; R, Williams 1961/1965, 1977; Williams and Orrom 1954) 'habitus' (see Bourdieu 1977; Bourdieu and Wacquant 1992) or 'local culture and sense of place' (Taylor *et al.* 1996: 4; see Massey 1994) are all constitutive of individuals and their environment. In other words, together they all form the experience of being in that place for that individual. That individual then reacts to that experience – and although people may react in different ways, in some sense the experience of being in that place always has at least some impact on how they respond to it. Presumably, when the feel of a place changes, the response by individuals within it also changes?

Change

Jennifer Davis's (1989) study of the history of one estate in north London could be taken as an argument that some things or some 'types of people' actually never change. The nineteenth-century Jennings Buildings examined by Davis later became the scene of the Broadwater Farm riots in the mid-1980s and of rioting in 2011. In fact the area had experienced entrenched patterns of criminality between 1850 and 1985 punctuated by episodic forms of large-scale public disorder. However, most places, and the social conditions within them, were not static. The working-class neighbourhoods mapped by Booth and others were not undifferentiated homogenous communities, as the previous chapters have shown, nor were those communities and their residents static in time – family fortunes changed, events intruded, aspirations came and went, new residents moved in and others left, the feel of places changed along with the physical infrastructure (see Ardener 1993):

> Proles Street was built, one imagines, at the height of the last trade boom of the nineteenth century. The front windows have bow sills, with a decorative iron rail to hold a window-box. There is a tiny garden in front of each house . . . all these attractions, it will be seen, were meant to catch the eye of small but flourishing tradesmen, quiet pensioners, commercial travellers, who sought a respectable neighbourhood . . . but Time brings its own judgement and before the century was out the housewives of Proles Street were feeling the pinch. By the end of the first decade of the new century, the slums to the south were encroaching perceptively, swallowing whole streets as a plague might.
>
> (*Benney 1936: 95–96*)

As the streets were affected by new contexts – the degentrification of Proles Street, for example – the way people felt within those spaces changed too: the experiences were linked and indivisible. Franco Ferrarotti, Professor of Sociology at Rome University, has discussed the meaning of place, but has also, as this chapter seeks to do, included the *passing of time* in his analysis of spatial conditions. I particularly liked the remark he made in 1990 when he himself was in his mid-sixties, that he 'had grown old with Italy. I have become old while a peasant and artisan country has, in the course of little more than two generations, become urban and industrial' (Ferrarotti 1990: 111). Certainly Italy was a different country in the 1930s to the Italy of the twenty-first century in the same way as penal-colony Australia was different from the same country in the 1940s, and, of course, British society in the 1880s was vastly different to Britain on the eve of World War II. Wouldn't all places have changed significantly over that time, and wouldn't the people who lived in those countries have changed too?

Ferrarotti is not the only researcher to connect personal autobiography and social change or to link place and time, of course. We could mention Henri Lefebvre (1991, 2004), Edward Soja (1996), Li-Fu Tuan (1977), Mike Davis (1992), Elias (1992), and others. Ferrarotti's work is more interesting to us, however, because (whereas some theories of space and time can seem curiously static) Ferrarotti unites the individual within space, with *change* over time. *Place matters*, but it is experienced differently by different actors with their individual characters, for example the stage of life one is at in any particular place, the activities and attitudes they enjoy in that space at that time, and their relationship with other people in that space. For us, in particular, we are interested in whether changes in environment over time changed offending behaviour. For example, criminologists and historians have noted the part that hope plays in reformation as a moral driver which supports desistance (Farrall 2002; Maruna 2005; Rowbotham 2009), and Farrall (2005) has explored how existential feelings of ontological security can also bolster desistance. Is it the case that a change for the better in the physical environment that offenders lived in could give them more hope for a better life – and might help them to stop offending? Moreover, was it the pace of change in these conditions which was the key to desistance from crime?

The dynamic periods of growth, as evidenced in, for example, impressive buildings springing up in quick succession, could provide real benefits, not least in employment opportunities but also in engendering a feeling of progress. The course of offenders' lives overlapped with different economic conditions, and rates of societal progress, with both booms and slumps. Offenders' attempts to stop offending are not one-offs; desistance from crime is a process, not an event. People moving away from crime make numerous, not single, decisions to offend or not offend that day, that minute, that moment, and people's experience of these economic rhythms and their interpretation of society's rate of progress at any particular time must have a bearing on their decision making. It may be that a faster rate of societal progress helped to magnify feelings of optimism and hope and to convince ex-convicts that it was worth making a personal commitment to change, given that their fortunes and society's fortunes could both quickly change together.

Pace of change

As historians, we are routinely interested in change within individuals, in structures (physical, bureaucratic, and mental), but we are also interested at the pace at which the progress of events unfolds – the *slowness* with which female suffrage was achieved, the *rapidity* with which World War I came to happen, and so on. As historians of crime, we are similarly interested in the speed that institutions progressed – how fast did the police professionalise, at what pace did the courts adopt more or less lenient sentencing patterns, and so on. The public, too, are deeply concerned with change within their lifetimes and how it affects them, and their views on the changes they witness routinely feature in everyday conversations, as Chapter 5 has demonstrated.[7] For example, the residents of Hyson Green high-rise high-crime estate in Nottingham were interviewed in the 1980s, immediately prior to their area being regenerated and reconfigured.

What is telling, however, is that many oral histories emphasise the pace of the changes they had experienced – the steep rapidity of the decline in manners, communities, civilisation – within their lifetimes, within their adult lives, and so on. As Ferrarotti (1990: 110[8]) said, 'Social change becomes an internalised experience . . . The course of life as biological time is reconnected to historical time dialectically.' In other words, people make sense of the changing world they live in by referencing what is happening to them and how they feel about it. As Chapter 5 has shown, this often means 'harking back' to past events and situations. People may feel better when things are generally going well – one gets a sense of 'well-being' when things are going well in society or with the economy – a 'feel good factor'. When things are grim, people feel gloomier about their lives. There is also the fact that people *do* enjoy greater chances of doing well, getting a job, getting a pay rise, when the economy is growing, so their perceptions are perfectly matched against real personal improvements. This is common sense, and this would most probably affect everyone, including ex-offenders. But how important is pace of change? How might an individual's conception of whether their part of the world, their neighbourhood, and/or their community is progressing quickly, or declining slowly, affect their behaviour?

Pace of change – testing the theory

How can we measure the impact of hope, or the pace of societal change, on the lives of individual offenders? One possible route into this is to reexamine the natural experiment in punishment and rehabilitation, the transportation of convicts to Australia – but rather than looking at the period when this process was ongoing, let us look at the longer term impacts in the 1880s and 1890s. Australian convicts seem to be the focus of an amazing amount of research, and some amazing research (on rehabilitation and recidivism, and on health, see Frost and Maxwell-Stewart 2001; Maxwell-Stewart 2008; Maxwell-Stewart and Hood 2001), but the post-convict period is lesser studied. However, as time went on, and the convict system petered out in Australia, convict and ex-convict groups still committed dispropor-tionate amounts of crime (given their numbers, respectively, in Western Australia and Tasmania). In Perth, in 1870, ten years after transportation had ended, they were responsible for about a third of all crimes, and they still figure disproportionately highly in the 1880s (albeit at a lower rate due to the declining number of surviving convicts and ex-convicts). In the main, a small number of ex-convicts were re-sponsible for a large amount of low-level disorder. Perhaps transportation hit many people so hard that all they were left with were a washed-up life, alcoholism, and drifting both through life and the colony (Godfrey and Cox 2008). The punish-ment of their criminal past impeded a criminal future, with many left incapable of carrying on a life of offending because they were physically incapable of doing so. This would be consistent with the findings of previous studies of habitual serious offenders in the nineteenth and twentieth centuries in England and Wales where long prison sentences or consecutive incarcerations tended to quash criminal ca-reers and lives in equal measure.[9] For many then, the transportation journey, and change of place, matched with a harsh penal regime (at least to start with) left them with a briefer and shallower criminal career. For others, their reformation was aided by the fact that convict labour was the foundation of social and economic policy in Western Australia and Tasmania:

> The integration of convicts into respectable society was not just a matter of getting married and finding a job. In other words, it took more than indi-vidual reactions to personal life changes to bring about a sustained change in behaviour and lifestyle. It also required respectable society to 'reach out' and incorporate and accommodate those who could be tolerated. Churches, workplace organizations and other agencies would have helped and so would political and trade union organizations looking for recruits. A population the size of the convict population would have just been too dangerous to leave outside of the political community or the working population for long (see essays in Nicholas 1988). Just as the working classes in Britain were incor-porated over the late nineteenth century, Australian convicts (at least a fair proportion of them) needed to be brought into society, brought into employ-ment, brought into social networks, brought into repute – in order for that society to progress.
>
> (*Godfrey and Cox 2008: 241*)

The enterprise of building the physical fabric of the colony was especially im-portant. The employment of convict labour helped to build social and financial capital in the labouring poor and emancipists. The changes it made to men and women were mirrored in the changes in infrastructure and the physical fabric of the colonies – changes which eventually brought them success – and made them flourishing and pleasant places to live – which again brings us back to the importance of 'place'.

The cumulative impact of the socioeconomic environment on convicts and emancipists we have been discussing would be differentiated by their personal characters and by the levels of social capital they could mobilise in their surroundings.[10] Ex-convicts, in Britain as well as in Australia, who were also skilled workers, or who could adopt skills that were needed in society at that time, were best placed to make new lives. A number of researchers (Farrall 2002; Mischkowitz 1994) have provided evidence that desistance is associated with gaining employment.[11] They were best placed to take advantage of their new environment and to form new relationships which also helped resettlement (Caddle 1991; Cusson and Pinsonneault 1986; Hughes, 1997, 1998; Irwin 1970; Jamieson *et al.* 1999; Laub *et al.* 1998; Leibrich 1993; Mischkowitz 1994; Parker 1976; Sampson and Laub 1993; Shover 1983; Trasler 1979; West 1982). The economic needs of the colony provided the preconditions for changes in their identity, status, and behaviour. Would it be possible to ask similar questions for England and Wales? Can we identify the impact of economic trends on individual behaviour?

Unfortunately, this is not such an easy task. The system of convict transportation to Australia really does offer a unique set of opportunities for researchers. Not only did it create a very detailed range of bureaucratic records on each offender (allowing us to recreate their experiences during, and, critically, after their convict detention), and accurate statistical information about trade and commerce, but it was also very geographically specific. The convict and non-convict populations of Tasmania and Perth were very stable between 1850 and 1914, allowing the possibility of linking individual and family records and specific socioeconomic circumstances to a hitherto unknown degree. The court and police jurisdictions of England and Wales were more permeable, people moved around more, and socioeconomic conditions varied considerably in different towns, cities, and regions over time. Recidivists were usually multiple recidivists (see Chapter 12) and they committed their offences over many years – also once they have started offending they are more likely to continue – therefore, a poor socioeconomic environment may have been the reason for a person's onset into criminality, but, once the criminal career had commenced, it may have continued through into better economic times. In order to really understand how societal and personal changes were combined within individual offenders' life trajectories we need to think again about the ways that space and time merge in the lives of hundreds if not thousands of individual offenders. Johnson, Godfrey, and Cox's ESRC-funded research on the speed of reconviction in different economic conditions in the lives of 650 British convicts between 1853 and 1940 has been one attempt to overcome these problems.[12] Williams' unpublished doctoral study of the impact of place on the offending histories of convict women in Liverpool and London is another. However, there is still considerable work to be done in this area. We have hardly scratched the surface.

Conclusion

The pace of societal change, as evidenced by the development of infrastructure and architecture, accelerated and heightened feelings of hope and optimism, which in turn supported people moving away from crime. Perhaps because concepts of time, place, and social change are still mainly the province of social theorists, and not of historians, these interconnections are underdeveloped. However, it seems clear that what is happening in society, and the pace at which it happens, either aids or inhibits individual offender's attempts to reform. The best way to investigate this hypothesis further may be to juxtapose ideas on spatial dynamics with biographical studies of offenders in a way which can improve our knowledge of spatiality and the meaning of *place*, the *passing of time*, and human agency or individual behaviour.

So far in this book we have discussed the importance of place in a number of chapters, even if only obliquely at times. In Chapters 2 and 3 we saw how the statistics of crime could be used to compare prosecution trends across international borders and also within individual countries – indeed, it would be possible to chart the number of prosecutions for individual offences across each town, city, borough, and county in England and Wales from 1857. The more intangible connections between crime, victimisation and place were taken up in Chapter 5. Quite clearly the way that people felt about their neighbourhood was integral to their feelings of safety and insecurity. Chapter 7 challenged us to think about where research itself takes place – in the archives or in cyberspace? In the following chapters, too, considerations of geography and spatiality are featured. Adopting new methods of policing or punishment changed the way that cities, towns, and for the first time suburbs, were viewed, watched over, and controlled. The policing of traffic extended the scope and range of police power over areas and parts of town that had seldom seen a uniformed officer, especially not one that was likely to prosecute respectable residents. Linking together information about offenders between various geographically dispersed policing and penal institutions connected the central Home Office to the periphery, casting the information net wide over known offenders and offering the possibility of tracking them after release from prison to anywhere in the country. Where once the prisons had collected and contained convicted offenders together, probation would now, for the first time in England and Wales, punish offenders in the community, altering our views of where punishment could now happen. All of these changes were embedded in and caused new spatial relationships to be formed. However, although we explore the spatial areas that change took place in, we must also remember the pace at which that change occurred.

10

NEW TECHNOLOGIES OF POLICE POWER

Sherlock Holmes (of 221b Baker Street) and George Dixon (of Dock Green) stand at either ends of our period as symbolic figures of authority embodying policing ideals. Conan Doyle wrote Holmes into existence in 1887, and Dixon was on TV screens from 1955. Holmes was a unique genius whereas George was universally genial; Holmes relished scientific forensic detective methods, whilst George let his knowledge of human nature guide him to the truth; Holmes was a Nietzschean superman, and George was an 'ordinary copper' as Jack Warner, the actor who played Dixon, tunefully sang:

> The C.I.D. are always in the headlines, but I prefer the ordinary scene.
> As an ordinary copper who's patrolling his beat, around Dock Green.
> Now I've been in the police force for a long time, more years than I care to think about.
> Sergeants come and go and inspectors come and go,
> But I'll stay on until they kick me out.
> I like the people I meet every day, as I go quietly whistling on my way.[1]

However, both were influential in reflecting back to the British public their own ideas about what was needed to control society, what the police were for, and what we should expect of them, but were either of them representative of what was happening on the streets? What was policing like during the 1880 to 1940 period? How did it face the new challenges of the twentieth century – political battles on the streets, mass industrial unrest, motorised crime, and the increasing competition for resources from more secretive police agencies?

Mobile and static policing

Chief Constable Percy Sillitoe, the man who would later become a noted 'gang-buster' and head of MI5, related in his memoirs how he had taken umbrage when one of his men was asked to move on by a local landowner (Bean 1981; Sillitoe 1955: 53):

> 'Don't you think it's damned foolish standing there like a big silly ass'
>   'I am here in execution of my duty, and such duty compels me to be here at the present time.'
>   'Are you tied to the damned gatepost?'
>   'I am at present, Sir, and for the time being intend to stay here'

Sillitoe prosecuted the landowner for his abusive language, but the magistrates were unsympathetic and the prosecution failed. Nevertheless, Sillitoe thought he was right to pursue it because he understood that he was defending the system as much as anything else. The whole of the beat system relied on individual policemen, such as that constable, being at particular places at specified times. Otherwise, like all of the other industries that operated with dispersed workers, all control was lost. Every fifteen minutes an officer on the beat had to be at a predetermined fixed point so that his sergeant could, if he so wished, meet him there to give him new orders or to check that he was where he was supposed to be. Those who failed in their duty could be punished:

> My father was a rugby player and if you played for the Metropolitan Police you were allowed half a shift off work. One Saturday my father was to play at Exeter, travelling by train from Paddington. My father was on early turn (6.am–2.p.m) and his sergeant grumbled about having to give Father time off. He was a miserable sergeant who then put my father on a beat which had a late lunch. My father asked the sergeant if he could change to a beat that had an early lunch otherwise, he would have to travel on an empty stomach. The sergeant said, 'No'. My father left his beat ten minutes early and travelled to Exeter, having eaten. That meal led to my father being fined two days pay and any promotion was blocked for three years. My father never left his beat early again.
>
> (*http://news.fitzrovia.org.uk/2011/08/17/tottenham-court-road-police-station-tales-from-the-early-1930s/*)

Between the quarter hours the officer walked with a measured pace, never deviating, so that he would arrive in time at the next point. 'Time, distance and social isolation ensured that each patrolling constable carried a mobile Panopticon within' (Brogden 1991: 36). In the 1920s the blue Dr Who–style 'TARDIS' police boxes allowed constables to receive a phone call at fixed times, relieving the senior officers of the burden of going out to meet them. When the station required the constable to call in, the blue light flashed on top of the box. Such occasions must have livened up the mandatory tramping the beat for hours on end carrying out the duties which were largely unchanged from the 1880s, or even the 1850s, policing drunks, checking doors, investigating accidents, and occasionally dealing with extraordinary events, like a burglary, or a medical emergency:

> It was one cold, damp, cheerless night in winter that I went on duty, and although it was only ten o'clock the streets were practically deserted. Here and there might be seen the solitary individuals muffled up to the throat, hurrying along the street seeking the shelter of their homes. I then commenced to work, peering into nooks and corners, entries and doorways to see what I could find. I tripped down the steps and was surprised to find the body of a man huddled in a heap at the bottom.
>
> (*PC Smethurst found the man had fallen down the stairs when drunk;*
> *Smethurst 1914: 29–30*)

Testing whether shop doors were locked overnight was a major job for the PC on his beat. Failing to do the door test could be punished. One morning a shopkeeper returned and found he had not locked his door (although nothing had been taken). Upset that the unlocked door had not been discovered, the shopkeeper complained to the Police Commissioner. The relevant constable was found and fined two days pay . . . In those days particular attention was paid when constables paraded for night duty: about twenty PCs went out at 10 p.m. from Tottenham Court Road. On parade the PCs had to hold up their whistle, notebook and reel of cotton for their sergeant to inspect. PCs used to tie cotton across doorways, steps, and alley entrances. If the cotton was broken then the policeman knew something was up.

> (*http://news.fitzrovia.org.uk/2011/08/17/*
> *tottenham-court-road-police-station-tales-from-the-early-1930s/*)

Saturday 3rd March 1934. At 6.10 am I was on duty in Northgate St when I heard a woman screaming lower down the street. I ran down Northgate St and found Mrs Doris Johnston aged 20 in the doorway of Chester United British Gas Company showrooms. She was in difficulties and I saw that she was about to give birth to a child the head of which was already born. She continued to scream and I gave her all the assistance I possibly could [she was taken by ambulance to her mother's house as she refused to go to the Maternity Ward of the local hospital] when I was carrying her along the footway in Trafford St. she gave birth to the child and it fell out onto my feet and the footway. Fortunately neither the mother or child (girl) were any the worse for their experience . . . (this child was killed in a street accident in Saltney, Chester on Friday 31st Jan 1940[2]).

> (*Diary of Albert Edward Wilcock, PC 39,*
> *Chester City Police Force*)

In one respect, of course, as already discussed, policing had changed. The rise in car numbers and the reorientation of policing away from the city centres towards straight pieces of road (so that the speed of passing cars could be tested) brought in a new focus for policing, with new rules and regulations of how to carry out systematic policing. Catching speeders required a set procedure to be adhered to, and so did other forms of 'active motoring policing' such as checking for red diesel (fuel which had not been taxed), which required specialist machinery.[3] Catching dangerous drivers, those whose vehicles were causing an obstruction, or who had left cars with lights or the engine running (which was illegal) were easily dealt with. It was also simple to deal with the thousands of vehicle owners who fell afoul of regulations such as displaying improper licence plates, not displaying the licence in a clear holder on the windscreen, not having brakes and lights in proper working condition, and so on. The point is, as Emsley (1993) and Taylor (2012) have pointed out, these cases (and the thousands of other similar cases that were investigated without any further police action) took a considerable amount of police time. Once the decision had been taken to address the regulation of motoring, and legislation had been passed, then it made sense to enforce them, and as the growth of car ownership grew, so did the number of prosecutions, and the amount of police resources consumed (see Figure 10.1).[4]

It has been suggested that the pressure on police budgets, particularly after World War I, forced the police to abandon the policing of low-level street offences. Taylor (1999) believes that the police learnt to play a political game in the twentieth century ('forging the job'), where serious offences were pursued in order to show the importance of the force, and motoring offences were pursued for the revenue that it created. There are several problems with this thesis. First of all, there is little documentary evidence that the Home Office or the chief constables had any intent to do this (see Chapter 3); the timescale is also odd, since the police had inserted

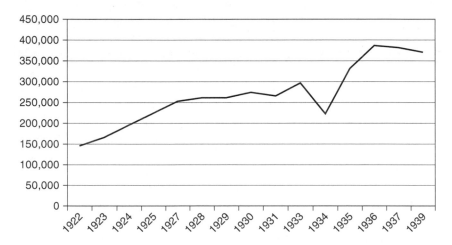

FIGURE 10.1 Motoring offences, England and Wales, 1922–1939 (figures taken from annually published judicial statistics)

themselves as the gatekeepers to prosecutions by the 1880s not in the post-World War I period, and the prosecution agencies had already taken over the prosecution of minor crime (NSPCC, truancy officers, market regulators, and so on) by that date too (see Chapter 4). Last, the decline of drunkenness and the rise of motoring prosecutions were not exclusive to the British experience. It was an international phenomenon, at least across Anglophone countries (see Figures 10.2 and 10.3).

However, despite this, the link between available resources and police activity is a real one. Although there were few explicit instructions from senior officers on how to cut costs, an emphasis on closely managing, if not reducing costs, was suffused throughout police practices. Magistrates and judges today are supposed to pay no attention to rising prison numbers and costs, but all sentencers are aware of the financial cuts in the public sector. The same can be said for everyone who works

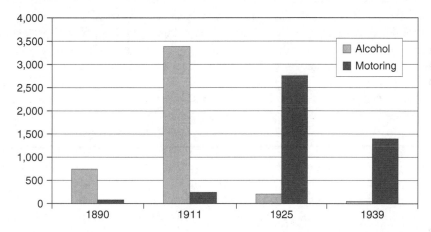

FIGURE 10.2 Prosecutions for alcohol and motoring related offences, Canada, 1890–1939[5]

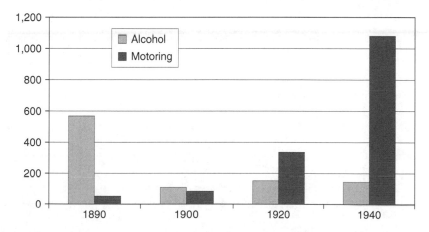

FIGURE 10.3 Prosecutions for alcohol and motoring related offences, Australia, 1890–1939[6]

in education, probation, health, libraries and archives and so on. In the first decades of the twenty-first century the culture of financial caution and prudence seeps into operational practices without explicit calls to watch costs having to be regularly reissued. That must surely also have been the case with police authorities a century earlier.[7] Although police numbers rather flatlined in the 1920s and 1930s, police budgets rose very dramatically after 1919 when the government sought to reduce police discontent (see later in this chapter), and motorised policing vastly inflated the costs (new Morris police cars were pricey). Taylor is probably right that the police used the growing number of motoring offenders to argue effectively for new resources (see Fig 10.4). Having secured them, they were then in a position to prosecute even more motorists. This seems more of an organic explanation of the growth of motoring as a police priority than does the attempt to raise revenue through motoring fines. Throughout the period, however, it was the case that 'stringent financial control has always driven police administrative practices' (Moylen 1929: 179).

In the nineteenth and twentieth centuries, budgetary control was exercised through the watch committees and standing joint committees (the Home Office ran the Metropolitan Police), and chief constables directed the resources they were allocated accordingly – sometimes arguing for more funding or to mitigate cut backs whenever they could.[8] In the police station, choosing to focus on either motoring or policing drunks was an operational decision made by inspectors and sergeants, and their decisions could have been influenced by costs and/or revenue streams. Once on the streets themselves, however, the amount of activity or zeal in carrying out their duties was up to the individual constables. Police cultural attitudes and values were therefore key. In part, police culture was made up of the natural common-sense conservatism shared by the kinds of officers they recruited, and partly through the routine practices of policing being passed down from established

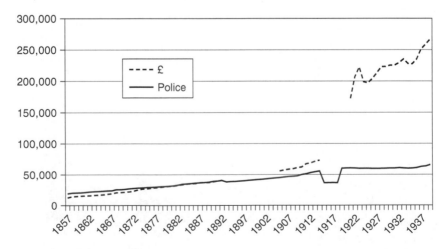

FIGURE 10.4 Police staffing numbers, and police budgets (in hundreds of £s; figures from annually published statistics)

sergeants to new officers in everyday contacts ('canteen culture'). The dominant cultures of policing determined what was worth bothering with and what was not. If something could be dealt with in a discretionary manner ('cuffing'), then it usually would be; if an officer thought some kind of behaviour was worth an arrest, then that is what happened:[9]

> if you went to trouble, you could clip a lad round the ear and tell him to behave and that was the end of the matter ... if you went to a domestic disturbance and the husband had clouted the wife, the policeman could deal with the matter and probably get hold of him and make it obvious to him that if he wanted a rough house he could have one, and that quietened things down.
> *(ex-policeman speaking of the interwar period,*
> *Nottinghamshire Oral History, tape 87d)*

If an incident involved someone who was already known to the police, or if the person involved was young or came from a bad area of town, then they were already on their way to being arrested:

> nine times out of ten, the people who caused you trouble, constantly caused you trouble, and so if you work in certain areas as I did, you are called, for example, the man that gives you trouble on Saturday nights by getting drunk and knocking the wife and kids about, was a regular performer. Well, you went and dealt with him. You knew the man who would accept a bat round the ear'ole himself, and the man who wouldn't it and would cause trouble, and therefore you had to lock him up.
> *(ex-policeman speaking of the interwar period,*
> *Nottinghamshire Oral History, tape 87d)*

Policing methods may have adapted to new situations between 1880 and 1940, but conceptions of what police work *was for* had not, nor had the targets at which it was *aimed*.

Police property

To an extent policing was impossible without violence. Policing by consent had its limits, and the officer on the streets had the discretionary power to set those limits. The policing of public space, on foot or on the road, brought police officers into daily contact with people who obstructed the footpath selling their wares, loitered on the streets 'looking for business', or were a bit tipsy and looking for trouble. Many of those people could be arrested, as they were breaking the law (soliciting, breaking bottles on the highway, urinating in shop doorways, obstructing the footpath, loitering with intent, and so on), but if they were amenable to being moved on, on and out of the area especially, then they would probably only be cautioned or warned off. However, if they caused the officer any trouble, or were within sight of respectable onlookers who demanded action, then there could be an arrest. As we saw in Chapter 1, Patrick Madden threatened and assaulted police officers (occasionally seriously), and it is no wonder that they sometimes used overpowering force to quell offenders if there was resistance to their authority, or if there was a challenge to their power. In the mind of the police, dealing with those who were 'known to them' (see Chapter 11), or who fitted a particular typology, meant there would always be the potential for trouble. Therefore, drunken men, youths 'giving cheek', groups of Irishmen or Italians, or 'foreign aliens', could all receive suspicion and rough treatment at the hands of the police. Constables on the beat emphasised both physical presence as a deterrent to crime, and coercive force as a normal tool of policing (used legitimately or not). But the police officer's view of their role in keeping order was not out of keeping with public expectations or attitudes towards those who were the policed, and that is why they were broadly supported:

> The majority of people who occupy these dens are idle loafers, who may be seen continually lounging about public-houses and beershops, and who send their mothers, wives and children out to beg and impose upon people with all sorts of pitiful tales, in order that they may be maintained in idleness and drunkenness, while there is abundance of work for them to do.
>
> (*Chadwick 1901/1974: 132*)

Those views are well established and can be seen in similar police opinions today:

> Most of us like a drink now and then. As a younger man, I had a few beers and rolled back home drunk more than once, but I never smashed all the car mirrors off in the streets on the way back, or attacked anyone with a baseball bat, or told the police to f**k off. I still enjoy a pint from time to time, but I don't go out and smack people in the face and puke over the pavement. I don't drink drive and I don't beat up my wife or kids or neighbours. I don't smash shop windows, or urinate in doorways, or use foul language at the top of my voice. I'm nothing special: there are millions of people who don't do any of those things, and you're probably amongst them.
>
> (*Gadget 2008: 37*)

The 'strong arms of the law' were tolerated by senior officers and politicians. Royal Commissions in 1908 and 1928 both substantially cleared the police of irregularities and overly violent policing, and they were backed up by conservative newspapers such as *The Times* which condemned the 'absurd lies and shallow slanders that maligned the reputation of the police' (Howgrave-Graham 1947: 3). Of course, the close relationship between press barons and senior police officers must have helped. Whilst Met Police Commissioner in the 1920s, Lord Byng, was trying to root out one or two 'Black Sheep', he persuaded the newspapers not to report police indiscipline for over two years on the grounds that it would be unfair to suggest there were a lot of 'rotten apples' in his force (Howgrave-Graham 1947: 17).

The middle classes did not know much about what life was like on the streets and would have tended to take the police officer's word at face value – certainly magistrates did in court (police prosecutions for drunkenness without civilian witnesses still had an almost 100 per cent conviction rate). The public were willing to let police officers make the decision whether or not force was necessary to subdue a suspect. When the middle classes started to come into contact with the police themselves, the deferential attitude adopted by many officers would have seen them quickly on their way – whereas other officers would have enforced the law much to the surprise of the respectable (but lawbreaking) motorist. Much depended on the attitude of both the middle-class motorist and the police officer who upbraided them.

The presence of a police officer was generally reassuring for the middle classes, but manufactured feelings of insecurity for the working-class boys and girls who were subject to police surveillance. In this way the police officer could still be presented in the media as a signal example of restraint and respect for law, order, and liberty. The bobby on the beat could be seen as a citizen on patrol, juxtaposed favourably against the jackbooted Nazi or Soviet officer strutting around. The police could congratulate themselves on being fair and impartial arbiters of the law, whilst giving a good physical account of themselves on the streets, where they were seen as an occupying force and an object of fear and hate by ordinary working-class communities.

Policing the young, youth culture, and gangs

Attitudes towards the police, expressed in private and in public, helped to establish one's place in society. Exchanging pleasantries about the weather in the street with the local Bobby screamed respectability; equally, the youth refusing to be moved on when requested shouted defiance and resistance. Far from carrying the world forward to a bright new twentieth-century dawn, many moral commentators were convinced that the seemingly dissolute and irresponsible nature of their young people would bring an end to the progress made over the previous century (Godfrey 2004). The colonising of public space by young people 'just hanging around' was a part of life in the Victorian period. The nascent youth culture that seemed to indicate the approaching collapse of society was not so developed or defined in the 1880s as it was in the 1920s and 1930s. Victorian working-class boys swore, larked about, smoked cigarettes, and had play or real fights in order to impress girls (Godfrey 2004). They also played street football, threw stones, obstructed the footpath, and won and lost money at pitch and toss. After World War I, young people did much the same, although there were attempts to take young men off the streets and into more controlled leisure activities, such as the scouting movement, Boys' Brigade, or Lads Clubs (Fowler 2008; Springhall 1983).

Concerns about how young people spent their time were partly conditioned by the worry that the children whose fathers had perished in the war were bereft of suitable male role models. They were not only deserving of state intervention, but they also needed to be controlled lest they fall into criminal behaviour. The 1920s saw something of a moral panic about juvenile delinquency (see Pearson 1983), but, in truth, the kinds of street-life that most normal working-class boys and girls participated in had always brought them to the attention of local police constables. Risk-taking behaviour undertaken by young men (climbing walls, having fights, cheeking authority figures) could easily be interpreted as criminality by residents and police officers, and, of course, juvenile shoplifting sprees (the new open counter layouts of Woolworth's were a key target) caused shopkeepers to constantly request police attention. As with today, youths did not commit the worst crimes, but as a demographic group they did commit a lot of crimes, and they were often condemned in the media. Police officers must have been influenced by the reports of youths out of control in the press, but on the streets they seem to have wanted to distinguish between problematic and non-problematic young people in their neighbourhoods (the penal system also institutionalised this kind of conceptual division for youths, see Chapter 12):

> In consequence of several purses being reported lost by females while doing shopping at the Colonial Stores, High St. I made enquiries and ascertained from the manager that he had noticed a girl repeatedly coming to the shop and leaving without making a purchase [he found and followed the girl] I saw her put her hand into a woman's pocket and take out a purse. I at once stopped her as she was making off . . . I then at once went in the company of PC Hill to the girl's home and found neither of the parents at home. I went to look for them, and in the King's Arms Inn West Street I found both of the parents. I called the Mother outside, and asked her if she knew where her daughter was, she replied 'No' I have not seen her since dinner time. I then told her she was locked up for picking pockets and she said 'Oh' but did not seem upset about it . . . while I was searching the house the Father came in and I told him what his daughter was charged with, and she said 'Oh, is that it?' and smiled.
>
> (*William Hoyle, detective, Exeter,*
> *occurrence book, 1907*)

The girl was sentenced to five years in an Industrial School in Coventry, which had the result of moving her hundreds of miles away in order to separate her from her parents' influence. Discretionary policing would not have allowed Detective Constable Hoyle to let the girl go unpunished, and an arrest was inevitable, but he also managed to get up a prosecution of the parents for neglect (which was successful). Indeed, many constables would seem to be just as happy imprisoning the parents for neglecting their duties as they would have been punishing their children. Something of the bile for feckless parents comes across in PC Smethurst's memoirs:

> the parents of these miserable young urchins were of a low type of human beings, selfish and ungrateful creatures who only worked at intervals, ate and drank like gluttons, wallowed in their filth and slept like hogs. The

gratification of their appetites and passions seemed to be their dominant trait, all other matters being of secondary consideration to them. They brought children into the world, caring very little how they grew up, or what became of them, so that they did not interfere too much with the life they wished to lead. It is no surprise to us who see the everyday life of such a class of people that their children turn into criminals for they are born, reared and steeped up to the life in sordid and filthy environments.

(*Smethurst 1914: 15*)

Shoplifters and gas-meter raiders were a nuisance that the authorities thought could be remedied with better parenting or a good birching for first-time offenders (as a deterrent to further offending). Those that could be rescued from imminent criminality could be detailed in reformatories and industrial schools (see Chapter 12), but violent gang fights seemed to pose more of a problem for the police (and society as a whole). Pearson (1983) has written on the reality and media portrayal of 'hooliganism', and Davies has extended our knowledge of the Manchester Scuttlers (Davies 1999, 2009, 2013). Although studies have shown that gang activity, and most juvenile offending, was often a temporary phase of life (the peak age of offending was fourteen for boys in this period, and most young offenders grew into respectable citizens; Godfrey, Cox and Farrall 2007), any sign of repeat offending, planning rather than youthful exuberance, and/or offending in groups all signalled to the authorities the development of a criminal career:

> Mrs Mossford Powell said she had just had a most disappointing morning in the Juvenile Court dealing with young offenders, some of whom had been before the magistrates three times since July. They were charged with breaking into empty houses and stealing the money from electricity metres. They admitted having gone round the town, examining estate agent's windows and making a list of empty houses. The Police Superintendent told the bench that it was the most appalling confession that he had heard from children. One of the worst features of the affair was the attitude of the children themselves, who entered the court as if it was a cinema – hands thrust into their pockets and grins on their faces.
>
> (*Crewe Chronicle, 22 January 1938*)[10]

The cinema was a telling reference, because, by the 1930s, U.S. gangster movies had taken over from the 'penny dreadfuls' as the supposed inspiration for juvenile crime (Springhall 1999). Eighty years before Anti-Social Behaviour Orders (ASBOs) magistrates put children on curfews and exclusion orders (banning them from the many local cinemas in every town and city) in order to lessen the (no doubt fictional) impact of pseudo-gangsterism.

The police were constantly engaged in the sifting and cognitive processing of situations and people. Was this person going to cause a problem or not? Was the person deserving of discretionary action or formal prosecution? Did the person come from a good home and a decent background? Was the person dangerous? The results of these deliberations caused some to find themselves clipped round the ear, arrested and prosecuted, or waved on their way with no further action. However, this might be suitable (perhaps?) for controlling the streets and dealing with public disorder, but this form of policing could not cope with real rather than pseudo-gangsters – the motor bandits, burglars, racecourse gangs, and organised criminals of the 1920s and 1930s.

Serious crime

The anticipated crime wave of returning soldiers desperate for material goods, brutalised by warfare, and prepared to use guns smuggled home from the front, was a damp squib (Emsley 2010: 21–22; 2013). There was no large-scale upsurge in serious crime caused by demobbed 'squaddies', but this was the period when serious property offending became more organised. Smash-and-grab robberies, speeding getaway cars, and shootouts captured the public imagination and made lurid splashes in the news media. Somehow linked to modernity, motor-car bandits seemed to speed around the major cities carrying out spectacular robberies. The Sabini Gang and the Brummagen Boys operated widespread networks of gambling dens and racecourse rackets, and like the Krays in the 1950s, they enforced their empire with violence. Too much for ordinary bobbies, detectives (who were not tied to a beat and therefore had more autonomy in their working methods, as well as cars, civilian clothes, and so on) were deployed to combat serious crime. The Flying Squad, so called because they were issued fast cars, was established after World War I in order to deal with gangs of car thieves, (Moylen 1929: 170):

> In the course of its short career the Flying Squadron has enjoyed more thrills than could ever be provided by any cinema theatre. Drama, comedy, tragedy, and pathos succeed each other with bewildering rapidity. Nothing will ever surpass, from the point of spectacular drama, the midnight fight in the Old Kent Road with a motor-car full of burglars speeding on their way to a robbery.
>
> *(Felstead 1923: 35)*

The poster boys of more reactive and robust mobile policing, they had a reputation for meeting violence with violence and, for some groups of officers, to be no more than street gangs themselves (indeed, many officers mixed socially, openly, with known offenders). Nevertheless, the Mobile Patrol Experiment (as the Flying Squad were originally called in 1919) seemed to be a successful model for the new fire-brigade style of policing of major incidents. By 1939, Lancashire had 140 wireless cars with VHF radios patrolling large areas of the north-west. Despite the crash-bang-wallop of the Flying Squad, the longest-term impact on crime was probably the development of insurance cover for burglaries and robberies.

Insurance against criminal victimization originated in England in the late eighteenth century but only in 1889 were there a large number of policies available (Michelbacker and Carr 1924). Originally the preserve of the rich, the insurance companies had many middle-class subscribers by the 1930s (Moss 2011), and this greatly elevated reported crime rates (insurance was only paid out on crimes reported to the police). As with the policing of industrial and political activism, it was the more subtle changes in policing or dealing with crime that had the longest-lasting effects.

Industrial and political strife

Policing crime was a routine task, but the police were also called in when industrial and political activity reached the capacity for large scale disorder, as they did in 1887 with the demonstrations of unemployed poor in Trafalgar Square on Bloody Sunday and the many serious industrial disputes and lockouts in South Wales, London, and the North-East just before World War I. Taken together, the heavy-handed policing of these disputes and protests reveal a uniformity of police approach towards those who caused obstructions in the streets, or who caused a breach of the peace by preventing employees from entering their place of work, or who demonstrated in public areas – all of whom were thought to be causing problems for the police which they thought needed to be forcibly dealt with. Keeping order during demonstrations or industrial disputes fitted in well with normal police duties and the natural inclinations of rank-and-file police officers. The strikes between 1910 and 1914 concerned structural industries such as shipbuilding and mining. After the war, however, the economic crises that followed the war affected all employees. The police officers who had served in the army and navy were also part of the generation of wartime heroes that felt let down by low wages, poor housing, and a vacillating weak government. When industrial disputes again began to spread in 1919 the police themselves decided to go on strike (supported by other unionists). The government felt that the threat of revolution was so strong that it was prudent to station a warship in the Mersey, and tanks and troops were deployed in Liverpool city centre. The government sacked all of the nearly 1,000 striking police officers from Liverpool, and their co-strikers in London and Birmingham were also dismissed. Not a single man was reinstated, and overall 2,300 police officers were sacked.[11] The Desborough Committee was set up in the aftermath of the strike, determined that police pay should be increased, and salaries were standardised across all 140 county and borough forces. They also established the Police Federation to represent police officers, but removed to this day the right to strike, making the federation something of a paper tiger. Nevertheless, the federation secured enhanced pension rights in 1921 and 1925, and they were effective enough in the 1930s for politicians to call for them to be disbanded (Reynolds and Judge 1968).

   The dismissal of all the police officers that had struck work in 1919 possibly skewed the police forces towards a more conservative base for a number of years. Certainly in 1926 the police played a full part in keeping industry (particularly transport) moving during the General Strike. Antagonism between police officers who had helped to defeat the strikers and working-class communities continued into the 1930s. The 'Battle of Cable Street' in 1936, which had started out as a fight between antifascists and Oswald Moseley's 'blackshirts' subsequently turned into prolonged battles between East End unionists and the police (Piratin 2006). The overt policing of industrial and political strife, essentially treating demonstrators in the same way as you would treat rioters, large drunken mobs, large juvenile gangs, or 'football hooligans', revealed not only prevailing conservative police attitudes but also the limitations of police tactics. In the 1930s the police, or rather new types of police agency, developed more subtle and secretive methods, building on a foundation of covert policing which had begun in the 1880s.

Secret policing

The current 'war on terror' has been presented as being without precedent, and certainly there seems very little social memory of the long tradition of bombing in this country. For example, Irish activists placed two bombs in March 1883 (one in the offices of *The Times*), another two were placed in October that year (one on the London Underground injured 60 commuters); two suitcase bombs failed to detonate at Paddington and Charing Cross station; in May 1884 a large bomb at the foot of Nelson's Column failed to go off, but the same evening a bomb exploded at Scotland Yard. Later that year the Tower of London and London Bridge were hit. In 1885 a bomb injured police officers at the Houses of Parliament. That Irish-American spree concluded in 1885 (and was not resumed until the IRA campaigns in London and Liverpool in 1939 and 1940). In response to the campaign, the Royal Irish Constabulary had been brought to London, but they were quickly replaced by the homegrown Special Branch (Moylen 1929: 185). The Branch saw themselves as a bulwark protecting British interests and citizens against Irish, Russian and Indian bomb makers, anarchist assassins, bolsheviks, and German spies. From its rather chaotic inception in 1909, Military Intelligence (MI5) was responsible for gathering information on the German war effort before and after 1914–1918, and quickly developed a sophisticated network of spies in Europe in the interwar period (Deacon 1980: 182).

At home, MI5 worked together with Special Branch and the Secret Intelligence Service in counterintelligence operations in the United Kingdom. They had some spectacularly misguided and catastrophic operations in Ireland in the postwar period, and, having learned some lessons, seemed to have worked hard against British leftists in London, Liverpool, and Glasgow to defeat any large-scale working-class movements with revolutionary capacity, including the 1926 General Strike. With reports from MI5 that the army was on the point of mutiny, and with the police strike of 1919 still within recent memory, the government raised military wages in 1926. They were then able to bring in the army to aid the police and to keep the country running, whilst MI5 ran successful 'red scares' which helped weaken the legitimacy of the British Left and rebrand the strikers as unpatriotic. Portraying both Leftist and Rightist groups as disloyal to the Crown was useful in undermining movements thought to be damaging to the British war effort (MI5 planned for war with Germany long before its outbreak in 1939). Oswald Moseley's British Union of Fascists fell into that bracket.

In 1934 at Olympia in London, stewards employed by Moseley beat up the hecklers and opponents of the 'blackshirt' movement. The public outcry caused the police to replace stewards at political meetings with their own officers, giving them a reputation as the protectors of right-wing orators. This was probably a little unwarranted, especially for senior officers who were solidly conservative rather than fascistic in character. The Olympia riots and clashes between unionists and fascists in the East End of London gave Special Branch the opportunity to police by more overt means. The 1936 Public Order Act allowed the police to ban meetings from happening if they were likely to end in disturbances, and to prescribe authorised routes for demonstrators to walk along – Moseley was no longer allowed to parade through Jewish areas of London, for example. The best form of policing political activity seemed to be preventative and covert. This was a lesson well learnt by both the Secret Services and the police in the latter half of the twentieth century as they balanced the use of police force against political demonstrators in the streets, with more subtle surveillance techniques.

All change?

At first glance, policing in the 1930s seemed to be carried on differently, had different priorities, used different methods, and was seen as being very different by the public, to policing in the 1880s.

The increasing professionalization of policing (the introduction of grades of constables, pension rights, better training, unionisation) and the better standard of police recruits encouraged new forms of policing. Technological advances (motorised policing and radio communication) were brought in to combat new challenges – criminals in fast cars, for example). The application of rigorous and systematic methods of detection (if not forensic investigation) came more and more to characterise policing in the public mind and in the media, if not in reality (see Chapter 11).

The secret world of undercover and covert policing was another real shift in the technologies of policing. The desire to control situations before they rose to become public order problems and to catch potentially dangerous subversives and terrorists had led to a significant break in traditional police methods from the 1920s onwards. With the partial withdrawal of police officers into cars, secret and covert forms of policing, and their concentration on dealing with serious and organised crime, the public came to understand less and less about what policing had become and what its new priorities were. This, together with the periodic media reports of corruption and 'third degree' tactics of police coercion weakened some trust in the police:

> A lot of people now will not accept, er . . ., a police officer's decision, whereas in the old days they would accept it because they believed then

that the policeman – I wouldn't say was infallible but they believed in his honesty and integrity and believed that he was a cut above the average man. But of course there's been that many policemen prosecuted for dishonesty and of course this has destroyed the illusion of the policeman being Mr. Perfect.

(ex-policeman speaking of the 1980s, Nottinghamshire
Oral History, tape 87d)

However, in working-class districts, particularly for youths, that trust relationship always had been very contested and strained. Indeed, despite the changes discussed earlier, in many areas there was only a slow evolution of police practices during this period. For example, the trend towards 'fire-brigade' policing (fast response from a centralised motorised police force) rather than general surveillance by beat bobbies became evident only really from the 1960s, not the 1930s. The public demand for visible policing, and the propensity for street-offences to occur on a regular basis, continued to draw the police back to the streets. Moreover, detective services developed slowly in the late Victorian period. Forensic science was basic and variable in quality until at least the second half of the twentieth century, although there was an increasing reliance on information sharing (see Chapter 11). It would be easy to replicate the teleological approach of Critchley (1970) and others who describe the progress of policing. However, although the growth of motoring and the severe public order challenges of the interwar period did, to a large extent, direct policy, we must remember that: first, normal 1880s-style beat policing continued until the 1950s and 1960s (and was then reified in Dixon of Dock Green, and re-introduced in community policing in the 1980s); second, traffic policing could have been hived off to a separate policing agency (perhaps coming under the remit of The British Transport Police, or even a private commercial company); third, information sharing had started in the 1870s but, as the following chapter shows, reliable computer-linked data were more than a century away; and last, secret policing, again, only came to dominate policing in terms of budgets and public awareness in the twenty-first century and the age of counterterrorism. Even today 1880s-style policing of drunken and abusive youths can be seen in British high streets every Saturday night (or daily on the TV channel Dave). These scenes of swearing teenagers having had too many 'alcho-pops' is a closer approximation of 1880s policing than to either Sherlock Holmes's or George Dixon's adventures.

11

PAPERWORK, NETWORKS, INFORMATION, CONNECTIONS, AND THEORIES

I like to think that Detective Constable William Henry Hoyle of Exeter was an optimistic man, maybe going about his business dressed in a brown derby hat, and with a bristling moustache. We don't actually know what he looked like because the staff records of detectives were not as detailed as the records of the offenders they sought.[1] Nevertheless he seemed a man of boundless energy who vigorously employed the three investigative options available to police officers at the start of the twentieth century: rounding up 'the usual suspects' and anyone else who was new in town, sending off fingerprint or other forensic evidence to New Scotland Yard, and tracking offenders (sometimes internationally) through the network of bureaucratic record keeping that developed from the 1870s.

From the 1870s onwards, criminal justice institutions became linked by bureaucracy and by the increasing need to share information (Thomas 2007). Habitual offender legislation (1869 Habitual Offenders Act and the 1871 Prevention of Crimes Act) required police and penal institutions to share information (something they had never done before). This in turn necessitated the Home Office and Scotland Yard to establish centralised systems to record and store information on released prisoners, until they became vast organisations that were only disbanded on the eve of World War II. This information could, in theory, be circulated to detectives whenever a crime had been committed. The vast amount of detailed personal and biometric data relating to thousands of former prison inmates that were collected also presented other possibilities. Eugenicists, who believed that hereditary characteristics caused certain forms of behaviour in individuals and that selective breeding could eradicate inherent weaknesses, consumed these kind of data with alacrity. It seemed to have the potential to reinforce their views about 'born criminals' and those who were predisposed to criminality through weakness of character. Aided by the new forensic techniques and a potentially universal database of fingerprints and anthropometric data, academics, scientists, medical and psychological experts working across Europe and the United States adapted eugenic foundations to a new 'science' of criminology. International organisations such as Interpol were formed, and police and penal experts met at international conferences in order to share ideas. So, after evaluating the usefulness of new detective techniques, this chapter will examine the flow of penal and policing policy around Europe and the wider world, and explore the eugenic roots of criminological theory in the United Kingdom.

The 'science' of detection

A crime had been committed. A watch had been reported as stolen after a fracas in a public street one Saturday night (20 September 1908). Detective Hoyle sprang into action using a well-worn established policing strategy: round up 'the usual suspects':

> I at once made enquiries and interviewed several of the men who were there when the disturbance took place but I could not get any information. I also made all possible enquiries at the Jewellers Pawnbrokers etc but failed to trace the missing property. Walter Pearson who is a base moulder at 'Willys' is suspected, and he is addicted to drink and his wife pledges at Lincott's. I searched the man, but without result. A sharp look out is being kept on these people.
>
> (*Exeter Detective Record Books,*
> *1905-08, Devon Archives*)

When that initial tactic failed (and it must be admitted that this crude strategy often did result in a conviction, even if the police did not get the real culprit; see later in this chapter) detectives turned to forensic evidence. Fingerprinting was the most well known of the new technologies in detective methods.

In 1880, Scottish physician Dr. Henry Faulds (1880) published a treatise on the usefulness of fingerprints for identification purposes. However, when he proposed his system to the Metropolitan Police, they were uninterested (Reid 2003). Hoping for a more sympathetic hearing, Faulds wrote to Charles Darwin who, though he was not willing to pursue it himself (he was quite old by this time), passed the letter to his cousin Francis Galton, an amateur anthropologist, who was much more interested in Faulds's theories (Cole 2001). After a decade of developing the original ideas, Galton (without crediting Faulds) published a detailed statistical model of fingerprint analysis and identification in *Finger Prints* (1892). It took Scotland Yard another decade to open up a Central Fingerprint Department (in 1901). In fact, the Home Office, which funded the Fingerprint Department, was backing two horses: the collection of fingerprints and anthropomorphic data collection. The Bertillon system of recording anthropometric data (various measurements were taken of parts of the prisoner's body) never really caught on in England in the same way it did in France and the United States, and in 1900 the Belper Committee finally came down in favour of fingerprints (see Beavan 2002; Knepper and Norris, 2009).

The other forensic tool that was used to identify suspects – photography – was the only rival to fingerprinting for a number of years.

The photographing of all convicted criminals received into county and borough prisons also came into force in 1871.[2] By 1873, approximately 30,000 photographs had been received by the Metropolitan Police, and 373 cases of positive identification had been made following examination of these photographs in the Habitual Criminal Office.[3] By 1900, they must have been knee-deep in photographs. The rate of accumulation and the similarity of facial features of the people in the photographs meant that there were too many of them for investigators to go through in any meaningful way (Ireland 2002; Jager 2001). They were useful for identifying repeat offenders by the prison authorities, however, as were the records of prisoners' tattoos. Together with the 'Register of Distinctive Marks' (including tattoos and scars, cuts, missing fingers, and so on) which was created in 1870, police officers and prison officers were more easily able to identify suspects (Stanford 2009: 54–81, 58–59). Metropolitan Police officers were regularly sent to local and convict prisons to inspect remand prisoners and convicts due for discharge respectively with a view to identifying known previous offenders (Stanford 2009: 67). However, by the time that Detective Hoyle was on duty in the 1900s, only fingerprinting seemed a viable and reliable means of identification, and even that, as Godfrey *et al.* (2010) noted, was never a 'silver bullet' against criminality.

Hoyle's records reveal the considerable optimism that local detectives invested in forensic evidence, and the ability of New Scotland Yard to identify perpetrators through their fingerprints. He frequently sent objects such as brass lamps and cutlery and so on to have 'dabs' identified by the Fingerprint Department. Invariably he was disappointed – 'no result' was usually the reply from New Scotland Yard, just as it was in the following case of a burglary of £73 from Mr Panter's Draper's shop in Exeter on 24 December 1908:

> On receipt of the information at the Police Station, I at once went to Sidwell St to make enquiries and examine the premises. I found that the front of the shop abuts on Sidwell St and the rear of the premises on the burying ground of Sidwell St Church being divided there from by a wall about 6" 6' high. Beside of this wall there are three large stone ornaments and I found marks on these stones, shewing (sic) where the thief climbed on to the wall at the rear of the yard. Entrance was affected to the interior of the premises, by means of the sitting room window, which was left unfastened, then through a short passage to the shops. Nothing had been broken open, except the cashbox, no inside doors having been locked. There were no fingerprints, boot prints, or other clues which would be likely to lead to the identification of the thief. I made a careful search of the churchyard and found the cashbox (broken open) with a few coppers in it, hidden away under a heap of leaves, the ground all around that spot being hard there were no footprints. I also made careful enquiry in the neighbourood and of PC Bradford who was on that beat, but could not get any information. For some time past, observation

has been kept on a house No. 51 Paul St occupied by a man called 'Hoare' (a suspected person) who, no doubt, has been concerned in several of the recent robberies in this city, and at 2–30am this morning PC Skinner, who is on Plain Clothes duty by night, found the marks on the door and stairs had been disturbed, and in consequence kept special observation during the night. but did not see 'Hoare'; He however left a note for me, saying what had occurred. After examining the premises at Sidwell St I immediately returned to the station and went with PC Walters and searched 'Hoares' house, but could not find anything to connect him with the robbery. I asked him what time he had come home the previous night, and he stated he did not return home until 2–10 as he had been working at the Gazette office. I afterwards found this to be correct. I then went to Black Boy Rd and made enquiries regarding a man called 'Bealey' but found he was home all night, and he is in constant work. It appears that a day or two previous to the robbery I met 'Barlow Bill' (a suspected person) previously convicted of shopbreaking and asked him what he was doing. He then informed me that he was out of work and had no money. On Boxing night about 11pm I saw 'Hill' in High St with another man called 'Hock' (a bad character) they were both very drunk. I kept observation and saw 'Hill' go down the street drunk on several occasions late at night. I made careful enquiries and found that a few weeks previous to Mr Panter's robbery 'Hill' had been at work on a roof at No. 31 Sidwell St, but as only money was stolen I was unable to get sufficient evidence to arrest 'Hill' but I hold very strong suspicions that he was concerned on this robbery.

Hoyle's willingness to pin this on one of his usual suspects – Hoares, Bealey, Hock, and Hill – is clear to see. Maybe he would have had a clearer focus for his investigation if some of the forensic evidence had stood up – identifiable marks on the stones at the point of entry, fingerprints on the cash-box, distinctive footprints, and so on. But, as on many occasions, whilst fingerprints could identify suspects (if they were already 'in the system'), there were also a huge number of occasions when it was impossible to find or collect fingerprints. However, despite the patchiness of results from forensic examination, it clearly had sufficient successes for detectives to continue to have faith in it. For example, a safecracker was convicted in 1938 because of the persuasive forensic evidence, which I have summarised below:

1.   Fibres found on the man's suit matched those found at the scene of the crime.
2.   His suit had residual traces of explosives on them.
3.   His suit had traces of enamel paint on them which matched the colour of the safe.
4.   Traces of a fuse were found on his suit, which matched the fuse used at the scene.
5.   Fragments of tissue paper in his trouser turn-ups matched those found at the scene.

6.   Pencil shavings (yellow) were found in the man's bedroom and also at the scene.
7.   Fibres from suit found in the ventilator which had been used as the access point.
8.   A tobacco tin taken from the scene of the crime was found in his suit pocket.

Impressive forensic evidence, which did lead to a conviction in this case, but I can't help but wonder what would have happened if he had taken his suit off either before or after the robbery? Although he sought to assert the importance of science in proving guilt in court, even former Clerk to the West Riding Justices, Ernest Pettifer, who described the preceding case in his memoirs, thought that forensics only aided and could never supersede the skills and experience of the investigating police officer (Pettifer 1940: 86). This view was shared by Sir John Fitzgerald Moylen, prominent barrister and private secretary to the permanent under-secretary of the Home Office, who largely saw policing as a battle of wits between detectives and crooks:

> The detective side of police work is . . . it must be admitted, a somewhat matter-of-fact occupation, in which hard work and a knowledge of the criminal classes are essential. Crime in real life is largely the work of professional criminals of poor intellectual capacity, no social accomplishments or charms, and little imagination, though they may have a great deal of low cunning. To cope with them successfully, powers of abstract reasoning and scientific knowledge or apparatus serve less than the more commonplace resources which may be summed up in the word "information".
>
> (*Moylen 1929: 178*)

Hunches, detective 'nous', and forensic evidence, were all useful weapons in the police armoury, but the key to catching offenders was simply the sharing of information, or so it appeared.

Spider's webs of information

A web of information began construction in the 1870s, designed to trap within it the habitual offender, and to make it impossible for them to continue a life of crime. The habitual offender acts subjected all those convicted of two felonies to be placed under police supervision for a maximum of seven years (Godfrey *et al.* 2010; Radzinowicz and Hood 1990: 1342). Convicts released on licence were also watched over. They had to report any change of address and were required to report to their district police station on a monthly basis. The Convict Supervision Office conducted visits to prisons, interviewing recently discharged prisoners with regards to their employment and residence and recording the data (Stanford 2009: 61). Registers were kept of those under supervision which recorded their name, aliases, prison and register number, date and place of birth, physical details, marks, peculiarities, offence, date of conviction, place of committal, sentence and date of conviction, date when prison sentence expired, date of liberation, and intended address and occupation, together with remarks concerning the offender. The records also had photographs of the prisoners attached to aid identification.

Originally, the task of compiling and maintaining the Habitual Criminal Register was given to the Commissioner of the Metropolitan Police. However, this responsibility was passed around like an unwanted gift. It moved from the Metropolitan Police to the Home Office in 1874, when there were then over 150,000 individuals listed, and then on again to the Prison Department in 1877. By 1879 the authorities were surely correct to conclude that the register and the whole bureaucratic structure had become unwieldy and unusable (Howard Association Annual Report 1875, quoted in Radzinowicz and Hood, 1990: 1348). The solution was to restrict the numbers of people being registered to those convicted under certain acts, and to create a new body responsible for coordinating the flows of information.[4] The Convict Supervision Office, created in 1880, helped to form a network of information which was unprecedented (Petrow 1994: 85–86), but it was still bedevilled by the same problems that everybody else had suffered. The primary tool of identifying likely suspects (either before or after a crime had been committed) was still the watchfulness, intuition, prejudices, and 'common sense' of the officers on the beat and the investigating detectives. As stated in the 1894 report into the best means available for identifying habitual criminals,

> It may at the outset be stated in general terms that the practice of the English police, though the details differ widely in different forces, is always dependent on personal recognition by police or prison officers. This is the means by which identity is proved in criminal courts; and, though its scope is extended by photography, and it is some cases aided by such devices as the registers of distinctive marks, it also remains universally the basis of the methods by which identity is discovered.
>
> (*1893–94 [C 7263] Identification of Habitual Criminals, Report of a Committee Appointed by the Secretary of State to Inquire into the Best Means Available for Identifying Habitual Criminals, p. 5*)

The usefulness of the habitual offender registers as a tool for helping officers identify offenders was poor because they were simply swamped with information. The authorities had become entangled in their own spider's web (Higgs 2004: 97). A mixture of too much information, and too little resource to properly manage it made it something of an expensive white elephant – but one which local detectives still believed in, and tried to use. For example, Detective Hoyle used the system to track an offender from Exeter to the Continent in 1905:

> *Wednesday 15th* one of the overseers came to the station at 3pm and reported to me that HC Scammall had absconded with a large amount of money beonging to the overseers which he: Scammall had collected and the fraud extended as far back as September 1902. I at once went with Mr Oliver to

the Bank and dispatched Det Martin to the Railway Station to make enquiries. I returned with Mr Oliver to the station and a warrant was granted on
his sworn instruction which was signed by T Linsworth JP. Det Martin traced
Scammall having left Exeter by the 9–15 train from St. Davids on Wednesday.
Also ascertained that a young woman called Tallsman with whom Scammall
had been keeping company also left St David's Station same morning by
10–20am booking for Bristol. Immediately sent telegrams giving full particulars to Liverpool, Southampton, and London police asking for enquiries to be
made at ports. I afterwards obtained full description of Scammall and Tallman
also their luggage and sent out about 100 informations to all principal towns
in the United Kingdom asking to have enquiries made at all shipping offices
Hotels and other likely places and if found to arrest Scammall.

   WANTED HERBERT CHARLES SCAMMALL a rate collector and
native of this City. About 28 to 30 years of age, 5 feet 8 inches high, rather
stout build, full face, pale complexion, clean shaven, rather large head which
he carries slightly forward. Has a rather excited manner when talking.
DRESSED when last seen in a blue lounge suit, motor cap with shiny peak,
carried a small brown hard bag with paper parcel strapped to it. Has also two
other suits of clothes with him viz:-A black frock coat and vest, black morning coat and vest, 2 pairs of grey trousers. Accompanied by a young woman
called "Tallman" 19 years of age, medium build and height, of good appearance. Dressed black coat and skirt (skirt tight fitting with pleats) blue felt hat
with oriental trimming. Has also 3 other costumes with her viz:-a brown,
blue, and dark green. Her luggage cosists of a medium size new black dress
trunk rounded top. Absconded on the 8th. inst. booking by the 10.15 a.m.
train, G.W.R. for Bristol. Will no doubt leave the country. Please cause immediate enquiries to be made at Shipping Offices, Hotels and other likely places
for this man and if found arrest and wire to THE CHIEF CONSTABLE,
CITY POLICE, EXETER.

   Det Martin then went to Scammall's house at 51 Roehampton St and
Miss Tallmans house at 19 Brunswick St, St Thomas and obtained a photo of
each. These I sent out to a photographer and had 5 copies of each made. I also
sent official letters to Bristol and Weston S. Mare police.

   Thursday 16th I sent out the 5 photos on descriptive forms and amended
informations to Liverpool, Southampton, London and other seaport towns.
I afterwards had an interview with the Town Clerk with reference to the
execution of the warrant outside the United Kingdom and was told that the
Council should not go to the expense of having Scammall arrested outside
of the United Kingdom. But he did not know if [the complainant] would go
to the expense.

   Friday 17th I had an interview with the Chairman of the Watch Committee with reference to Scammall being extradited. he also informed me
that the council would not go to the expense. I obtained information that
two letters bearing East Dulwich postmarks had been received by Scammall's

mother since he absconded. Also that 3 packages of luggage had been sent away in January 27th addressed Hotel Monmore in Marmood Rd, London. I at once sent full particulars by wire to Scotland Yard asking for urgent enquiries to be made at that address. Det Martin made enquiries at the Railway Goods Dept and was informed that the order was received at Bombay Rd Collecting office, but from whom Mr Taylor (who is in charge at the office) could not say. He could not identify Scammall's photograph.

Saturday 18th a telephone message was received from Bath police asking for a photo of Scammall as there was a man answering his description. I at once forwarded by Express letter by passanger train the photo of Scammall and Tallsman. On 20th I forwarded photo of Scammall with Postal Order to the editor of the Police Gazette, Scotland Yard with a footnote that Scammall was not to be arrested outside the United Kingdom 'as per instructions received'.

(photo appeared in the Police Gazette February 24th 1905 case 31)[5]

Again Detective Hoyle had missed his man, despite his best efforts. The system could not be relied upon to identify or track offenders; however, as a tool for enabling local police officers to press down on the nerves of those that they, very literally, watched over, it was much more surefooted (Godfrey *et al.* 2010). Together with the other bureaucratic records designed to collate information on offenders and ex-prisoners by the start of World War I, there was a layered matrix of very detailed information compiled and stored by yet another body, the Criminal Record Office (CRO; formed 1913, it took over from the Habitual Offenders Registry who had picked up this responsibility in 1905). By 1924 the records of 770,000 people were kept in a card index, and some claimed that this was a superbly run system for 'Catching Thieves On Paper' (as the booklet on the system published by Metropolitan Police in 1936 was titled). When a gruesome murder was committed by Frederick Guy Browne in Essex, the investigating officer asked the CRO for their list of suspects capable of such a crime. The first name on their list was Frederick Guy Browne (Thomas 2007: 14–15). In truth, however, the CRO was already being wound down around World War I, but the cultural legacy lingered in police operations into the 1920s and 1930s:

One great handicap a man like myself has to face, assuming he means to go straight, is this: I am known to the CID and may be 'picked up' any day and sent to gaol. There is a law known as The Law of the Suspected Person [. . .] Whenever I am on a charge I am given a thorough look-over in the police court reception room by any detective officers who are hanging around. After one or two convictions I am thus 'known' to a fair number of them. I am walking through the West End one day when one officer sees me. I am picked up . . . I am put up against the wall in a quiet corner and quickly 'run over' for anything that may be on me at the time. At the station I am charged with being a suspected person, searched, and my fingerprints are taken. In the Court the next morning the evidence of the officer is somewhat as follows ... "We saw the prisoner acting suspiciously, so we followed him [...] he tried the handles of some parked cars [...] We asked him what he was doing, and where he was going, and, not getting satisfactory replies, told him he would be charged ...

Magistrate: 'Is the man working? No'.
'What are his means of livelihood? Apparently none'.
'How long has he been out of work? Weeks. Possibly months.'
There then follows the inevitable question which will damn him:
'*Is this man known?* Yes, and he has had several convictions. He has been known to the police for several years, is an associate of bad company, and a pest to society ...'
"Three months hard labour. Next, please.'

(*Allen 1932: 236–238*)

By this point the recording system was disintegrating, and the ease with which offenders and ex-prisoners could move around the country in cars and on trains probably meant that the system was largely inoperable.[6] The longest-lasting impacts of the system were twofold. First, the links established between penal and police agencies from the 1870s on became a model (albeit one which has never been achieved) for greater systematic cooperation within the U.K. criminal justice system; and second, it provided an impetus for greater international co-operation. We could say that transnational policing originated in Rome at an international meeting designed to counter terrorism, but only formally began in 1914 at the First International Congress of Judicial Police in Monaco. There already existed a series of International Penal and Penitentiary Congresses which ran from 1872 to 1950, and a long history of police collaboration, especially between France and Germany and between Germany and the United States (Deflem 2002). In 1923, the first Interpol office opened in Vienna, but it was really no more than an exchange bureau for police-related information (and not a very effective one at that). Like most national police agencies, Interpol only really started to become effective as a transnational policing agency, rather than an information clearinghouse, in the 1980s (see Chapter 10). As Emsley noted (2007: 181–199) these European conferences also facilitated debates around the nature and causes of criminality in the 1890s.

From eugenics to scientific criminology

It would be a huge exaggeration to say that these international conferences fostered a spirit of collaboration immediately. However, the glue that held the various highly opinionated and very nationalistic experts together in the conference sessions were, first, Lombrosian-inspired theories of 'born criminals' and, later, their common adherence to pernicious and virulent theories around eugenics.

In the last quarter of the nineteenth century, Cesare Lombroso theorised that some people in society had not evolved to the same level as others. These atavistic subhumans would exhibit both lower levels of civility and physical characteristics which would mark them out. He devised his theories through examination – measuring (the angle of the forehead, size of ears and nose, length of arms, how close the eyes were together, and so on) of prisoners in Italy. His follower Enrico Ferri coined the term *born criminal* as a classification for habitual offenders who were destined to commit crime through their very nature. Helpfully, Lombrosians proposed that 'physical stigmata' could be used to identify particular types of offenders. Thieves, rapists, and murderers all bore their own physical markers and so could be easily identified once police officers understood the code. When it appeared that some types of offender did not, in fact, bear these physical markers, Lombrosians were forced to adapt their theories somewhat. They accepted that 'criminaloids', moral imbeciles, or infrequent offenders might have been influenced by environmental factors. Poverty, for example, might have pushed a non-criminal type into an act of desperation that belied their usual civilized state.

Lombrosio's theories persisted longer in Germany than they did in France or England (Broberg and Roll-Hansen 1996; Pick 1989). The First International Congress of Criminal Anthropology in Rome in 1885 saw the Lombrosian School dominate, but only until the French (notably the criminologist and social-psychologist Gabriel Tardee) challenged Lombroso's findings at the next meeting of the Congress in Paris four years later (Wetzell 2000: 44–48). Charles Goring, who used Lombroso's statistics themselves to undermine anthropomorphism, published *The English Convict* in 1913. His book challenged the scientific validity and rationale that underpinned this kind of anthropomorphic research. The 'ideal criminal' of Lombrosian imagination was not credible.[7] Neither did Goring, in his large-scale statistical study, find any links between criminality and unemployment, environment, poverty, or stress. Like many others, he was persuaded by the emerging school of eugenic thought.

Eugenics simply applied the principles of Darwinian evolution and animal husbandry to explain why, and how, society could be threatened by degeneracy if mentally unfit people were allowed to outbreed normal, decent citizens. Influenced by Lombroso and Havelock Ellis, eugenicists such as Galton (who had moved from fingerprints to eugenics) favoured the sterilization of habitual offenders and the cleansing of society in order to impose a moral hygiene. Alcoholics, the medically unfit, and the mentally ill were all included in this list of people thought to have inherently weak characters and to be suitable for sterilization, segregation, or containment in some way (Clouston 1906; Norwood East 1936: 352–364; Seliger *et al.* 1946; see Searle 1976: 104–105). Reverend Osborne Jay proposed an imaginative scheme:

> There is only one solution. Education has failed, religious work, the Poor Law and prison systems are alike ineffective, and universal charity cannot rightly be considered a real factor in the case. The only method, I think, is to stop the supply of persons born to be lazy, immoral, and deficient in intellect. This can only be done by sending the present stock of them to what I will call a

penal settlement, for life. In many respects it would resemble a prison, only, of course, larger and far less gloomy. It should be possessed of gardens, covered promenades, a gymnasium, and baths, recreation rooms, reading rooms, and even a theatre and concert room. In such a place there would necessarily be the possibility of recourse to punishment, solitary confinement, or even an application of corporal punishment. To the submerged temperament such a place would be the best home they had ever known.

(*The London, 12 March 1896*)

Eugenics drew on a new kind of liberalism. The rational choice theory favoured by classical and positivist criminologists and those who saw crime as a moral failing was ebbing away, to be replaced by the idea that people were incapable of choosing to commit crimes, or getting regularly drunk, because they were fatally undermined by their intrinsic inherited weaknesses of character. They were, as Wiener (1990: 191–192) stressed, now at the mercy of a brutal kind of protective care and control model that incarcerated those labelled mentally weak or incapable in the asylums as much as it did the prisons.

Eugenics was a 'religion' which made priests of scientists, but which appealed to the cultural and academic elite (Childs 2001: 3–13). Galton had inspired the Eugenics Education Society, (founded in 1907 and changed to the Eugenics Society in 1926[8]) which then attracted a wide range of prominent followers.[9] Thomas Smith Clouston, for example, was president of the Medico-Psychological Association (formed in 1888). John Maynard Keynes founded an new economic theory which was dominant in the United States and Britain in the 1940s, and 'Keynsian economics' is still influential today. As with other members of the Eugenics Society, Keynes was concerned with creating jobs for useful workers, and he saw both the control of money supply, and the control of population numbers, as a way of guaranteeing that society ran efficiently. His ideas were at their most influential at the same time as he was the director of the Eugenics Society (from 1937 to 1944). Marie Stopes, influential campaigner for birth control and family planning, was a member, as were several prominent politicians including future prime ministers Balfour and Chamberlain. William Henry later Lord Beveridge, was an economist who authored the influential *Beveridge Report* which became the blueprint for the postwar welfare state. His earlier work is lesser referenced. In 1906 he had penned a pamphlet entitled *The Problem of the Unemployed*, which suggested that unemployable men (rather than unemployed men) should be paid an allowance for food by the state, but, in return, would not be allowed to reproduce. Beveridge was the director of the London School of Economics (LSE) and Political Science from 1919 to 1937, and he was succeeded in that post by another prominent member of the Eugenics Society. The LSE had actually been founded in 1895 by social commentators, campaigners, Fabian Society members and eugenicists, Beatrice and Sidney Webb. The LSE also employed the academic Richard Titmuss, professor of Social Administration, who advocated family planning, and the restriction of numbers of children to be born into poor families (the society was a strong supporter of abortion rights). Eugenics was popular with Oxbridge undergraduates (Searle 1976:

12–13). There was also strong representation in Liverpool, where members of the University participated in the Eugenics Alliance (Starkey 2000: 62–65).

The Sociological Society (founded in 1903) became the Institute of Sociology in 1930, with its own journal *The Sociological Review*. Sympathetic to eugenics, the journal seemed to have no difficulty in associating sociology with eugenics. The two disciplines were comfortable bedfellows in the 1920s and 1930s. The London School of Economics taught eugenics in its sociology courses, alongside economics, anthropology, and demography.[10] The eugenic emphasis on the young as a site of hereditary disorder then fed into nascent psycho-criminological theories of delinquency even when the eugenic movement itself was in decline (Abel and Kinder 1942). In the 1920s eugenics tended to lose its veneer of scientific rigour and diffused into a generally more widespread, lazy, and casual anti-Semitism. In the 1930s and beyond, race rather than criminality became a focus for those obsessed with uncovering inherent weaknesses in individuals and in society as a whole. Hahn Rafter (1997) describes the impact of eugenics in the United States, where, arguably, eugenic thinking had its longest run, with physical characteristics and criminality still being linked in the 1950s. Of course, racial profiling was always, and continues to be, very evident in U.S. law enforcement strategies.

Criminology in the United Kingdom has been criticised for its willingness to be the handmaiden of the State in defining problematic behaviour and refining techniques of dealing with it (Hillyard *et al.* 2004). The science or pseudoscience of criminology must be seen as a willing partner to a eugenic programme until the 1930s, even when it moved away from eugenics very quickly to embrace environmental, not hereditary, causes of criminality.[11] Nevertheless, the possibility of identifying criminal predispositions through fingerprinting was still being discussed in the 1970s and again in the 1990s (Cole 2001: 115–116) and research on the genome has given a new twist to eugenicistic-type research (Duster 2003; Galton 2002).

Conclusion

So, how to sum up eugenics and its influence? As Major Leonard Darwin stated, 'Eugenics is always in some danger of being used as a dumping-ground for cranks' (Eugenics Education Society Annual Report 1912–13: 5–6). In the United Kingdom, it attracted more than cranks; it also attracted some of the leading academic theorists and thinkers from the right and left of the political spectrum. In the end, eugenics never took a full grip in Britain for the same reasons that we find it hard to find a coherent strategy for policing (see Chapter 10). The criminal justice system, with its various institutions working to their own agendas, was reactive and pragmatic in its operation. It never really engaged with a dominant ideology, although it was swayed in part by different concepts and theories from time to time (especially those concerning recidivism, see Chapter 12). However, neither Lombrosianism nor eugenics (nor criminology for that matter) ever constituted a coherent programme for action in the same way that they did in Continental Europe or the United States.

In a discipline which teaches that crime is a social construct in the first introductory lectures, it is hard to understand how measuring how close someone's eyes are, or looking for criminal characters, came to be so well developed. However, these theories seemed to be able to explain recidivism in the 1880s and 1890s, and the inability of the institutions of justice to effect reform through imprisonment. They also offered a way of differentiating between the large number of apparent nuisances in society (petty recidivists and drunks) and the small hard-core of serious offenders. Once these putative groups were identified, penal theory and sentencing regimes could be adjusted to deal with them (as we will see in the following chapter).

12

A JUST MEASURE OF PUNISHMENT

A Fair Measure of Reformation

In Thursday's announcement, the Ministry of Justice said that six prisons would be closing, as well as one of the three jail facilities on the Isle of Wight that have been amalgamated with each other. The prisons that are to close are Bullwood Hall in Essex, Canterbury, Gloucester, Kingston in Portsmouth, Shrewsbury, and Camp Hill on the Isle of Wight. The UK's oldest working prison, Shepton Mallet, in Somerset, is also among those to be shut. The Ministry of Justice said the closure of the seven prisons this year would result in the loss of 2,600 places from prisons and was expected to save £63m per year in running costs.

BBC News (11 January 2013)

The closure of a number of prisons in 2013 creates a curious echo of the prison closure programme enacted a century earlier when thirty-six prisons were shut down between 1900 and 1931. Perhaps some of the recently closed prisons that were built in the Victorian period will reopen as gaol museums or hotels? (See Chapter 8.) How had the situation arrived whereby a rising tide of recidivists on short custodial sentences threatened to swamp the prison estate in the 1880s and 1890s yet an extensive programme of closure was brought in just thirty years later? How did the prison population fall to its lowest ever level in an era of industrial and political strife (the suffragette movement, the industrial struggles of the 1910–1913 period)? We explore some of the turbulence in ideas around reform and sentencing that took place in this period, and examine some of the alternatives to custody, especially for youths, that denuded the prison population.

The rising tide of recidivism

The Lombrosian and eugenics theories discussed in the last chapter had refocused attention away from the idea of a criminal class. Rather than fixing on a hard-core criminal community of serious offenders lurking in the heart of the mid-Victorian city, legislation and social policy looked towards weak-minded individuals in a residuum of poor souls at the bottom of the class system. Those who dwelt in the depths with the residuum were thought to have resisted, or not been able to take advantage of, the benefits that late-Victorian capitalism was providing. As with most social policy, it started with the idea that 'something must be done', and the first thing to do was to assess the dimensions of the problem. Social surveys by Charles Booth (in 1886), Seebohm Rowntree (1901), and others provided information on the lives of the poor, some of whom, as Booth acknowledged, had criminal convictions. Criminality, alcohol-dependency, immorality, dirtiness and lack of hygiene and perceived hereditary weaknesses were by now all jumbled together and viewed as a kind of criminal incontinence (continually getting drunk and breaking the law). The judicial statistics provided more information on the apparent rising tide of recidivists in the prison system (see Figure 12.1).

The 1880s and 1890s were something of a crisis point. It was always likely that the number of recidivists would increase as soon as convict transportation ended (once sent to Australia, offenders could hardly reoffend in Britain). As transportation had largely ended in the 1850s, by the 1880s a significant number of ex-prisoners were racking up a number of convictions. The crisis seemed most acute in the 1880s, and again in the early 1900s, however, when the number of committed prisoners who had served time before overtook the number of first time prisoners. The annually published criminal statistics (see Chapter 2) seemed to provide very visible proof that the prison system was incapable of rehabilitating the people in its charge.

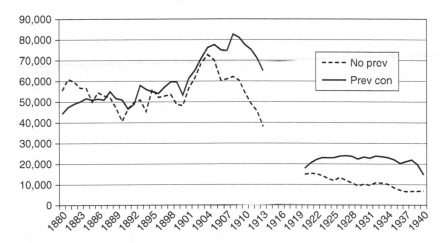

FIGURE 12.1 Recidivists convicted, England and Wales, 1880–1938

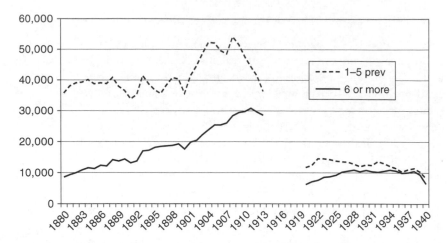

FIGURE 12.2   Number of convictions per recidivist, England and Wales, 1880–1938

Indeed, as can be seen in Figure 12.2, the prisons seemed to manufacture recidivism since the numbers of people with six convictions or more rose inexorably from 1880 to World War I.

When it comes to considering penal policy in this period, we should, as Victorian and Edwardian policy makers and legislators did, always keep the 'recidivist problem' in the back of our minds.

Short sentences and never-ending ones

Most people who ended up in prison in this period were only there for a short time, six months or less (in fact about two-thirds of the prison population was made up of prisoners serving less than a fortnight's custody), and the majority found themselves spinning round and round in the revolving doors of the prison system. This was not only an expensive system, but an ineffective one too, and few commentators defended short sentences, not even those in the prison system that administered them (Quinton 1910: 132). Discussion of what could be done to prevent reoffending, and the appropriate length of the prison sentence that would both deter and rehabilitate, and the type of prison regime that could accomplish a measure of reform were widespread, varied, and, in some cases very imaginative[1]:

> Towards the turn of the twentieth century there were many contentious debates about the possibility of finding proportionate sentences suited to the severity of the offence. This could be long sentences of penal servitudes which would deter future offending, or, alternatively, indeterminate sentences might keep society safe from persistent offenders until they were safe to be released back into the community. The first proposal for preventative detention was proposed in 1904 but was soundly criticized and withdrawn. In

1908 a redrafted Act was passed which Radzinowicz and Hood described as 'a landmark' that had 'no analogy in contemporary European law'.

(*Godfrey, Cox, and Farrall, 2010*)

The Prevention of Crime Act 1908 (8 Edw7 c.69) stipulated that, after serving no less than five years and no more than ten years in a convict prison, the offender could be released to a more reformative regime at Camp Hill Prison on the Isle of Wight. The regime there was based upon a stepped system of rewards for good conduct, hard work (on the prison farm, in the gardens, in the educational classes, or in the industrial workshops) and good behaviour. In many ways it echoed the nineteenth-century Australian convict probation system. If the treatment at Camp Hill was well received by the prisoner, and they were responsive to it, the Secretary of State could order an inmate's conditional release on licence.

However, the low-level habitual offender came more and more to dominate the government's thinking in the late nineteenth century. William Tallack, secretary of the Howard Association, was just one of those who distinguished between 'weak and indolent' habitual offenders and 'wilfully brutal ruffians' (Tallack 1899: 165). Those few serious offenders should, Tallack believed, be sent to specially adapted institutions, similar to an internal gulag or a British penal colony (see Chapter 11). However, because the numbers of professional criminals appeared to have shrunk, intellectual resources were now redirected towards treating, rehabilitating, or (through eugenics) eradicating habitual offenders (Quinton 1910: 7). There were many arguments about the type of recidivists could come under the provisions of any kind of act which was capable of detaining some offenders for a period longer than would have been merited had they simply been first-time offenders. There were more discussions about which kind of regime could combine a component that deterred future offending in individuals and that could generally deter first time offenders from continuing a life of crime and a regime that could encourage habitual offenders to return to making an honest living. For serious offenders, the policy was fairly clear by 1908, there was a desire to incapacitate the dangerous offender with very long penal sentences. For the low-level repeat offenders who committed many offences which, in themselves, did not merit prison sentences but which together defined a persistently criminal life, what sort of sentence would be suitable for them? These were difficult issues that continued to confound penal theorists well into the twentieth century, and which are still unresolved today (see Godfrey *et al.* 2010; Radzinowicz and Hood 1971: 1288, 1309–1313, 1321–1327).

'Prison property'

So, by 1908, a twin-track approach to sentencing was established, at least in theory. The hardened serious offender would be diverted into preventative detection and incapacitated by long prison sentences. The weak-willed, habitual low-level offender would be incapacitated by short prison sentences (as there was little alternative until World War I, as we will see later in this chapter). The organisation of the prison system reacted to this conceptual recategorisation of different types of offenders and developed the system of classification they had begun in 1877. Start class denoted first-time prisoners, and together with juveniles, they were kept separate from recidivists. Wakefield Prison received local prisoners that were serving longer sentences, and they were trained in industrial crafts whilst there. Wormwood Scrubs was reserved for first-time prisoners and was meant to have a less-repressive atmosphere in order to encourage rehabilitation. Liverpool and Wandsworth collected weak-minded local prisoners, and Dartmoor was chiefly used for habitual convicts (Gillin 1931: 221–222, 225). In truth, the hard-core recidivists who committed serious offences such as robbery or murder were dwarfed by the huge numbers of small-time, low-level habitual offenders who washed in and out of the prisons and the courts.

The regular stock-in-trade of the magistrates court (until motoring offences took off in the 1930s; see Chapter 4) were working-class and unemployed low-level offenders often caught up in legislation designed to incapacitate the habitual drunk (for example, the Habitual Drunkards Acts of 1879, 1894, 1898). There were not enough inebriates institutions to house all these alcohol-dependent men and women, and therefore, they ended up in prison on short sentences, serving time away not only from drink, admittedly, but also from families and from employment, but with no real chance or support to help them change their ways,[2] they were back in prison again very shortly after release. The ranks of the poor, dishevelled, hung-over defendants trailing through the courts time and time again proved a visceral image of the 'residuum', or the 'underclass', or other unhelpful labels. Court scenes were given colour by reports in the local newspapers to be consumed by those that did not watch proceedings in the public gallery or for those who wanted to relive the experience. The magistrates were normally described as sometimes bemused, sometimes amused, and often stern figures of local justice (Parry 1912: 95). They were described as gentlemen who could arbitrate the disputes of the 'lower orders' such as an incorruptible and fair-minded cricket umpire. In other words, 'gentleman more or less experienced in the way of the world, sufficiently well-educated, one who was willing to listen to the baffling problems of their work and life, and to advise them in their difficulties – a man available to the poor' (Waddy 1925: 2). Laden with class-ridden assumptions and eugenic overtones that the poor led disorganized chaotic lives, and needed the advice of wise councils to guide them, the magistrate had occasionally to play the disciplinarian; like children, the poor were thought to need things 'spelling out to them':

> 'You are a drunkard' said he in the course of his address. I must tell you that your brazen manner and bearing on the eight occasions you have been before me, have given me the lowest opinion of you. . . . Drunken men like you are a *pest* and a *nuisance*. We can do without you. *We don't want you.* You are an *encumbrance*, and a constant source of expense and danger. Go away, and take care you don't make an appearance here again.
>
> (*Liverpool Review, 28 February 1885,*
> *quoted in Godfrey 2003*)

Despite the messages of moral condemnation towards the defendant in the dock, the real audience were reading court reports in the newspapers, or sitting in the public galleries (on the expressive court, see Carlen 1976; D'Cruze 1998; Garfinkle 1956). Those galleries were often filled to capacity with sometimes more than a hundred people, particularly if the trial involved local 'celebrities', or might involve entertaining accounts of neighbourhood disturbances (Giles 1964: 117). This was a good opportunity for local magistrates to issue warnings, or advice, or condemnation of the people they saw as being no different from those they were already dealing with in the dock:

> This is the peculiar sort of atmosphere they (the non-descript loafers who are powerfully represented therein) create and are enveloped in. This is the peculiar sort of atmosphere generated by dirt which has won for a certain class the name of the 'great unwashed'. They are here of both sexes and all ages, some of them with bandaged heads, and others with battered and plastered faces, and all bearing an aversion to soap and water, and with the air of people who habitually sleep in their clothes. These are the friends, witnesses, relations of those who are about to appear before Mr Raffles [the Magistrate] and are waiting their turn to appear in court . . . The atmosphere as well as the inhabitants of this *locus* is redolent of positive immorality, and in a sanitary point of view it is amazing that a plague does not emanate from it. The air is thick, and is composed of a villainous compound of smells – of decomposed tobacco, whisky fumes, animal exhalations, rotten fruit, bits of mouldy bread, and many other things. The court is large enough for its purpose, but if the unwashed crowd outside in the hall was packed into it, it would simply be as bad a fever den as any in the lower quarters of Liverpool.
>
> (*The Porcupine, 5 December 1868*)

Until the 1930s and 1940s, the court could still attract a substantial audience looking for entertainment; even for many Victorians and Edwardians, a visit to the courts was as entertaining as a trip to the zoo or to the theatre (Rich 1932: 232–233). However, the courts' appeal as a venue of entertainment declined rapidly in the face of the growth of easily obtainable alternative leisure activities – radio first, then television. As Godfrey (2003) stated, that trend continued and now the pronouncements of the magistrates reverberate around virtually deserted courtrooms. Nevertheless, at the same time as policy makers and legislators were passing acts to keep the right sort of people inside prisons in the early twentieth century, an altogether better class of prisoner was causing the authorities something of a headache.

A better class of prisoner

From the first years of the twentieth century to World War I, approximately 1,000 suffragettes were imprisoned in England for offences of disorder. Using tactics of disruption and mainly nonviolent forms of protest, campaigners for the female vote came into contact with the police in the same way as striking workers and the unemployed would do in the 1910s and 1920s, and political agitators would in the 1930s (see Chapter 10). Some campaigners chained themselves to railings on public streets and were imprisoned for public order offences and their subsequent failure to pay outstanding fines. The first suffragette was imprisoned in 1906, and typically, this was for a low-level public order offence. Despite the prosaic nature of the offences they were sent there for, the women demanded to be treated as political prisoners. When that request was refused, some of the women went on hunger strike. The artist Marion Wallace Dunlop had been sentenced to be imprisoned for a month in Holloway for vandalism in 1909, and she was the first hunger striker.[3] The prison authorities were directed by government to force-feed the suffragettes, strapping them down by force and using a tube that was inserted in the prisoner's nostrils. It should be remembered that many of these women came from respectable families, and fearing criticism from the social elite, and the growth of public sympathy for the suffragettes, the government brought in The Prisoners (Temporary Discharge for Ill Health) Act of 1913. Known as the 'Cat and Mouse Act', the legislation allowed the temporary release from prison for hunger strikers when their health began to diminish, only for them to be readmitted to custody when they regained their health. The experiences of the incarcerated suffragette, therefore, mimicked the lives of short-term recidivist prisoners, and it would be interesting to see if prison conditions would have been improved more quickly if the imprisonment of middle- and upper-class women had continued. As it was, the British government gave an amnesty in 1914 with the outbreak of the war and released all of the prisoners who had been imprisoned for suffrage activities (Geddes 2008: 81; Purvis 1995: 103). Of course, the rise in the prison population caused by the incarceration of suffragettes had been negligible, but how did the prison population fluctuate over this period, given the changes in legislation that we have described?

The numbers game

The trend in local prison numbers (for males) was fairly steady between 1856 and 1880 (the average daily population never lower than 12,000 or higher than 16,000). After falling to 18,000 in 1891, the population rose to over 23,000 by 1904, before a dramatic fall to 13,000 at the end of World War I; between 1919 and 1945 the male population then moved upwards from 6,068 to 10,136 whereas female incarceration continued to fall. The total number of committals to prison followed a similar trend but with a marked upwards sweep of committals for men until World War I, before falling rapidly until the early 1920s and thereafter being relatively stable until the 1940s.

There was an acute crisis in penal capacity when convict transportation was coming to an end in the late 1860s (the last transport ship arrived in Western Australia in 1868). Subsequently, penal capacity always exceeded actual numbers although the population always hovered between 80 per cent and 90 per cent of capacity, meaning that prisons in nineteenth and twentieth centuries were

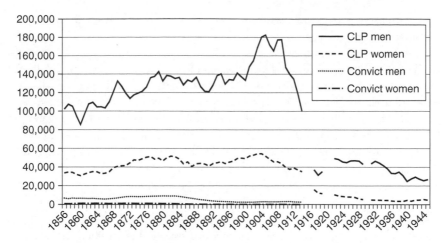

FIGURE 12.3   County local prison (CLP) and convict prison committals, 1856–1945

always near, if not in, crisis, and had to manage their populations carefully. A supply-side explanation for prison numbers would be that it simply mirrored the amount of crime being committed. Throughout the period the vast numbers of offences were dealt with summarily in magistrates' courts. Broadly there was a growth in offending at summary level from 1857 to the start of the twentieth century, a drop during World War I, and a rise again until World War II. In each year the number of summary offences (more minor offences dealt with in the magistrates' courts) committed eclipsed numbers of indictable crimes (the more serious offences dealt with in higher courts, see Chapter 3). As Figure 12.4 shows that although the number of summary offences prosecuted each year did have a relationship with prison numbers, from around the turn of the twentieth century

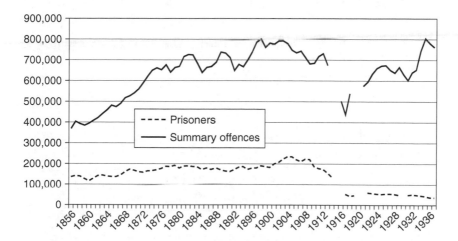

FIGURE 12.4   Summary offences and prison populations, England and Wales, 1857–1937

the relationship is extremely weak, and, in fact, the two trends are divergent to a considerable degree.

The prison population did not swell by an increase in the number of months in the average prison sentence. The average length of prison sentences actually fell for indictable cases from 1876 whereas, for summary cases, the average sentence length rose from about the same point. Between 1858 and 1911 the average only fluctuated between 0.7 and 0.8 months. Between 1918 and 1938 the average varied between 1.1 and 1.3 months. However, because of the fall in convicted offenders, the rise in average sentence length had little effect on the numbers inside prison. For example, the 70,740 people convicted in 1901, had they received the average sentence, contributed 54,469 months of prison sentence. In 1938, despite the average sentence being 1.3 months, the 24,802 only contributed 24,802 months – approximately half the prisoner/month numbers of 1901. It seems clear that the downward fall in custodial sentencing was not simply due to fluctuations in the number of offences committed, or to the rises and falls in average sentence length, or to conviction rates. The dominant factor was the proportion of offenders who began to receive noncustodial disposals rather than prison sentences (especially for summary offences); see Figure 12.5.

Figure 12.5 demonstrates the proportionate sentencing trends from 1857 to 1938 for summary offences. The chart shows the increasing growth in the use of fines, which is consistently replacing custodial sentencing for summary offences over this period, to the point at which fines represent around 80 percent of all disposals for these crimes. Similarly, Figure 12.6 examines proportionate sentencing

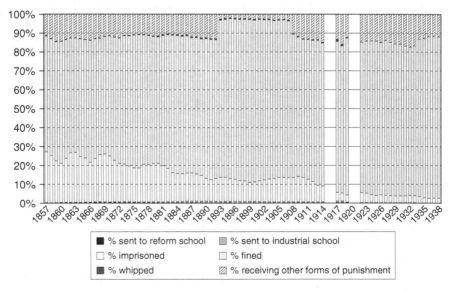

FIGURE 12.5 Proportion of sentencing disposal (summary offences), England and Wales, 1857–1938

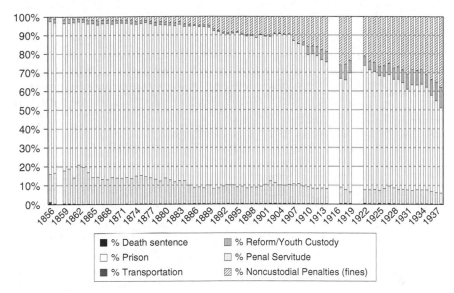

FIGURE 12.6 Proportion of sentencing disposal (indictable offences), England and Wales, 1857–1938

trends for indictable offences; again, similar to summary offences, the picture illustrates how noncustodial penalties grow in popularity over the years – at the expense of the custodial population which decreases dramatically from 81 percent in 1956 to 45 percent in 1938.

The introduction of preventative detention in 1908 had no appreciable impact. It never could have after Winston Churchill had his say on the legislation. Home Secretary Winston Churchill ensured that the 1908 act was transformed into a comparatively weak, and very little-used, damp squib. He had feared that the judiciary would impose longer sentences to compensate for the 'softer' reformative stage of the sentence and that, therefore, prisoners would serve even longer than they would normally on a sentence of penal servitude. He ensured that the number of hoops that needed to be jumped through before a preventative order was imposed dissuaded judges from using them. It worked. In 1910, fewer than 200 offenders were sentenced under the act, the following year it was an even smaller number. Just fifty-seven were sentenced under the act after Churchill's interventions (McConville 1995: 156, 165). Between 1922 and 1928 an average of thirty-one criminals were sentenced to preventative detention each year. By 1928, then, there were about five hundred people who had been sentenced under the act – just 483 criminals from a prison population of 52,695, fewer than 1 percent of the prison population, or about one person serving preventative detention for every 800,000 people in England and Wales. With such small numbers of offenders coming under the system, it was inevitable that the system would be seen as 'hav[ing] failed in its object' (1934 Report of Convict Prisons). The prison commissioner conclusively announced in 1928 that 'Preventative Detention can have no appreciable effect on the problem of recidivism'. The Report of the Committee on Persistent Offenders (1932) also condemned the dual track system as unfair, ineffective, largely inoperative, and largely unused – only nineteen of the 542 offenders who were sentenced to penal servitude in 1933 were also subject to preventative detention. The system limped along at a low ebb until the Home Secretary's Advisory Council finally condemned the act in 1963, and it was formerly ended in 1968 (Brown 2003: 127; Godfrey *et al.* 2010; Radzinowicz and King 1977: 238).

Decarceration and divergence

It appears that neither changes in legislation nor changes in the average length of prison sentences imposed, actually had an impact on the size of the prison population. Instead, the introduction of a series of diversionary programmes and some changes to the way that court fines could be paid first stabilised the prison population and then caused it to fall. The Prison Act of 1898 had allowed offenders to pay any part of a fine and have a proportion of their prison sentence proportionately removed, but the act did not have much of an impact, unlike the Criminal Justice Administration Act of 1914 which gave convicted offenders time to pay their fines rather than face immediate imprisonment if they could not dredge up the requisite shillings to pay their debts. This change diverted thousands of convicted men and women away from the prison gates, as did the mental deficiency acts passed in 1913. Brought into existence as a result of eugenic reasoning (see Chapter 11) they were seen by prison governors; Thomas Holmes (1908: 48), the secretary of the Howard Association; and various psychiatrists (such as the anonymous author of *Psychology in Court by a Doctor* published in 1933) as a means of diverting the weak-minded into institutional care. Quinton thought that habitual criminals were disproportionately subject to mental conditions that gave them a reckless approach to offending and to their lives. He was convinced that they carried out silly petty offences to give their lives a bit of colour and to get some money to spend on drink. Their mental powers were insufficient for them to plan a big job that would set them up for life or to plan a desistance route into a successful nonoffending life (Quinton 1910: 91). After the 1913 acts were passed, those the courts decided were idiots, imbeciles, feeble minded, or moral imbeciles (imbecility with criminal tendencies) could be placed into mental health institutions rather than prisons. Forensic criminologist Norwood East (1949: 125) was convinced that offenders were transparent to any trained psychiatrist and that the psychotic and psychopathic offenders could be weeded out of the general offender population and dealt with separately, and eventually 65,000 were diverted away from the prisons until the acts were repealed in 1959.

Slower to take effect, but more important over the longer term, the Probation of Offenders Act passed in 1907 meant that sentencers could impose unsupervised or supervised periods of probation on trivial offences or on offenders that would benefit from it (and for whom prison would be unsuitable because of their age, character, health, mental condition, or because they were lightly convicted). The probation officers largely took over from the police court missionaries that had been a feature of the courts mainly in the metropolitan cities (Gard 2007; Vanstone 2007; see Stokes [1950] for a street-level view of the work of a probation officer). Page (1992) described the effectiveness of the London probation service as a social service, finding homes for homeless offenders, reuniting them with family, helping them to secure employment (and other forms of practice and emotional help). In that sense they worked in a similar way to the government-subsidized Discharged Prisoners' Aid societies (DPAs). In the 1920s, the DPAs helped about 40,000 discharged prisoners a year. About a third of the people that applied to them were placed into employment, and this kind of practical help was provided for most prisoners, even if it was just providing a pair of boots and a first night's accommodation after release (Gillin 1931: 241). This service was also open to those released from youth institutions. The development of the discipline of psychology and the belief that young minds were most susceptible to positive influence had a huge impact on the treatment of young people convicted of offences in the twentieth century.

The Gladstone Committee of 1895 had originally recommended that youths should be separated from experienced offenders in prison (and in 1908 this principle would extend to youths appearing as defendants in the courts too). In 1902, Evelyn Ruggles-Brise introduced a system at Borstal in Kent which confined children in secure accommodation. The Borstal regime was disciplined, highly regulated, and had an authoritarian feel, but was designed to educate and train the young people as much as punish them for their crimes, giving them skills that would help them lead 'an honest and industrious life'. Those very words were used in the 1907 Probation Act, and the Borstal system shared a similar philosophy. Keeping children away from adult offenders and providing them with basic skills would give those who could reform, the chance to do so. A lot of people invested their hopes in the Borstal system (Quinton 1910: 125) and it developed on a national basis and it was formalised in the 1908 Prevention of Crime Act (the same act that brought in preventative detention). The Borstal system was championed by reformers and by disciplinarians at the same time. After World War I, ex-prison governor Cecil Rich thought that young men back from the trenches had suffered disillusion with postwar society and the lack of jobs for ex-servicemen. He therefore advocated a separate system for all young offenders, although he also decried any soft approach to reforming children and any semblance of a less-disciplined approach to offending youths: 'You do not want to make Borstal into a crèche and wet-nurse the inmates' (Rich 1932: 90–91, 106, 109).[4] In 1933 the Children and Young Persons Act removed the distinction between reformatory and industrial schools that had been established in the nineteenth century (the reform schools had taken in children who had committed impressionable crimes, but both industrial and reform schools provided discipline and training in craft and technical skills). As can be seen in Figure 12.7, the Borstal system seems to have swept up the same number of youths that otherwise would have been sent to reform schools.

By this date the courts were told that they should regard the welfare of the child as paramount. The prisons and the whole burgeoning youth justice system were

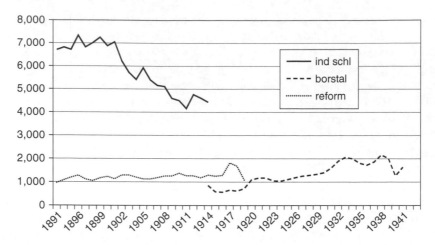

FIGURE 12.7 Children housed in industrial schools, reform schools, and Borstal, England and Wales, 1891–1941

now instructed to provide the same level of care and training for the child as would a wise guardian, and also treat the child as responsible for their criminal actions. As Elkin (1946: 106–107) acknowledged, some courts took more easily to guardianship, whilst others took more easily to punishing criminality. Ruck (1946: 15–17), the assistant director of the Borstal Association and social surveyor, thought that probation for juveniles was undermined by overuse and that, although it should not be considered a failure, it was not as effective as he hoped. In 1938, for example, only 4 per cent of sentenced adult offenders received probation, but about half of all children left court under the supervision of a probation officer (Norwood East 1946: 177). Others lamented that it was not used enough. Serious crimes could be dismissed in youth court because probation officers were not available, even when the child needed supervision. It was 'cheaper to dismiss a large number of cases than appoint more probation officers (Elkin 1946: 109).[5]

Despite the rhetoric, the Borstals and the other institutions created to care for troubled children employed some officers who clearly did not act as wise guardians. Some children experienced their time inside the institutions as a brutalising and brutal time of their lives, intimidated by bullies and a system of care which did not seem to care. Although some children left the institutions never to offend again, many others left with a legacy of deep psychological damage (Humphries 1981: 209–240).

Reforming the postwar prison

Three influential studies of the prison system were published in the early 1920s. Evelyn Ruggles-Brise originally wrote *The English Prison System* for the postponed 1915 International Prison Congress, and it was eventually published in 1921; the Fabian Socialists, the Webbs, published *English Prisons Under Local Government* in

1922; and their nephew Stephen Hobhouse and his colleague Fenway Brockway published the most critical of the three reports, *English Prisons Today,* in the same year. Partly as a result of Hobhouse and Brockway's critical assault on the last vestiges of retributive Victorian penal policy, the prison system was reformed (insofar as the internal regimes were relaxed and rehabilitation was more strongly promoted). In 1937, hard labour, was finally removed (the Prison Act of 1898 had already removed some kinds of labour such as oakum picking and the crank). Rules on clothing, haircuts, and visits were all relaxed. Warders, now renamed prison officers, were there to assist prisoners to reform. Convict heads were no longer shaved, the broad arrows had disappeared from prison uniforms, and local prisoners did not have to undergo a period of separation on reception into prison. Between 1914 and 1922, twenty-four prisons were closed because of the drop in prisoner numbers, five more were closed in 1922 because of severe economic cutbacks, and seven more were closed between 1925 and 1931 for the same reason (Brodie *et al.* 2002: 170–171). It was the smaller prisons that had felt the axe, as the larger gaols were felt to be more economical and to have the facilities that suited the new penal philosophies: the surviving prisons had training rooms and educational facilities. The smaller number of prisons and a more centralised control over them also enabled new modern penal philosophies to be put in place more easily – independent-minded governors who clung to out-of-date Victorian penal cultures were replaced over time. So the prison estate was much reduced after World War I, and a more reformative culture established. Why then did the prisons continue at all? Surely the rehabilitation of offenders would gradually wean habitual offenders away from their lives of crime? Instead, the reconviction rate is just as quick for released prisoners as it ever was, and the prisons are still variously attacked for being too soft, too harsh, too expensive, and too ineffective. Let us examine the case against the prisons. Who leads the case for the prosecution?

Punishment on trial?

Let right-wing commentator Peter Hitchens lead the charge. He thinks that 'modern prisons are the result of idealist projects to improve the world, like most other human mistakes and disasters ... No matter how many times they have failed in their task, the utopians tried and tried again' (Hitchens 2003: 111). He is, of course, right, but for the wrong reasons. The prisons could never achieve what was expected of them. They can simply punish. They have incapacitated some very serious offenders. For example, the local community were probably glad when Patrick Madden was inside some prison or other because that prevented him from preying on vulnerable men and women (see Chapter 1), but none of the sentences he received, in local or in convict prisons, had any rehabilitative effect on him (or, it would appear, did anyone else). The reforms that were introduced simply reduced the punitive element of prison life to a degree (quite a significant degree, in fact), but doing less harm should not be confused with doing good. The reforms that were designed to achieve more of a rehabilitative framework following the penal crisis of the 1890s 'reshaped rather than relaxed social control' (Wiener 1990: 337). Alyson Brown agrees with Wiener that 'fundamentally, the changes that were implemented constituted not a decisive shift in philosophy or penal practice but the amelioration of some existing practices and the development of others' (Brown 2003: 111). They could never be anything else because penal and legislative reform was inclusive of seemingly contradictory and divergent philosophies. Debates about punishment were really arguments about whether people were 'deserving' or not. Were the people coming before the courts deserving of sympathy or harsh treatment? Were the youths deserving of discipline, training, and/or care? In this chapter we have described the numerous attempts to sharpen a diagnostic tool that could be used to separate out the moral from the immoral; the mentally weak from the hardened offender; the youths with potential to change their lives for the better from the youth heading for a life of crime. Those fortunate enough to fall into a category which enabled them to avoid imprisonment (a youth that was thought capable of 'growing up good', a convicted man who could afford to pay the court fine promptly, a weak-minded woman sentenced under the mental deficiency acts) might have avoided one type of punitive environment only to suffer another (in Borstal or an asylum). Hitchens was right to the extent that utopian reform can have unintended consequences. He was also right that the prisons are failures. I suspect that he would not agree with the majority of professional criminologists that agree that we have to find better alternatives to custody than those that the Victorians and Edwardians developed.

13

THE SUBMERGED CRIMINAL JUSTICE 'STATE'

It is easy to draw some quick sketches of the differences between the 1880s and the late 1930s. This was when modernity seemed to arrive in a rush. The 1880s were the start of a Second Industrial Revolution, with a massive influx of immigrants into London, the expansion of the British Empire into Africa, and the development of new chemical and manufacturing industries; skyscrapers rose in the United States, and the London Underground system expanded to link people across London. Mobility was enhanced for ordinary people by motor buses and trains as well as the London tube. Roads were covered in tar, and after World War I, faster cars began to use them. By the end of the 1930s, Britain had experienced severe boom and bust economic conditions, political and social upheaval, the stirrings of youth culture, and consumer culture. The second war with Germany in twenty years would bring about another raft of technological and socioeconomic changes. The pace of change in society was accelerating, and this was true in the cultural and intellectual realm.

In the 1880s, eugenics was becoming a mainstream idea, after which the new biologically based doctrines of criminology insisted that we could understand the scientifically measurable processes by which people were brought into crime. From counting crimes and measuring heads, the 'environmental criminology' (the Chicago School) offered new perspectives in the 1920s and 1930s, as did new perspectives about criminality over the life course (Glueck and Glueck 1934, 1937, 1940, 1943). Psychology was also brought into the courts in this period (especially in youth justice). These new methodologies and means of analysis encompassed the idea of hidden thoughts, subconscious motivations, hereditary or socially transmitted dispositions to crime, and delinquent psychologies of offending permeating through into action. Now understanding criminality was not a simple affair, easily seen as the wrongdoing of immoral people; criminality was no longer on the surface.

Had Patrick Madden (the convict we were introduced to in Chapter 1) started his criminal career twenty years later, he may have had very different experiences of the criminal justice system, and of life. Certainly his offending would have been explained in different ways. The simplistic view that he was one of the brutish criminal classes that skulked in the inner-city rookeries was really more a feature of the 1850s and 1860s than the 1880s and 1890s. His offences would also be treated quite differently in court. His indictable offences would have brought him under the habitual offenders' acts and, after serving an extended prison sentence, he would have been subsequently supervised by the police. Whether that would have deterred him or just brought him back to prison on an even more frequent basis is unclear.

Had he started offending another twenty years on from that, in the early twentieth century, the maelstrom of juvenile adolescent development may have been put to the judge as an explanation for his onset into crime; probation officers may have supported him to stop offending; and if he hadn't, then he may have been one of the few hundred people sentenced to preventative detention (or he could even have been sent to Broadmoor Criminal Lunatic Asylum given his serious violence towards women). Of course he would have had the opportunity of joining the armed forces in the 1914–1918 period if he had been the right age. So, with Patrick, as with everyone else, place and time mattered. The date that defendants went before the courts, and the prevailing notions of rehabilitation, retribution, and criminality, determined how offenders were 'seen', and how they were dealt with.

Anyway, our counterfactual take on Patrick's personal history can be put to one side because, in reality, he began his life of crime in the 1860s and 1870s, which escalated in the 1880s and 1890s. This period was a time when the criminal justice system was focused on habitual offenders. Between the 1860s and 1890s, the criminal justice system seemed to narrow its focus to habitual offenders, serious dangerous criminals, and the juvenile delinquent (later the troubled adolescent) whilst also expanding its focus in other areas – to the motorist, for example. Moreover, as probation became a viable sentencing option in the early twentieth century, the system seemed to be deepening and lengthening its involvement with offenders who before would simply have paid fines and carried on with their lives. The development of a unified criminal justice system was impossible given these contradictions. Policies designed to address criminality vacillated between narrowing and expanding their conception of who they were controlling, at times the habitual low-level offender whose short sentences in gaol boosted the gaol population in the 1880s and 1890s or the habitual offenders who were to be preventatively detained, at other times the youths who hung around street corners or the irresponsible motorist causing obstructions or driving recklessly. Policy was incoherent, and apart from some using some broad brushstrokes, it is difficult to get a true picture of the intentions of the criminal justice system in the 1880–1940 period because there were many competing centres of influence and institutional need driving the agenda forward in a haphazard manner. However, the directions taken by the institutions of control that made up much of the criminal justice system itself – now linked in a bureaucratic chain from prison, to habitual offender registry, to police station, to probation officer – are easier to determine. They tended to become more and more covert, and more marginal to the public, than was previously the case.

Processes of street policing and sentencing were comparatively open to public view in the eighteenth and mid-nineteenth centuries (although prisons were not). However, in the 1880 to 1940 period, policing and penal power became more submerged and hidden. In the 1880s courtrooms were often thronged with hundreds of people for important trials or notorious defendants. Even the local magistrates' courts had a fairly large audience watching defendants answer to everyday offences. By the 1930s, however, courtrooms no longer held their audience as other attractions vied for public attention. The prisons had, of course, always been private spaces but were beginning to be built away from the centres of town and made to look more like normal local authority buildings rather than as castles or palaces of terror (Jewkes and Johnston 2007; Pratt 2002).

Beat policing continued throughout this period as a routine practice, as it had done since the 1850s, however, the beats were directed more towards the areas of town thought to be criminogenic, and overwhelmingly this was the poorer districts where people such as Patrick Madden lived and worked. So, normal public order policing carried on in the normal way, and so did detection (in the sense that the usual suspects and strangers new in town were the first port of call for enquiries to be made) but only for a small section of the nonrespectable working class who felt the full force of police surveillance. Those same people were also subject to various regulatory bodies which joined the police to impose a level of civility (sending the children to school, keeping the yard clean, and so on) so that 'policing' was now undertaken by a variety of semiofficial agencies in addition to the police. Like the police, these agencies operated mainly in the poorer districts, but their activities were not as overt as the police even in these areas. Even more secret agencies also joined the panoply of policing services. MI5 and Special Branch devoted themselves to detecting and dealing with dangers to the British state before they became visible to the British public. For the majority of the public, the only visible forms of policing were the rare occasions when black cars sped by, with blue lights flashing and loud bells ringing, on their way to a burglary or the traffic officer directing traffic after an accident or stopping a motorist for having faulty equipment on their car. Seeing a police officer carrying out their duty therefore, for most of the public, became extraordinary. For the public, the criminal justice system became so submerged during this period that we are surprised when it resurfaces (usually during the policing of disturbances) and why, collectively, we have been so fascinated to peek into this hidden world (on television or in gaol museums).

In order to glimpse something of the submerged world, Victorians and Edwardians read the same newspapers (trial reports, editorials, reprints of criminal statistics) that modern historians now access (either digitally or in archives). However, today, we have access to many more historical sources in addition to newspapers. We know not only more about the workings of key criminal justice agencies than we ever have done, but also more about the lives of offenders and their experience of being policed or appearing in court. Moreover, because the history of crime continues to be a vibrant area of debate within academic circles, we now have a number of theories we can use to explain those experiences, at least for the period up to World War I. The historiography of postwar crime is smaller, but is also likely to grow considerably in the next decade or two (especially given that the centenary of the war will encourage publications focussing on that period). The conditions both for the emergence of new academic theories and for the development of new crime histories are largely conditioned by availability of sources. As Chapters 3 and 4 have shown, historians of crime have moved over time from studies shaped by statistical and quantifiable records generated by the criminal justice institutions (indictments, statistical government returns), through to more qualitative sources such as Quarter Sessions depositions and newspaper reports, and on to literature and pictorial representations. Chapter 5 confirmed that the scale and availability of large oral history collections must inevitably, in time, have a say in shaping academic debate and (given oral history's appeal to nonprofessional historians) also popular opinion. The revolution in new digital media will continue to shape new visions of the past (see Chapter 7) and create its own impact (Chapter 8).

I think it is almost impossible to overstate the privileged position that modern crime historians have. The Victorians and Edwardian public could never visit a nineteenth-century prison, but we can (as dark tourists). We cannot possibly understand what it was really like to be imprisoned for years in a dark cell, but neither could the public nor the policy makers of the 1880–1940 period. We only have a shadowy and imperfect view of real events that happened a hundred or so years ago. How could we have anything else? We have no direct experience of prison conditions that were in place a century ago. However, historians today may actually have a far better view than the majority of people who lived in the nineteenth and twentieth centuries did.

Perhaps because some of the concepts of time, place, and social change discussed in this book are still mainly the province of social theorists, and not of historians, the spatial and bureaucratic interconnections examined in Chapters 9 through 12 remain under-researched. This is a shame, for, as historians of crime, what *we* have at our fingertips and under *our* gaze is *all* time and every place. Aided by the new digital media, our reach is wide and deep. So we should, as a community of scholars, be able to juxtapose ideas on spatial dynamics together with biographical studies of offenders in a way which improves our knowledge of spatiality and the meaning of *place*, the *passing of time*, and human agency or individual behaviour. Or we can use our skills to interpret the interactions between criminal justice agencies, the bureaucratic information nexus that enables surveillance, and the meaning of crime to local communities. Finally, we can explore the usefulness of crime historians as knowledge generators for dark tourists, for policy makers, for academic researchers, librarians, archivists, and (perhaps most important) the public.

NOTES

Chapter 1: A convict's story

1. Presumably the Bible had been repatriated to Britain when the colonial transportation system ended.
2. Interview with resident, b. 1898, Ironbridge, tape no. 75.

Chapter 3: Statistics and the 'capturing' of crime on paper

1. The place and displacement of crime is discussed later in the book, and we should also remember the crimes that happened in prisons (a considerable number was never officially recorded in judicial statistics; see ESRC project RES-062–23–3102).

Chapter 4: From policeman state to regulatory control

1. Diary of Albert Edward Wilcock, PC 39, Chester City Police Force.
2. The first speeding offence in the United Kingdom was on 28 January 1896 when Walter Arnold was prosecuted for travelling at 8 mph in 2-mph zone. He had been caught by a fit policeman on a bicycle and was fined one shilling and costs.
3. Organisations opposing the increasing regulation of motoring also originated in this period. The Royal Automobile Club (founded 1897) and The Automobile Association (founded 1905) defended the interests of the motorists against the new regulations (Brendon 1997; Sheppard 2005).
4. For example the report in *The Illustrated Police News* for Saturday, 12 January 1889, shows that the society followed up reports made to them about possible cases, appointed solicitors to prosecute the case, and removed the children to their refuges if necessary. Aurbach (2012) shows that resistance to the new regulatory bodies could also cause cases to come to court, see Jackson (2000) for a history of the work of the NSPCC.

Chapter 5: Talking about crime

1. For example, in Australia, the National Library has three main archival holdings (the New South Wales Bicentennial Oral History Collection, the Hazel de Berg Collection, and the Cultural Context of Unemployment collection) which contain together many

thousands of transcribed interview hours. The South Australian Library at Adelaide has large oral history collections dealing with, for example, the experiences of World War I veterans and the lives of Australians alive in 1938. Western Australia too is served by a large collection of transcribed tapes at Perth. Details of these repositories and their oral history collections (including detailed catalogues) are now available online.

2. Nottingham Local Studies Library has three main oral history collections. Collection A were collected as part of the Nottinghamshire Oral History Project, which looked at people's working lives between 1900 and 1950. The interviews, which contribute to this and other chapters in this book, have been transcribed and are available for loan. Collection B was produced by the Hyson Green Project and consists of interviews with people who lived or worked on the Hyson Green flats in the years prior to their demolition in 1988. Again these tapes have been transcribed and are available for loan. Collection C is made up of interviews with major figures in political and social life in Nottingham. Further information on all of these collections can be found in Information Sheet No. 7.

3. Discourse analysts who have, on the whole, tended to criticise the transcript as an imperfect copy of the spoken word have attempted to find better reproductive methods (Kitzinger 1998) or abandon the attempt altogether (Coates and Thornborrow 1999). They may be right to do so. However, discourse analysts may be fixated with a different set of research and methodological priorities to those historians who analyse large numbers of transcripted oral histories.

4. Indeed, life histories form a conceptual conversation between individual and society, in which both dialogues are structured by the other. For example, images from national culture are mobilized to imbue an individual's story with meaning and this story keys into dominant narratives of culture – both experienced at a conscious level, (often) to claim particular qualities for a nation and at the unconscious level.

5. Of course, other narrative motifs frequently appear in life-stories – the 'rags to riches' story or the physical decline of the body, for example.

6. As Damousi (2001: 3) states, 'Trauma, grief and loss are not experienced as frozen, timeless emotional states. These emotions have a history, and are ever-changing as they are rewritten from the perspective of the present.' Talking about people who have died is a way of legitimising their lives, ensuring that others understand that 'here was somebody worth remembering'; it also justifies the relationship, 'here was someone who was connected to me'. There are many cultures worldwide that seek to incorporate ancestors into the lives of their descendants, from South American Days of the Dead, to ancestor consultation in the Far East, and it may be that talking about the deceased performs some function for those living in more secular societies.

7. This account says something about how the oral tradition has preserved crime 'stories'. Similarly, a patricide carried out in 1890 ensured that Back Lane in Hough (Cheshire) is still known locally as 'Murder Lane'.

8. The golden age is a common trope well known to police history researchers (McLaughlin 2006).

Chapter 6: An ethical conversation?

1. Some of these issues were explored in 2003, and it is interesting to revisit some of our thoughts now that a decade of use of oral history transcripts has passed and the ethical use of research data has generally become so much more a topic of debate. See Godfrey and Richardson (2004) and Richardson and Godfrey (2003).

2. The latter of these is included in the guidelines of the 'Bringing them Home' project (an oral history project also carried out by the National Library of Australia [NLA] to collect and preserve the stories of those involved in the removal of children from indigenous people).

3. In one Australian repository I was not allowed to view oral interviews undertaken with prisoners carried out in 1991 until I had the written permission of each interviewee – the

names of which had already been anonymised and were therefore virtually untraceable, or traceable but dead.

4. The 1988 Copyright Act gave oral history interviewees the right to be named as the 'authors' of their recorded words if they are published or broadcast; and publishers and broadcasters are obliged not to subject their words to 'derogatory treatment' by, for example, editing, adapting, or making alterations which create a false impression. These rights are retained by interviewees, whoever owns the copyright. The right to be named needs to be 'asserted' (i.e., stated formally, preferably in writing) by the interviewee in order to have legal force. However, except in cases in which interviewees have asked not to be identified, it is recommended that interviewers and custodians should ensure that informants are credited whenever their words are made public.

5. Freemantle Prison Oral History Project OH2230/28, J.S. Batty Library, Perth, Western Australia.

6. Surname deleted by the author.

7. Interview with John Thompson, OH2230/5 Freemantle Prison Oral History Project, J.S. Batty Library, Perth, Western Australia, recorded by Arthur Tonkin, 14 May 1990, p. 27.

Chapter 7: New digital media

1. Gatrell and Hadden's 1972 essay remains a wonderful introduction to many of the sources used by crime historians; see also Godfrey (2011b), Fowler and Paley (2005), Hawkings (2009), and Wade (2009).

2. One book is so graphic that it must, in my opinion, be close to breaching legislation on obscene material.

3. The photographing of all convicted criminals received into county and borough prisons also came into force in late 1871, and by 1873 an official investigation reported that within a little more than twelve months of the act being enforced, some 30,463 photographs had been received by the Metropolitan police, and that during the same period of 2 November 1871 to 31 December 1872.

4. In general the rule which is usually adopted by county records offices (where most lower court records are kept for this period) is a thirty-year closure which is designed to protect the identity of people convicted in that period. Some insist on a 75- or even 100-year-closure period for reasons which are hard to determine let alone understand – the courts have always been open to the public, and trials are written up by newspapers (which are not restricted in any way). There is more reason for the closure of youth court records because youth courts are not open to the public, and it seems sensible to protect youth from their indiscretions which might damage their chances of gaining employment as an adult. Most archivists take a sensible line and will allow reasonable access to bona fide researchers so long as the names of people named in the records are anonymised, or (occasionally) as long as any images taken by digital camera are transcribed and then destroyed. The time it takes to negotiate access to records should not be underestimated.

5. In 1879 the Register was restricted to only those persons who had been discharged from a sentence of penal servitude and those who had been sentenced under Section 7 of the Prevention of Crimes Act of 1871 (such offenders had been convicted of an indictable crime after a previous conviction had been proved).

6. It is also possible to purchase the *Police Gazettes*, although they are very expensive, see http://www.adam-matthew-publications.co.uk/digital_guides/police_gazette_part1/Editorial-Introduction.aspx.

7. The website contains images and transcriptions of all surviving editions of the Old Bailey Proceedings from 1674 to 1913.

8. I have slightly trimmed the transcript, but the full version is available at http://www.oldbaileyonline.org/browse.jsp?id=t19120319–16-offence-1&div=t19120319–16#highlight.

9. The records of female licences (1853–1871, 1883–1887) are searchable by name at www. ancestry.com, and the male licences can be found on the website supported by The National Archives (www.findmypast.co.uk).

10. Another example of comments about prisoners includes 'Bone Idle; a Manchester Prison regular; Hopeless individual; has work to go to but shirt in rags; Wife will not have him back'.

11. King (1999) has provided a guide to navigating the various sources that can be explored (on the web, in bibliographic databases, and in journals, for example).

12. The 'whole-life' methodology has now begun to be taken up by a cohort of postgraduate crime history researchers, and in time, a number of publications will follow which will show how they have used, adapted, and progressed this methodology.

13. The closure of the National Archives on Mondays has coincided not only with the economic crisis, but also with the movement of large amounts of archival material online.

Chapter 8: Impact

1. It was the Royal Institute of Chartered Surveyors Project of the Year for 2007.

2. It may be that he was the H.R.P. Dunn discharged from military service on medical grounds in 1919, *British Army WWI Pension Records 1914–1920*, available on Ancestry. com.

3. The last hanging at the Shire Hall, Nottingham (the site of the Galleries of Justice Museum) was actually in 1799.

4. The most compelling contradictory narrative I have seen was in Alcatraz, of all places, where the final room that visitors pass through is dedicated to the idea of restorative justice and questions the need for prisons at all.

5. In Australia, by contrast, historical debates around the impact of colonization on indigenous peoples – characterised as 'black armband' versus 'white blindfold' history – are often highlighted in the media. Both Labour and Conservative administrations claimed versions of Australian history to suit their own ideological purposes (see Attwood and Foster 2003; Elder 1998; Finnane 2005; Manne 2003; McIntyre and Wehner 2004; Windschuttle 1996).

6. See Hitchens's (2003) use of the history of crime to critique contemporary politics, and in defence of libertarian values. Some historians embrace right-wing agendas, of course; witness David Starkey's controversial explanation of the 2011 London riots (www.bbc .co.uk/news/uk-14513517).

7. *Finding Your Roots* broadcast in the United States and occasional one-off special shows in the United Kindgom, for example, *Meet the Izzards* are beginning to use DNA to add a genetic element to researching ancestors.

8. It isn't.

9. The earliest site might be Madam Tussauds. When it opened in 1835, one of the main attractions was the Chamber of Horrors. This part of the exhibition included victims of the French Revolution and newly created figures of murderers and other criminals.

10. Although there are websites dedicated to remembering the event, see, for example, www.chicagotribune.com/news/politics/chi-chicagodays-valentinesmassacre-story,0,1233196.story.

11. The information 'signage' and interpretation at these Tasmanian convict sites are of a very high standard and are helpful both to the casual tourist and to the experienced researcher.

Chapter 9: Time, place, and space

1. Since the early 1800s, members of his family had been steeped in the frontier experience, participating in the Mexican–American War and the American Civil War. Wyatt himself

was too young to enlist in that bloody 1860s conflict which resulted in the death of three quarters of a million combatants (Hacker 2011), but he had seen his share of violence. As Earp bounced around the U.S. boom towns, sometimes gambling, drinking, and being arrested (he had once escaped from a local gaol) he picked up work acting as deputy city marshall in Wichita and assistant marshal in Dodge City before he accepted the position of lawman in Tombstone. Courtwright (1998) believed that the men who had survived the Civil War, or who had been implicated in the brutal suppression of native peoples in the drive westwards, had been inculcated into an essential theme of violence in American society – that the wild country had bred wild men.

2. The study was divided into three sections: poverty, industry, and religious influences. Research on the 'unoccupied classes' was also included in his study, and this included some valuable data on the inmates of workhouses and pauper institutions.

3. Interestingly Charles Booth's maps have now been added to by some in order to add to their theories on the identity and operations of Jack the Ripper; see, for example, www .casebook.org/victorian_london/maps.html. Also see Gray's (2010) interesting take on modern and historical conditions in the East End of London.

4. In 1847, the commissioners appointed to inquire into the state of the criminal law of the Channel Islands reported against the practice in question. The Jersey Civil Law Commissioners of 1859 also stated that strong representations had been made to them of the hardship to which the poorer classes who were not natives of Jersey were liable – of being at once removed from the island to the place of their birth if they should become chargeable on the rates. That was, they added, a great hardship not only on the labouring classes, by whose industry the island had for a long series of years been benefited, but also on the port of Southampton, to which these paupers usually found their way. He had placed himself in communication with the authorities of Southampton, and by a letter from the clerk to the Board of Guardians, dated the 1 June, 1864, it appeared that there was no doubt that since July 1861 to December 1863, no fewer than thirty-two persons either under sentence of banishment, or paupers who had no settlement in Jersey, had in this way been deported . . . Another gentleman, who had published a work on the laws of Jersey, wrote to him stating that banishment from Jersey meant simply transportation to England and that though the law had in practice been somewhat modified, so far as the severer penal cases were concerned, yet it might be revived and put in force at any time. That gentleman also mentioned an instance of some persons from Jersey being sent to the English hulks, where they were disposed of according to the English practice and at English expense *(HC Deb 24 June 1864 vol 176 cc277–9; HC Deb 18 May 1904 vol 135 c163)*.

5. Jersey Heritage Centre, D/AF/A1/1 Police Photograph album of criminals 26/06/1909 – 01/05/1920; D/Y/G3/273, Depositions in the case against Albert (surname removed by author) and Yves Marie (name removed by author) accused of burglary, 01/08/1911– 05/08/1911; D/Y/G3/318 Depositions (witness statements) in the case against Yves Marie accused of burglary and attempted theft, 10/10/1912–12/10/1912.

6. Because of the period, when no censuses are available, and newspapers for Jersey and France have not yet been digitised, it is difficult to assess the long-term impact of banishment. However, as Chapter 7 demonstrated, we now at least have the advantage of digital sources to help us answer these questions for other offenders.

7. In *Marxism and Literature* Raymond Williams (1977) insisted that structures of feeling could only be understood in terms of past and future aspirations.

8. See also his perceptive comment, that '[i]f it is true that every individual is a singular universe, one must also recognise that the life history of an individual is also a universal history in miniature' (Ferrarotti 1990: 107).

9. Work by Meisenhelder (1977) and others (e.g., Hughes 1998; Shover 1983) has revealed that some of those repeatedly incarcerated say that they have become tired of prison and feel that they can no longer cope physically and emotionally with the experiences of prison life. In effect, some offenders reach a point in their lives when they can 'take no more' from the criminal justice system and 'burn out'.

10. Social capital equates to the amount of influence, protection, or other forms of advantage that can be mustered by individuals participating in networks or relationships within local societies, see Putnam (2000).
11. Although recent studies have described the quality of employment, with the possibility of career progression and status acquisition, as being more important than the fact of employment per se (Godfrey, Cox and Farrall 2007).
12. This technique compares the common characteristics of a historical group in order to uncover hidden truths about the lives of occupational groups, or in this case groups of convicted offenders.

Chapter 10: New technologies of police power

1. 'An Ordinary Copper' written by Darnell and Warner.
2. This last sentence in parenthesis was obviously added in 1940.
3. For catching speeders '[a]n ideal trap is a measured distance of at least 400 yds. A to A, a man at each end to signal the passing his point, B a uniform man further on to stop by signal offending cars, and two men handling one tested stop watch in unison, these two being in such a position as enables them to see A-A and B and to signal to B if necessary – two men at one watch are much less open to criticism than two watches' (Instructions to Superintendents from Chief Constables, 1905).
4. There was also the concomitant growth in accidents involving motor vehicles with which to contend. There had been fewer than 40,000 car accidents at the end of World War I, but it was five times higher than that by 1945.
5. Based on data from Hamilton, Ontario, magistrates' courts, Hamilton Archives.
6. Based on data from Adelaide magistrates' courts, South Australian Archives.
7. Not least because the police service suffered a severe reduction in the numbers of available officers during World War I (see Chapter 3).
8. Bradford's Watch Committee refused to pay for long truncheons (replacing them with short batons) in the 1880s. The chief constable encourage his officers to prosecute every minor assault on them, until the Watch Committee relented and allowed the police the long truncheons they then used to 'protect' themselves from assaults.
9. Discretionary policing allowed officers on the beat to decide whether a matter was serious enough to make an arrest, and the system of custody sergeants either proceeding with the charge or refusing it was another checkpoint in the process, as noted in Chapter 3.
10. For some reason Mrs Powell's call for the children to be birched was reprinted the other side of the world in Perth in *The Daily News* (Saturday, 26 March 1938).
11. The 1885 crime act had made it illegal for anyone to interfere with the police in the execution of their duty – this gave the police a lot of the discretion on the streets that we have already discussed. However, it was also used in 1919 to dismiss any officer who persuaded another to down tools.

Chapter 11: Paperwork, networks, information, connections, and theories

1. Although they can be usefully used to build up a picture of the people who put on the blue uniform in this period, see Klein (2010).
2. Captain Walter Crofton, chairman of the directors of convict prisons in Ireland had originally proposed this in the 1860s.
3. Photographs of criminals. Statements of the number of photographs of convicted criminals sent from the prison of each county and borough to London, 1873 (289): 6.
4. The district conference scheme established in 1918 also facilitated the flow of information between police forces and the Home Office.

5. The Exeter City Police Felony Report Book, 1905 to 1908, reported the case of Herbert Charles Scammall, a rate collector wanted for the embezzlement of £640 in February 1905.
6. At least until computerisation in the 1970s and 1980s perhaps (see Chapter 10).
7. The means of carrying out an English version of a Lombrosian study was in place long before 1913. Standardised prison forms were introduced by Griffiths in the 1870s (Griffiths 1905: 265–267). These forms included not only detail of height, weight, colour of eyes, hair colour and so on, but also information on inherited disease, weaknesses (heart, lungs, mental, etc.) and so could have been used for a Lombrosian or a eugenics-style study. However, after the forms had been filled in, it seems that no-one then collated or analysed the information they contained.
8. The Eugenics Society changed its name again in 1989 to the 'Galton Institute' which is still in operation today.
9. Perhaps something of the influence of the Eugenics Society can be seen in a list of the journals that were edited by its members: *Behaviour Research and Therapy*, *Brain*, the *British Heart Journal*, the *British Journal of Clinical Practice*, the *British Journal of Inebriety*, the *British Journal of Psychology*, the *British Journal of Psychiatry*, *Economic Journal*, *Ibis*, the *International Journal of Sexology*, the *Journal of Asian Demography*, the *Journal of Biosocial Sciences*, the *Journal of Medical Genetics*, *Mankind Quarterly*, *Medical Digest*, *Prenatal Diagnosis*, the *Prison Medical Journal*, *Quarterly Journal of Medicine*; the *Realist*, *Samajaswathya*, *Sociological Review*, and *Women's Own*.
10. Galton bequeathed money to London University for them to continue researching eugenics.
11. Even great advocates for eugenics, such as Charles Darwin's son, Leonard, were forced to admit that environment and situation played a part. A bad home and the temptation to offend were listed alongside 'bad natural qualities' in 'What Is Eugenics' (Darwin 1928: 50).

Chapter 12: A just measure of punishment

1. The purpose of sentencing was subsequently debated by key sociological thinkers in the twentieth century (Duff 1986; Durkheim 1964; Feinberg 1994; Garland 1990; Mead 1934).
2. The Inebriates Act of 1898 had been designed to eradicate those addicted to alcohol filling up the gaols on short sentences, but in lieu of any institution in which to treat them (aside from a few Inebriates Homes for women dotted around the country), the prisons were not relieved (Quinton 1910: 112–113, 116).
3. Until 1900 all local prisons had female accommodation, but in 1902 Holloway became a female-only prison, and the female wings elsewhere began to be closed down.
4. Rich (1932: 138) also fancied a return of the 'cat' for degenerate child sex offenders and could not be confused with being a do-gooder in any respect.
5. The 1936 *Departmental Committee on the Social Services in connection with the Courts of Summary Jurisdiction* acknowledged that probation officers were overworked, as did Cecil Rackham (1946), vice-chairman of the Howard League for Penal Reform.

BIBLIOGRAPHY

Abel, T. & Kinder, E. (1942) *The Subnormal Adolescent Girl*, New York: Columbia University Press.

Allen, T. (1932) *Underworld. The Biography of Charles Brooks, Criminal*, London: Newnes.

Allen B. & Montell, L. (1981) *From Memory to History: Using Oral Sources in Local Historical Research*, Nashville: American Association for State and Local History.

Anderson, D. & Killingray, D. (Eds.) (1991) *Policing the Empire: Government, Authority and Control, 1830–1914*, Manchester: Manchester University Press.

Apter, T. (1996) 'Expert Witness: Who Controls the Psychologists' Narrative?' In R. Josselson (Ed.), *Ethics and Process in the Narrative Study of Lives. Vol. 4. The Narrative Study of Lives*, Thousand Oaks, CA: Sage, 22–44.

Ardener, S. (1993) *Women and Space. Ground Rules and Social Maps*, Oxford: Bloomsbury.

Arksey, H. & Knight, P. (1999) *Interviewing for Social Scientists. An introductory resource with examples*, London: Sage.

Arnot, M.L. & Usborne, C. (Eds.) (1999) *Gender and Crime in Modern Europe*, London: UCL Press.

Attwood, B. & Foster, S. (2003) *Frontier Conflict: the Australian Experience*, Canberra: National Museum of Australia.

Aurbach, S. (2012) '"The Law Has No Feeling for Poor Folks Like Us!": Everyday Responses to Legal Compulsion in England's Working-Class Communities, 1871–1904', *Journal of Social History 45*, 3, 686–708.

Bailey, L. (2002) *Bisbee. Queen of the Copper Camps*, Tucson, AZ: Westlorne Press.

Bailey, L. (2004) *"Too Tough To Die." The Rise, Fall, and Resurrection of a Silver Camp; 1878 to 1990*, Tucson, AZ: Westlorne Press.

Barham, R. (1837) *The Life and Letters of the Rev. Richard Harris Barham, Author of the Ingoldsby Legends, Vol. 1*, London: Richard Bentley.

Bean, P. and Melville, J. (1989) *Lost Children of the Empire*. London: Unwin Hyman. PUT IN

Beavan, C. (2002) *Fingerprints. Murder and the Race to Uncover the Science of Identity*, London: Fourth Estate.

Benney, M. (1936) *Low Company. Describing the Evolution of a Burglar*, London: Peter Davies.

Bennett, J. (1981) *Oral History and Delinquency. The Rhetoric of Criminology*, Chicago: University of Chicago Press.

Beveridge, P. (1957) *Inside the C.I.D.*, London: Evans Brothers.

Blee, K. (1998) 'Evidence, empathy and ethics. Lessons from oral histories of the Klan', re-printed in R. Perks & A. Thomson (Eds.) *The Oral History Reader*, London: Routledge, 333–344.

Boddy, J, Boaz, A., Lupton, C., & Pahl, J. (2006) 'What Counts as Research? The Implications for Research Governance in Social Care', *International Journal of Social Research Methodology*, *9*, 4, 317–330.

Borland, K. (1991) '"That's Not What I Said": Interpretative Conflict in Oral Narrative Research'. In S. Gluck & D. Patai (Eds.), *Women's Words. The Feminist Practice of Oral History*, London: Routledge, 63–77.

Bornat, J., (2001) 'Reminiscence and Oral History: Parallel Universe or Shared Endeavour?', *Ageing and Society*, 21, 219–241.

Bornat, J. (2002) 'A second take: revisiting interviews with a different purpose', paper presented at the XII International Oral History Conference, Pitermaritzburg, South Africa, 24–27 June 2002.

Brendon, P. (1997) *The Motoring Century. The Story of the Royal Automobile Club*, London: Bloomsbury.

Briggs, J. Harrison, M. McInnes J. and Vincent, D. (1996) *Crime and Punishment in England*, London: UCL Press.

Bourdieu, P. (1977) *Outline of a Theory of Practice*. Cambridge: Cambridge University Press.

Bourdieu, P. & Wacquant, L. (1992) *An Invitation to Reflexive Sociology*, Chicago: University of Chicago Press.

Bourke, J. (1994) *Working-Class Cultures in Britain, 1890–1960*, London: Routledge.

Box S. (1987) *Recession, Crime and Punishment*, London: Macmillan.

Brodie, A., Croom, J. & O'Davies, J. (2002) *English Prisons. An Architectural History*, Swindon: English Heritage.

Broberg, G. & Roll-Hansen, N. (1996) *Eugenics and the Welfare State. Sterilization Policy in Denmark, Sweden, Norway, and Finland*, East Lansing: Michigan State University Press.

Brogden, M. (1991) *On the Mersey Beat. Policing Liverpool between the Wars*, Oxford: Oxford University Press.

Brown, A. (2003) *English Society and the Prison. Time, Culture and Politics in the Development of the Modern Prison, 1850–1920*, Woodbridge, Suffolk: Boydell Press.

Brown, A. & Barton, A. (2012) 'Prison Tourism and the Search for Authenticity', paper presented to the 'Modern Activism' Conference, Liverpool, June 27, 2012.

Buckland, G. (2001) *Shots in the Dark*, Boston: True Crime Pictures.

Burke, P. (1980) *Sociology and History*, London: Allen and Unwin.

Burke, P. (1989) *New Perspectives on Historical Writing*, Oxford: Blackwell.

Caddle, D. (1991) 'Parenthood Training for Young Offenders: An Evaluation of Courses'. In *Young Offender Institutions, Research and Planning Unit Home Office Paper 63*, London: HMSO, 1–45.

Caminada, J. (1895) *Twenty-Five Years of Detective Life*, Manchester: John Heywood.

Carlen, P. (1976) *Magistrates' Justice*, London: Martin Robinson.

Carr, E. (1961) *What is History?* London: Vintage.

Carrabine, E., Lee, M., South, N., Cox, P., & Plummer, K. (2008) *Criminology: A Sociological Introduction*, London: Routledge.

Carter Wood, J. (2004) *"The Shadow of Our Refinement": Violence, Custom and the Civilizing Process in Nineteenth-century England*, London: Routledge.

Carter Wood, J. (2008) '"Mrs. Pace" and the Ambiguous Language of Victimization'. In L. Dresdner & L. Peterson (Eds.), *(Re)Interpretations: The Shapes of Justice in Women's Experience*, Cambridge: Cambridge Scholars Press, 79–93.

Certeau, M. de (1984) *The Practice of Everyday Life,* Berkeley: University of California Press.

Chadwick, W. (1901/1974) *Reminiscences of a Chief Constable*, London: Longendale Amenity Society.

Chainey, S & Ratcliffe, J. (2005) *GIS and Crime Mapping*, Chichester: Wiley-Blackwell.

Chamberlain, K. (2012) 'Prostitution in Inter-War Liverpool', unpublished thesis, Keele University.

Chase, M. and Shaw, C. (1989) The dimensions of nostalgia. In M. Chase and C. Shaw (eds.) *The Imagined Past – History and Nostalgia*. Manchester: Manchester University Press. pp.1–17.

Chesney, K. (1972) *Victorian Underworld*, London: Penguin.

Childs, D. (2001) *Modernism and Eugenics*, Cambridge: Cambridge University Press.

Clark, A (1987) *Women's Silence, Men's Violence; Sexual Assault in England, 1770–1845*, London: Pandora.

Clarke, B. (2004) *From Grub Street to Fleet Street: An Illustrated History of English Newspapers to 1899*, Aldershot: Ashgate.

Clouston, T. (1906) *The Hygiene of the Mind*, London: Methuen.

Cohen, S. and Taylor, L. (1992) Escape Attempts: The Theory and Practice of Resistance in Everyday Life: The Theory and Practice of Resistance to Everyday Life, London: Routledge.

Cole, S. (2001) *Suspect Identities. A History of Fingerprinting and Criminal Identification*, Cambridge, MA: Harvard.

Conan Doyle, A. (1921) *The Coming of the Fairies* (available online at Project Gutenberg: www.gutenberg.org/).

Conboy, M. (2004) *Journalism: A Critical History*, London: Sage.

Courtwright, D. (1998) *Violent Land: Single Men and Social Disorder from the Frontier to the Inner City*, Harvard, Mass.: Harvard University Press.

Cox, P. (2002) 'Race, Delinquency and Difference in Twentieth Century Britain'. In P. Cox & H. Shore (Eds.) *Becoming Delinquent: British and European Youth, 1650–1950*, Dartmouth: Ashgate, 159–179.

Cox, P. & Shore, H. (Eds.) (2002) *Becoming Delinquent: British and European Youth, 1650–1950*, Aldershot: Ashgate.

Courtwright, D. (1998) *Violent Land: Single Men and Social Disorder from the Frontier to the Inner City,* Harvard, Mass.: Harvard University Press.

Critchley, J. (1967) *History of Police in England*, London: Constable.

Crossick, G. (1977) *The Lower Middle Class in Britain, 1870–1914,* London: Croom Helm.

Critchley, J. (1970) *Conquest of Violence. Order and Liberty in Britain*, London: Constable.

Crouzet, F. (1982) *The Victorian Economy*, London: Routledge.

Cusson, M. & Pinsonneault, P. (1986) 'The Decision To Give Up Crime'. In D. Cornish & R. Clarke, (Eds.) *The Reasoning Criminal*, New York: Springer-Verlag, 72–82.

Damousi, J. (1999) *The Labour of Loss: Mourning, Memory and Wartime Bereavement*. Cambridge: Cambridge University Press.

Damousi, J. (2001) *Living with the Aftermath. Trauma, Nostalgia and Grief in Post-War Australia*. Cambridge: Cambridge University Press.

Dannhauser, W. (1995) Nietsche and Spengler on Progress and Decline. In A. Melzer, J. Weinberger and M. Zinman (eds) *History and the Idea of Progress,* London: Cornell. pp.117–136.

Darwin, L. (1928) *What Is Eugenics*, London: Watts and Co.

Davies, A. (1992) *Leisure, Gender and Poverty. Working-Class Culture in Salford and Manchester, 1900–1939*, Buckingham: Open University.

Davies, A. (1999) 'These viragoes are no less cruel than the lads: Young women, gangs and violence in Late Victorian Manchester and Salford', *British Journal of Criminology, 39*, 1, 72–89.

Davies, A. (2009) *The Gangs of Manchester*, Preston: Milo Books.

Davies, A. (2013) *City of Gangs: Glasgow and the Rise of the British Gangster*, London: Hodder & Stoughton.

Davis, J. (1989) 'From "Rookeries" to "Communities": Race, Poverty and Policing in London, 1850–1985', *History Workshop Journal, 27*, 1, 66–76

Davis, M. (1992) *City of Quartz: Excavating the Future in Los Angeles*, London: Vintage.

Dayan, C. (2011) *The Law is a White Dog. How Legal Rituals Make and Unmake Persons*, Princeton, NJ: Princeton University Press.

D'Cruze, S. (1998) *Crimes of Outrage. Sex, Violence and Victorian Working Women*, London: UCL Press.

Deacon, R. (1980) *A History of British Secret Service,* London: Grafton.

Deflem, M. (2004) *Policing World Society: Historical Foundations of International Police Cooperation,* Clarendon Series in Criminology, Oxford: Oxford University Press.

De Groot, G. (1996) *Blighty. British Society in the era of the Great War,* London: Longman

Dell, S. (1997) *The Beat of Western Dartmoor,* Tavistock: Devon and Cornwall Constabulary.

Dendrickson G. & Thomas F. (1954) *The Truth about Dartmoor*, London: Victor Gollancz.

Detotto, C. & Otranto, E. (2012) 'Cycles in Crime and Economy: Leading, Lagging and Coincident Behaviors', *Journal of Quantitative Criminology, 28*, 295–317.

Dickens, C. (1839) *Oliver Twist* (available online at Project Gutenberg: www.gutenberg.org).

Dickens, C. (1860) *Great Expectations* (available online at Project Gutenberg: www.gutenberg .org).

Doyle, P. (2005) *City of Shadows. Sydney Police Photographs, 1912–1948*, Sydney: Historic Houses Trust.

Doyle, P. (2009) *Crooks like Us*, Sydney: Historic Houses Trust.

Duff, R. (1986) *Trials and Punishments*, Cambridge: Cambridge University Press.

Durkheim, E. (1964) *Rules of Sociological Method*, New York: Free Press.

Duster, T. (2003) *Backdoor to Eugenics*, London: Routledge.

East, N. (1949) *Society and the Criminal*, London: His Majesty's Stationery Office.

Eisner, M. (2001) 'Modernization, Self-Control and Lethal Violence. The Long-term Dynamics of European Homicide Rates in Theoretical Perspective', *British Journal of Criminology 41*, 4, 618–638.

Elias, N. (1992) *Time: An Essay*, Oxford: Blackwell.

Elkin, E. (1946) 'The Treatment of the Juvenile Delinquent'. In Radzinowicz, L. & Turner, J. *Penal Reform in England. English Studies in Criminal Justice, Volume 1*, London: Macmillan and Co., 106–118.

Elder, B. (1998) *Blood on the Wattle: massacres and maltreatment of Aboriginal Australians since 1788,* Sydney: New Holland Press.

Elton, G. (2002 ed) *The Practice of History,* London: Wiley-Blackwell.

Elwood, S. (1988) 'Not so Much a Programme, More a Way of Life: Oral History and Spanish Fascism', *Oral History, 16*, 2, 57–66.

Emsley, C. (1991) *The English Police. A Political and Social History*, Harlow: Longman Pearson.

Emsley, C. (1993) '"Mother, What Did Policemen Do When There Weren't Any Motors?" The Law, the Police and the Regulation of Motor Traffic in England, 1900–1939', *The Historical Journal, 36*, 2, 357–381.

Emsley, C. (2007) *Crime, Police and Penal policy. European Experiences 1750–1940*, Oxford: Oxford University Press.

Emsley, C. (2010) *Crime and Society in England 1750–1900*, Harlow: Longman Pearson.

Emsley, C. (2013) *Soldier, Sailor, Beggarman, Thief. Crime and the British Armed Services since 1914*, Oxford: Oxford University Press.

England, J. & Bacchini, S. (2012) 'Perspectives on working with archived textual and visual material in social research, *Special Issue: Dilemmas in archiving contemporary material: the example of the British Library, International Journal of Social Research Methodology, 15*, 4, 263–269.

Farrall, S. (2002) *Rethinking What Works with Offenders*, Cullompton: Willan Publishing.

Farrall, S. (2005) 'On the Existential Aspects of Desistance from Crime', *Symbolic Interaction*, *28*, 3, 367–386

Faulds, H. (1880) 'On the Skin-Furrows of the Hand', *Nature 22*, 574, 605.

Feinberg, J. (1994) 'The Expressive Function of Punishment', in R. Duff (Ed.) *A Reader on Punishment*, Oxford: Oxford University Press, 71–92.

Felstead, S.T. (1923) *The Underworld of London*, London: John Murray.

Fentress, J. & Wickham, C. (1992) *Social Memory. New Perspectives on the Past*, Oxford: Blackwell.

Ferrarotti, F. (1990) *Time, Memory, and Society*, Westport, CT: Greenwood Press.

Finch, J. (1984) '"It's Great to Have Someone to Talk to": The Ethics of Interviewing Women'. In C. Bell & H. Roberts (Eds.) *Social Researching: Politics, Problems, Practice*, London: Routledge and Kegan Paul, 70–87.

Finnane, M. (2005) 'Crimes of Violence, Crimes of Empire?'. In B. Godfrey & G. Dunstall, *Crime and Empire: Criminal Justice in Local and Global Context, 1840–1940*, Cullompton: Willan, 43–57.

Fishman, S. (2002) 'Absent Fathers and Family Breakdown: Delinquency in Vichy France' in P. Cox and H. Shore (Eds.), *Becoming Delinquent: British and European Youth 1650–1950*, Aldershot: Ashgate Publishing, pp.141–157.

Foucault, M. (1991) *Discipline and Punish. The Birth of the Prison*, London: Penguin.

Fowler, R. & Paley S. (2005) *Family Skeletons: Exploring the Lives of Our Disreputable Ancestors*, London: National Archives of England.

Friedlander, P. (1995) 'Theory, method and oral history'. In Perks, R. and Thomson, A. (eds) *The Oral History Reader*. London: Routledge. pp. 311–319.

Frost, G. (2004) '"She Is but a Woman": Kitty Byron and the English Edwardian Criminal Justice System', *Gender & History*, *16*, 3, 538–560.

Frost, L. & Maxwell-Stewart, H. (2001) *Chain Letters. Narrating convict lives*, Melbourne: Melbourne University Press.

Gadd, D. (2012) "In-Depth Interviewing and Psychosocial Case Study Analysis." In D. Gadd, S. Karstedt, S. Messner (Eds.), *The SAGE Handbook of Criminological Research Methods*, London: Sage, 36–49.

Gadget. I. (2008) *Perverting the Course of Justice*, London: Monday Books.

Galton, D. (2002) *Eugenics. The Future of Human Life in the 21st Century*, London: Abacus.

Galton, F. (1892) *Finger Prints*, London: Macmillan and Co.

Gans, H. (1988) 'Sociology in America: The Discipline and the Public', Presidential Address to the American Sociological Association, Atlanta, GA, February 1.

Gard, R. (2007) 'The First Probation Officers in England and Wales 1906–14', *British Journal of Criminology, 47*, 6, 938–54.

Garfinkle, H. (1956) 'Conditions of successful degradation ceremonies', *American Journal of Sociology*, LXIV, 420–24.

Gariglio, L. (2006) *Portraits in Prison*, Rome: Contrasto.

Garland, D. (1987) *Punishment and Welfare. A History of Penal Strategies*, London: Gower.

Gatrell, V.A.C. (1992) 'Crime, Authority and the Policeman State.' In F.M.L. Thompson (Ed.), *Cambridge Social History of Britain*, *III*, Cambridge: Cambridge University Press, 243–310.

Gatrell, V.A.C. & Hadden, T.B. (1972) 'Criminal Statistics and their Interpretation'. In E.A. Wrigley (Ed.), *Nineteenth Century Society: Essays in the Use of Quantitative Methods for the Study of Social Data*, Cambridge: Cambridge University Press, 26–99.

Geddes, J. (2008) 'Culpable Complicity: The Medical Profession and the Forcible Feeding of Suffragettes, 1909–1914', *Women's History Review 17*, 1, 79–94.

Giles, F. (1964) *Open Court. Pages from the notebook of a London Magistrates' Clerk*, London: Cassell.

Gillin, J. (1931) *Taming the Criminal. Adventures in Penology*, New York: Macmillan Company.

Glueck, S. & Glueck, E. (1934) *One Thousand Juvenile Delinquents: Their Treatment by Court and Clinic*, City: Publisher.

Glueck, S. & Glueck, E. (1937) *Later Criminal Careers*, New York: The Commonwealth Fund.

Glueck, S. & Glueck, E. (1940) *Juvenile Delinquents Grown Up*, New York: The Commonwealth Fund.

Glueck, S. & Glueck, E. (1943) *Criminal Careers in Retrospect*, New York: The Commonwealth Fund. New York: The Commonwealth Fund.

Godfrey, B. (2003a) 'Counting and Accounting for the Decline in Non-Lethal Violence in England, Australia and New Zealand, 1880–1920', *British Journal of Criminology*, *43*, 2, 340–353.

Godfrey, B. (2003b) 'Sentencing, Theatre, Audience and Communication: The Victorian and Edwardian magistrates' courts and their message'. In B. Garnier (Ed.), *Les Témoins devant la justice*, Rennes: Presses Univ. de Rennes, 161–171.

Godfrey, B. (2003c) '"Dear Reader I Killed Him": Ethical and Emotional Issues in Researching Convicted Murderers through the Analysis of Interview Transcripts', *Oral History*, *31*, 1, 54–64.

Godfrey, B. (2004) 'Self-Identity, Empathy and Sympathy in Reading Transcripts'. In B. Roberts (Ed.), *Narrative, Memory & Identity: Theoretical and Methodological Issues*, Huddersfield: University of Huddersfield, 59–67.

Godfrey, B. (2006) 'Community 'Law', Policing, and the Structures of Legitimacy', *Crime, History and Society/Crime Histoire et Societe*, *10*, 1, 77–93.

Godfrey, B. (2008) 'Changing Prosecution Practices and Their Impact on Crime Figures, 1857–1940', *British Journal of Criminology*, *48*, 2, 171–190.

Godfrey, B. (2012a) 'Discipline', In M. Hewitt (Ed.), *The Victorian World*, London: Routledge, 415–431.

Godfrey, B. (2012b) 'The "Convict Stain": Desistance in the Penal Colony'. In J. Rowbotham, M. Muravyeva & D. Nash (Eds.), *Shame, Blame and Culpability*, London: Routledge, 96–109.

Godfrey, B & Cox, D. (Eds.) (2005) *Cinderellas and Packhorses: the Shropshire Bench*, Shrewsbury: Logaston Press.

Godfrey, B. & Cox, D. (2008) 'The "Last Fleet": Crime, Reformation, and Punishment in Western Australia after 1868', *Australian and New Zealand Journal of Criminology*, *41*, 2, 236–258.

Godfrey, B. & Cox, D. (2013) *Policing the Factory. Theft, Private Policing and the Law in Modern England*, London: Bloomsbury.

Godfrey, B. Cox, D. & Farrall, S. (2007) *Criminal Lives: Family, Employment and Offending*, Clarendon Series in Criminology, Oxford: Oxford University Press.

Godfrey, B., Cox, D. & Farrall, S., (2010) *Serious Offenders*, Clarendon Series in Criminology, Oxford: Oxford University Press.

Godfrey, B. & Dunstall, G. (2005a) 'Introduction'. In B. Godfrey & G. Dunstall (Eds.), *Crime and Empire: Criminal Justice in Local and Global Context, 1840–1940*, Cullompton: Willan, 135–145.

Godfrey, B. & Dunstall, G. (2005b) 'The Growth of Crime and Crime Control in Developing Communities: Crewe and Timaru'. In B. Godfrey & G. Dunstall (Eds.), *Crime and Empire: Criminal Justice in Local and Global Context, 1840–1940*, Cullompton: Willan, 135–145.

Godfrey, B., Emsley, C. & Dunstall, G., (2003) '"Do You Have Train Spotters in New Zealand": Issues in Comparative Crime History at the Turn of Modernity'. In B. Godfrey, C. Emsley & G. Dunstall (Eds.), *Comparative Histories of Crime*, Cullompton: Willan Press, 1–36.

Godfrey, B. & Lawrence, P. (2005) *Crime and Justice, 1750–1950*, Cullompton: Willan Press.

Godfrey, B., Lawrence, P. & Williams, C. (2007) *History and Crime*, London: Sage.

Godfrey, B. & Richardson, J. (2004) 'Loss, Collective Memory and Transcripted Oral Histories', *The International Journal of Social Research Methodology*, 7, 2, 143–155.

Gosling, J. (1959) *The Ghost Squad*. London: W.H. Allen.

Gray, D. (2010) *London's Shadows: The Dark Side of the Victorian City*, London: Continuum.

Griffiths, A. (1905) *Fifty Years of Public Service*, London: Cassell and Company.

Griffiths, P. (1996) *Youth and Authority: Formative Experience in England 1560–1640*, Oxford: Oxford University Press.

Gurr, E. (1981) 'Historical Trends in Violent Crime: A Critical Review of the Evidence', *Crime and Justice. An Annual Review of Research*, 3, 295–353.

Gurr, T.R., Grabosky, P.N. & Hula, R.C. (1977) *The Politics of Crime and Conflict: A Comparative History of Four Cities*, Beverly Hills, CA: Sage.

Hacker, D. (2011) 'A Census-Based Count of the Civil War Dead Volume', *Civil War History*, 57, 4, December.

Hahn Rafter, N. (1997) *Born Criminals*, Chicago: University of Illinois Press.

Halbwachs, M. (1925) *On Collective Memory*, Chicago: University of Chicago Press.

Hamilton, P. (1994) 'The Knife Edge: Debates about memory and history'. In K. Darian-Smith & P. Hamilton (Eds.), *Memory and History in Twentieth-Century Australia*, Oxford: Oxford University Press, 9–32.

Harrison, R. (1956) *Crime Doesn't Pay, This Is Why: The CID and the FBI*, London: Corgi.

Hawkings, D. (2009) *Criminal Ancestors: A Guide to Historical Criminal Records in England and Wales*, London: The History Press.

Hay, D. and Snyder, F. (Eds.) Policing and Prosecution in Britain, 1750–1850, Oxford: Oxford University Press.

Heaton, J. (2004) *Reworking Qualitative Data: The Possibility of Secondary Analysis*, London: Sage.

Henry, J. (1952) *Who Lie in Gaol*, London: Victor Gollancz.

Higgs, E. (2004) *The Information State in England: the Central Collection of Information on Citizens Since 1580*, Basingstoke: Palgrave Macmillan.

Hills, S., Ryland, T. & Dimsdale, N. (2010) 'The UK Recession in Context – What Do Three Centuries of Data Tell Us?', *Q4 Quarterly Bulletin*, V, 277–291.

Hillyard, P., Sim, J., Tombs, S. & Whyte, D. (2004) 'Leaving a "Stain upon the Silence": Contemporary Criminology and the Politics of Dissent', *British Journal of Criminology*, 44, 3, 369–90.

Hitchens, P. (2003) *A Brief History of Crime: The Decline of Order, Justice and Liberty in England*, London: Atlantic Books.

Hobbs, D. (1988) *Doing the Business. Entrepreneurship, the Working Class, and Detectives in the East End of London*, Oxford: Oxford University Press.

Hobsbawm, E. (1997) *On History*, London: Weidenfield and Nicolson.

Hodgkin, K. & Radstone, S. (2003) *Memory, History, Nation: Contested Pasts*, London: Transaction Press.

Holmes, R. (1915) *My Police Court Friends with the Colours*, Edinburgh: William Blackwood.

Holmes, T. (1900) *Pictures and Problems from the London Police Courts*, London: Thomas Nelson.

Holmes, T. (1908) *Known to the Police*, London: Edward Arnold.

Hood, R. and Joyce, K. (1999) 'Three Generations: Oral testimonies on Crime and Social Change in London's East End', *British Journal of Criminology*, 39, 1, 136–61.

Houlbrook, M. (2001) 'Towards a Historical Geography of Sexuality', *Journal of Urban History*, 2, 4, 497–504.

Howell, P. (2009) *Geographies of Regulation: Policing Prostitution in Nineteenth Century Britain and the Empire*, Cambridge: Cambridge University Press.

Howgrave-Graham, H. (1947) *Light and Shade at Scotland Yard*, London: Wyman and Sons.

Hubbard, P. (1999), *Sex and the City: Geographies of Prostitution in the Urban West*, Aldershot: Ashgate.

Hudson, P. (1992), *The Industrial Revolution*. London: Edward Arnold.

Hughes, M. (1997) 'An Exploratory Study of Young Adult Black and Latino Males and the Factors Facilitating Their Decisions to Make Positive Behavioural Changes', *Smith College Studies in Social Work*, *67*, 3, 401–414.

Hughes, M. (1998) 'Turning Points in the Lives of Young Inner-city Men Forgoing Destructive Criminal Behaviours: A Qualitative Study', *Social Work Research*, 22, 143–51.

Humphries, S. (1981) *Hooligans or Rebels? An Oral History of Working-Class Childhood and Youth 1889–1939*, Oxford: Blackwell.

Ireland, R. (2002) 'The Felon and the Angel Copier: Criminal Identity and the Promise of Photography in Victorian England and Wales'. In L. Knafla (Ed.), *Policing and War in Europe*, Westport, CT: Greenwood Press, 53–87.

Irwin, J. (1970) *The Felon*, Englewood Cliffs, NJ: Prentice Hall.

Jackson, L. (2000) *Child Sexual Abuse in Victorian England*, London: Routledge.

Jackson, L. (2006) *Women Police: Gender, Welfare and Surveillance in the Twentieth Century*, Manchester: Manchester University Press.

Jackson, L. (2010) 'The Geography of Everyday Life: Spatial and Ethnographic Approaches to the History of Crime and Policing', paper presented at British Crime Historians Symposium 2, Sheffield, September 2–3.

Jackson L. & Bartie, A. (2011) '"Children of the City": Juvenile Justice, Property and Place in England and Scotland 1945–1960', *Economic History Review*, *64*, 1, 88–113.

Jager, J. (2001) 'Photography: A Means of Surveillance? Judicial Photography, 1850 to 1900', *Crime, Histoire et Societies/Crime, History and Societies*, *5*, 1, 27–51

Jamieson, J., McIvor, G. & Murray, C. (1999) *Understanding Offending among Young People*, Edinburgh: The Stationary Office.

Jamieson, R. & Grounds, A. (2002) *No Sense of an Ending. The Effects of Long-Term Imprisonment amongst Republican Prisoners and Their Families*, Monaghan: SEESYU Press.

Jeremy, D. (1998) *A Business History of Britain 1900–1990s*, Oxford, Oxford University Press.

Jewkes, Y. and Johnston, H. (2007) 'The Evolution of Prison Architecture'. In Y. Jewkes (Ed.), *Handbook on Prisons*, Cullompton: Willan, 174–196.

Johnson and Monkonnen (1996) *The Civilization of Crime: Violence in Town and Country since the Middle Ages: Violence in Town and Country Since the Middle Ages,* Chicago: University of Illinois.

Jones, D. (1998) 'Distressing Histories and Unhappy Interviewing', *Oral History*, *26*, 2, 49–54.

Josselson, R. (Ed.) (1996) *Ethics and Process in the Narrative Study of Lives. Vol. 4. The Narrative Study of Lives*, Thousand Oaks, CA: Publisher.

Joyce, S. (2003) *Capital Offenses. Geographies of Class and Crime in Victorian London,* Charlottesville: University of Virginia Press.

Kidd, A. and Nicholls, D. (1999) *Gender, Civic Culture and Consumerism: Middle Class Identity in Britain 1800 to 1940: The British Middle Classes, 1795–1939,* Manchester: Manchester University Press.

King, P. (1999) 'Locating Histories of Crime: A Bibliographical Study', *British Journal of Criminology*, *39*, 1, 161–174.

King, P. & Noel, J. (1993) 'The Origins of "the Problem of Juvenile Delinquency": The Growth of Juvenile Prosecutions in London in the Late Eighteenth and Early Nineteenth Centuries'. *Criminal Justice History: An International Annual*, 14, 198–207.

Klein, J. (2010) *Invisible Men: The Daily Lives of Police Constable in Manchester, Birmingham and Liverpool*, Liverpool: University of Liverpool Press.

Klockars, C. (1974) The Professional Fence, New York: New York Free Press.

Knepper P. and Norris, C. (2009) 'Fingerprint and photograp. The early history of surveillance technologies in the manufacture of suspect identities' in P. Knepper & J. Shapland (Eds.) *Urban Crime Prevention. Surveillance and Restorative Justice: Effects of Social Technologies*, Boca Raton, FL: Taylor and Francis, pp. 70–100.

Koonz, C. (1986) *Mothers in the Fatherland: Women, the Family, and Nazi Politics*, New York: St. Martin's Press.

Langley-Smith, E. (1998) *Convict Prison Freemantle*, Perth: Perpetua.

Laub, J.H. & Sampson, R.J. (1993) 'Turning Points in The Life Course: Why Change Matters to the Study of Crime', *Criminology, 31* (3) 301–325.

Laub, J., Nagin, D. & Sampson, R. (1998) 'Trajectories of Change in Criminal Offending: Good Marriages and the Desistance Process', *American Sociological Review, 63*, 225–238.

Law, J. (1889) *In Darkest London: Captain Lobo*, London: Salvation Army.

Lawrence, P. (2000) '"Images of Poverty and Crime". Police Memoirs in England and France at the End of the Nineteenth-Century', *Crime, Histoire et Sociétés / Crime, History and Societies, 4*, 1, 63–82.

Lawrence, P. (2003) 'Scoundrels and Scallywags, and Some Honest Men . . .' Memoirs and the Self-Image of French and English Policemen, c.1870–1939'. In C. Emsley, B. Godfrey &G. Dunstall (Eds.), *Comparative Histories of Crime*, Cullompton: Willan Press, 125–144.

Lawrence, P. (2012) History, Criminology and the 'Use' of the Past. *Theoretical Criminology*, 16(3).

Lawrence, P. & Donovan, P. (2008) 'Road Traffic Offending and the Courts in England, 1913–1963', *Crime, Histoire et Sociétés / Crime, History and Societies, 12*, 2, 119–140.

Leeson, B (1934) *Lost London. The Memoirs of an East End Detective*, London: Stanley Paul and Co.

Lefebvre, H. (1991) *The Production of Space*, Oxford: Oxford University Press.

Lefebvre, H. (2004) *Rhythmananalysis, Space, Time and everyday Life*, translated by and with an introduction by Stuart Elden, London: Continuum.

Leibrich, J. (1993) *Straight to the Point: Angles on Giving Up Crime*, Otago, New Zealand: University of Otago Press.

Lennon, J. & Foley, M. (2010) *Dark Tourism. The Attraction of Death and Disaster*, Andover: Cengage.

Levi, L. (1885) *Wages and Earnings of the Working Classes*, Shannon: Irish University Press.

Lidstone, K., Hogg, R. and Sutcliffe, F. (1980) Prosecutions by Private Individuals and Non-Police Agencies, Royal Commission on Criminal Procedure, London: HMSO.

Lieblich, A (2002) 'Narrative Research Is Always Delicate', paper to Oxford Sociology Department, May 10.

Lloyd-Baker, T.B. (1860) 'Abstracts and Inferences Founded upon the Official Criminal Returns of England and Wales for the Year 1854–1859, with Special Reference to the Results of the Reformatories', *Transactions of the National Association for the Promotion of Social Science*, December, 427–429.

Loader, I, and Mulcahy, A. (2003) Policing and the Condition of England: Memory, Politics and Culture, Clarendon Studies in Criminology, Oxford: Oxford Univerity Press.

Loader, I. and Sparks, R. (2010) *Public Criminology?* London: Routledge.

Logan, W. & Reeves, K (Ed.) (2009) *Places of Pain and Shame*, London: Routledge.

London, J. (1903) *The People of the Abyss*, London (available online at Project Gutenberg: www.gutenberg.org).

Lowenthal, D. (1989) Nostalgia tells it like it wasn't. In Chase, M. and Shaw, C. (eds) *The Imagined Past – History and Nostalgia*. Manchester: Manchester University Press, pp. 18–32.

Lyon, S. & Thurgood, G. (2007) 'It's Open to Interpretation: Telling Porkies – Narrating and Rewriting Life History and the Use of Dramatic Licence'. In B. Roberts (Ed.), *Narrative and Memory*, Huddersfield: University of Huddersfield, 43–52.

Mackenzie C. (1937) *"Chokey" by Red Collar Man*, London: Victor Gollancz.

Macintyre, S. & Clark, A. (2004) The History Wars, 2nd edn, Melbourne: Melbourne University Press.

Mahoney, B. & Anderson B. (2011) *Faces*, Dublin: True Crime Publishing.

Maguire (2002) Criminal Statistics: The 'Data Explosion' and its Implications' in M. Maguire, R. Morgan and R. Reiner (ed) *The Oxford Handbook of Criminology*, Third Edition. Oxford: Oxford University Press, 322–76.

Manne, R. (ed.) (2003), *Whitewash: on Keith Windschuttle's fabrication of Aboriginal history*, Melbourne: Black Inc. Agenda.

Manning, P. (2011) *The Technology of Policing: Crime Mapping, Information Technology, and the Rationality of Crime Control*, New York: New York University Press.

Marshall, H. (1933) *Slum*, London: Heinneman.

Maruna, S. (2005) *Making Good: How Ex-convicts Reform and Rebuild Their Lives*, Washington DC: American Psychological Association.

Massey, D. (1994) *Space, Place and Gender*, Cambridge: Polity.

Maxwell-Stewart, H. and Hood, S. (2001) *Pack of Thieves? 52 Port Arthur Lives*, Port Arthur, Tasmania: Port Arthur Historic Site Management Authority.

Maxwell-Stewart, H. (2008) *Closing Hell's Gates*, London: Allen and Unwin.

Mayhew H. (1851–61) *London Labour and London Poor* (available online at Project Gutenberg: www.gutenberg.org.).

Mayne, A. (1993) *The Imagined Slum. Newspaper Representation in Three Cities 1870–1914*, Leicester: Leicester University Press.

McConville, S. (1995) *English Local Prisons, 1860–1900*, London: Routledge.

McCormack, C. (2000) 'From interview transcript to interpretative story: part 2 developing an interpretative story', *Field Methods*, 12, 4, 298–315.

McLaughlin, E. (2006) *The New Policing*, London: Sage.

Mcneill, F. (2005) Remembering probation in Scotland. *Probation Journal*, 52, 1, 23–38.

McRae, S. (1997) 'Household and Labour Market Change Implications for the Growth of Inequality in Britain', *British Journal of Sociology*, 48, 384–405.

Mead, G. (1934) *Mind, Self and Society*, London: University of Chicago.

Mearns, A. (1883) *The Bitter Cry of Outcast London* (available online at Project Gutenberg: www.gutenberg.org.).

Meisenhelder, T. (1977) 'An Exploratory Study of Exiting from Criminal Careers', *Criminology*, 15, 3, November, 319–334'. http://onlinelibrary.wiley.com/doi/10.1111/j.1745-9125.1977.tb00069.x/abstract

Mellaerts, W. (1997) 'Dispute Settlement and the Law in Three Provincial Towns in France, England and Holland, 1880–1914', unpublished PhD thesis, University of East Anglia.

Michelbacker G. & Carr L. (1924) *Burglary, Theft and Robbery Insurance*, New York: Lawrence.

Miller, R. (2000) *Researching Life Stories and Family Histories*. London: Sage.

Minichiello, V., Aroni, R., Timewell, E. & Alexander, L. (1990) *In-Depth Interviewing*, Sydney: Addison Wesley Longman.

Mischkowitz, R. (1994) 'Desistance from a Delinquent Way of Life?' In E.G.M. Weitekamp & H.J. Kerner (Eds.), *Cross-National Longitudinal Research on Human Development and Criminal Behaviour*, Boston: Kluwer-Nijhoff, 10–22.

Misztal, B (2003) *Theories of Social Remembering*, Milton Keynes: Open University Press.

Monkkonen, E. *Murder in New York City*, Los Angeles: University of Californian Press, 2001

Morris, R. (2000) 'Lies, damned lies and criminal statistics: Reinterpreting the criminal statistics in England and Wales', *Crime, Histoire et societies/Crime, History and Societies*, vol, 5, no.1, 111–27.

Morse, J. (2000) 'Researching Illness and Injury: Methodological Considerations', *Qualitative Health Research*, *10*, 4, 538–546.

Moss, E. (2011) 'Burglary Insurance and the Culture of fear in Britain, c.1889–1939', *The Historical Journal*, *54*, 1039–1064.

Mountain, T. Whyte (1930) *Life in London's Great Prisons*, London: Methuen.

Moylen, J. (1929) *Scotland Yard and the Metropolitan Police*, London: G.P. Putnam's Sons.

Nead, L. (1997) 'Mapping the Self: Gender, Space and Modernity in Mid-Victorian London'. In R. Porter (Ed.), *Rewriting the Self*, London: Routledge, 167–185.

Nevill, William Beauchamp (1903) *Penal Servitude*, London: William Heinneman.

Nietzsche, F. (1883) *Thus Spoke Zarathustra* (available online at Project Gutenberg: www.gutenberg.org.)

Norwood East, W. (1936) *Medical Aspects of Crime*, London: J and A Churchill.

Oakley, A. (1981) 'Interviewing Women: A Contradiction in Terms'. In H. Roberts (Ed.), *Doing Feminist Research*, London: Routledge and Kegan Paul, 30–62.

Ogborn, M. (1998) *Spaces of Modernity: London's Geographies, 1680–1780*, New York: Guilford.

Olick, J. (1999) 'Genre Memories and Memory Genres', *American Sociological Review*, *64*, 381–402.

Oral History Society: Ethical Guidelines for Interviewers and Custodians of Oral History Recordings and Related Material. (http://www.nmgw.ac.uk/~ohs/ethics.html).

Orwell, G. (1933) *Down and Out in Paris and London*, London: Penguin.

Orwell, G. (1937) *Road to Wigan Pier*, London: Penguin

Orwell, G. (1948) *1984*, London: Penguin.

Page, M. (1992) *Crimefighters of London. A History of the Origins and Development of the London Probation Service 1876–1965,* London: Inner London Probation Service Benevolent and Educational Trust.

Pamphilon, B. (1999) 'The Zoom Model: A dynamic framework for the analysis of life histories', *Qualitative Inquiry*, 5, 3.

Paris, E. (2000) *Long Shadows: Truth Lies and History*, London: Bloomsbury Publishing.

Parker, H. (1976) 'Boys Will Be Men: Brief Adolescence in a Down-Town Neighbourhood'. In G. Mungham & G. Pearson (Eds.) *Working Class Youth Culture*, London: Routledge, 27–47.

Parker, T. (1994) *Life after Life*, London: Harper Collins.

Parry, E.A. (1912) *What the Judge Saw, being Twenty-Five Years in Manchester by one who has done it*, London: Smith Elder and Son.

Patai, D. (1991) 'US Academics and Third World Women: Is ethical research possible?' In S. Gluck & D. Patai (Eds.), *Women's Words. The Feminist Practice of Oral History*, London: Routledge, 137–153.

Pearson, G. (1983) *Hooligan. A History of Respectable Fears*, London: Macmillan.

Peneff, J. (1990) Myths in life-stories. In R. Samuel and P. Thompson (Eds.), *The Myths We Live By.* London: Routledge, pp. 36–48.

Perkins, J. & Thompson, J. (1998) 'The Stockman, the Shepherd and the Creation of an Australian National Identity in the Nineteenth-Century'. In D. Day, (Ed.) *Australian Identities*, Melbourne: Melbourne University Press, 15–26.

Perks, R. and Thomson A. (1998) *The Oral History Reader,* London: Routledge.

Petrow, S. (1994) *Policing Morals: The Metropolitan Police and the Home Office 1870–1914*, Oxford: Clarendon Press, Oxford University Press.

Pettifer, E. (1940) *The Court is Sitting*, Bradford: Clegg and Son.

Pick, F. (1989) *Faces of Degeneration. A European Disorder c.1848 c.1918,* Cambridge: Cambridge University Press.

Piratin, P. (2006) *Our Flag Stays Red: An Account of Cable Street and Political Life in the East End of London*, London: Lawrence & Wishart Ltd.

Plummer, K. (1983) *Documents of Life. An Introduction to the Problems and Literature of a Humanistic Method,* London: George Allen & Unwin.

Portelli, A. (1997) The Battle of Valle Giulia. Oral History and the Art of Dialogue. Madison: University of Wisconsin Press.

Pratt, J. (1997) *Governing the Dangerous,* Sydney: Federation Press.

Pratt, J. (2002) *Punishment and Civilization. Penal Tolerance and Intolerance in Modern Society,* London: Sage.

Priestley, P. (1985) *Victorian Prison Lives. English Prison Biography, 1830–1914,* London: Methuen.

Prins, G. (1991) 'Oral History'. In Burke, P. (Ed.), New Perspectives on Historical Writing, Oxford: Blackwell.

Purvis, J. (1995) 'The Prison Experiences of the Suffragettes in Edwardian Britain', *Women's History Review 4,* 1, 103–133.

Putnam, R. (2000) *Bowling Alone: The Collapse and Revival of American Community,* New York: Simon and Schuster.

Quinton, R. (1910) *Crime and Criminals 1876–1910,* London: Longmans, Green and Co.

Rackham, C. (1946) 'The Probation System'. In L. Radzinowicz & J. Turner (Eds.), *Penal Reform in England. English Studies in Criminal Justice, Volume 1,* London: Macmillan and Co., 118–128.

Radzinowicz, L. (1939) 'The influence of economic conditions on crime', *Sociological Review, 33,* 139–53

Radzinowicz, L. (1948) *A History of English Criminal Law and its Administration from 1750. Volume 1 the Movement for Reform,* London: Stevens.

Radzinowicz, L. (1971) 'Economic pressures'. In L. Radzinowicz & M. Wolfgang (Eds.), *Crime and Justice, Volume 1, The Criminal in Society,* New York: Basic Books, 542–565.

Radzinowicz, L. & Hood, A. (1990) *A History of English Criminal Law and its Administration Since 1750, Vol. V: The Emergence of Penal Policy,* Oxford, Clarendon Press.

Reid, D. (2003) 'Dr. Henry Faulds – Beith Commemorative Society', *Journal of Forensic Identification, 53,* 2, 15–30.

Reiner, R. (2011) *Policing, Popular Culture and Political Economy: Towards a Social Democratic Criminology,* Aldershot: Ashgate.

Reynolds, G. & Judge. A (1968) *The Night the Police Went on Strike,* London: Weidenfeld and Nicolson.

Rhodes, H. (1937) *The Criminals We Deserve,* London: Methuen.

Rich, C. (1932) *Recollections of a Prison Governor,* London: Hurst & Blackett.

Richardson, J. & Godfrey B. (2003) 'Towards Ethical Practice in the Use of Archived Transcripted Interviews', *The International Journal of Social Research Methodology, 5,* 4, 347–357.

Rich, C. (1932) *Recollections of a Prison Governor,* London: Hurst and Bracket.

Riesman, D. (1953) *The Lonely Crowd, a study of the changing American Character,* New Haven, CT: Yale.

Roberts, B. (2002) *Biographical Research,* Buckingham: Open University Press.

Roberts, E. (1984) *A Woman's Place: An Oral History of Working Class Women, 1890–1940,* Oxford: Oxford University Press.

Rock, P. (2005) Chronocentrism and British criminology. *British Journal of Sociology,* 56 (3). 473–791.

Rook, C. (1899/1979) *The Hooligan Nights: Being the Life and Opinions of a Young and Impertinent Criminal Recounted by Himself and Set Forth by Clarence Rook with an introduction by Benny Green,* Oxford: Oxford University Press.

Rose, M. (1973) 'The Success of Social Reform? The Central Control Board (Liquor Traffic) 1915–21'. In M. Foot (Ed.), *War and Society,* London: Harper Collins, 71–84.

Ross, E. (1982) '"Fierce Questions and Taunts": Married life in Working-Class London' *Feminist Studies,* 8, 3, 575–602.

Rowbotham, J. (2009) 'Turning away from Criminal Intent: Reflecting on Victorian and Edwardian Strategies for Promoting Desistance amongst Petty Offenders', *Theoretical Criminology, 13,* 105–119.

Rowntree S. (1901) '*Poverty: A Study of Town Life*', New York: H. Fertig.

Rubin, H. & Rubin, I. (1995) *Qualitative Interviewing. The Art of Hearing Data,* London: Sage.

Ruck, S. (1946) 'Developments in Crime and Punishment'. In L. Radzinowicz & J. Turner, (Eds.), *Penal Reform in England. English Studies in Criminal Justice, Volume 1,* London: Macmillan and Co., 1–17.

Sampson, R.J. & Laub, J.H. (1993) *Crime in the Making: Pathways and Turning Points Through Life,* London: Harvard University Press.

Samuel, R. (1998) 'Perils of the transcript'. In R. Perks and A. Thomson (Eds.), *The Oral History Reader,* London, Routledge.

Samuel, R. (1991) *East End Underworld. Chapters in the Life of Arthur Harding,* London: Routledge and Kegan Paul.

Samuel, R. (1994) *Theatres of Memory. Past and Present in Contemporary Culture,* London: Verso.

Samuel, R. & Thompson, P. (1990) (Eds.) *The Myths we Live By.* London: Routledge.

Santos, R. (2012) *Crime Analysis with Crime Mapping,* London: Sage.

Savage, M. & Warde, A. (1993) *Urban Sociology, Capitalism and Modernity,* Basingstoke: Macmillan.

Searle, G. (1976) *Eugenics and Politics in Britain 1900–1914,* Leiden, the Netherlands: Noordhoff International Publishing.

Seliger, R., Lukas, E. & Lindner, R. (1946) *Contemporary Criminal Hygiene,* Baltimore: Oakridge Press.

Sellin, T. (1951) 'The Significance of the Records of Crime', *Law Quarterly Review, 65,* 498–504.

Sharpe, J.A. (1989) *Crime in Early Modern England 1550–1750,* London: Longman.

Sheppard (2005) *From Little Acorns: A History of the Automobile Association 1905–2005,* Calcutta, Media World/BestBooks.

Shore, H. (1999) Artful Dodgers: *Youth and Crime in Early Nineteenth Century London,* Woodbridge, Suffolk: The Boydell Press.

Shore H. & Cox, P. (2002) (Eds.) *Becoming Delinquent: British and European Youth, 1650–1950,* Aldershot: Ashgate.

Shover, N. (1983) 'The Later Stages of Ordinary Property Offender Careers', *Social Problems, 31* (2), 208–218.

Sibley, D. (1995) *Geographies of Exclusion,* London: Routledge.

Sigler, J. (1974) 'Public prosecution in England and Wales', *Criminal Law Review,* 642.

Sindall, R. (1990) *Street violence in the nineteenth century: Media panic or real danger?* Leicester: Leicester University Press.

Sillitoe, P. (1955) *Cloak without Dagger,* London: Cassell and Company.

Silverman, D. (2000) *Doing Qualitative Research,* London: Sage.

Smethurst, T. (1914) *A Policeman's Notebook,* Bolton: Aurora Publishing.

Smith, M. (1994) *Social Science in the Crucible: The American Debate over Objectivity and Purpose, 1918–1941,* Raleigh, NC: Duke University Press.

Smythe, W. & Murray, M. (2000) 'Owning the Story: Ethical Considerations in Narrative Research', *Ethics and Behavior, 10,* 4, 311–336.

Soja, E. (1996) *Thirdspace. Journeys to Los Angeles and Other Real-and-Imagined Places,* Oxford: Blackwell.

Spierenburg (1998) (Ed.), *Men and Violence. Gender, Honor, and Rituals in Modern Europe and America*, Columbus, Ohio: Ohio State University Press.

Springhall, J. (1999) *Youth, Popular Culture and Moral Panics: Penny Gaffs to Gangsta Rap, 1830–1996*, London: Palgrave Macmillan.

Starkey, P. (2000) *Families and Social Workers. The Work of Family Service Units 1940–1985*, Liverpool: Liverpool University Press.

Stedman Jones, G. (2013) *Outcast London: A Study in the Relationship between Classes in Victorian Society*, London: Verso.

Stokes, S. (1950) *Court Circular. Experiences of a London Probation Officer*, London: Pan Books.

Strauss, L. (1987) *Qualitative Analysis for Social Scientists*, New York: Cambridge University Press.

Sutherland, E. (1924) *Principles of Criminology*, Chicago: University of Chicago Press.

Sutherland, E. (1937) The Professional Thief, Chicago: University of Chicago Press.

Tallack, W. (1899) *Penological and Preventive Principles, with Special Reference to Europe and America*, London: Wertheimer, Lea and Co.

Taylor, D. (2012) *Hooligans, Harlots, and Hangmen. Crime and Punishment in Victorian Britain*, Santa Barbara, CA: Praeger.

Taylor, H. (1998a) 'Rationing crime: The political economy of criminal statistics since the 1850s', *Economic History Review*, 49, 3, pp. 569–90.

Taylor, H. (1998b) 'The politics of the rising crime statistics of England and Wales', *Crime Histoire and Societies: Crime, History and Societies*, 1, 2, pp. 5–28.

Taylor, H. (1999) 'Forging the Job: A Crisis of "Modernisation" or Redundancy for the Police in England and Wales, 1900–39', *British Journal of Criminology*, 39, 1, pp. 113–136.

Taylor, I., Evans, K. & Fraser, P. (1996) *A Tale of Two Cities. Global Change, Local Feeling and Everyday Life in the North of England*, London: Routledge.

Thomas, D. (1998) *Victorian Underworld*, New York: New York Press.

Thomas, T. (2007) *Criminal Records. A Database for the Criminal Justice System and Beyond*, Basingstoke: Palgrave Macmillan.

Thompson, J. (2007) *Probation in Paradise. The Story of Convict Probationers on Tasman's and Forestier's Peninsulas, Van Diemen's Land, 1841 – 1857*, Hobart, Tasmania: Artemis Publishing.

Thompson, P. (1977) *The Edwardians: The Remaking of British Society*, London: Routledge.

Thompson, P. (2000) *The Voice of the Past*, Oxford: Oxford University Press.

Thompson, P. (2003) 'Towards Ethical Practice in the Use of Transcribed Oral Interviews. A Response', *International Journal of Social Research Methodology*, 6, 4, 357–361.

Tobias, J.J. (1972) *Nineteenth-Century Crime. Prevention and Punishment*, Newton Abbot: David & Charles.

Tomes, N. (1978) 'A Torrent of Abuse: Crimes of Violence Between Working-Class Men and Women in London, 1840–1875' *Journal of Social History*, 11, pp. 328–345.

Tonkin, E. (1990) History and the myth of realism. In R. Samuel and P. Thompson (eds) *The Myths we Live By*, London: Routledge., pp. 25–35.

Trasler, G. (1979) 'Delinquency, Recidivism and Desistance', *British Journal of Criminology*, 19, 4, 314–322.

Tuan, L.-F. (1977) *Space and Place*, Minneapolis: University of Minnesota Press.

Turner, S. & Turner, J. (1990) *The Impossible Science: An Institutional Analysis of American Sociology*, London: Sage.

Van, I. & Garson, G. (2001) 'Crime Mapping and its Extension to Social Science Analysis', *Social Science Computer Review*, 19, 4, 471–479.

Vanstone, M. (2004) *Supervising Offenders in the Community: A History of Probation Theory and Practice*, Aldershot: Ashgate.

Verne, J. (1870) *20,000 Leagues under the Sea* (available online at Project Gutenberg: www. gutenberg.org.).

Waddy, H. (1925) *The Police Court and its Work*, London: Butterworth.

Wade, S. (2009) *Tracing Your Criminal Ancestors*, Barnsley: Pen & Sword Books.

Waites, B. (1987) *A Class Society at War: England 1914–1918*, Leamington Spa: Berg Publishing.

Walker, N. (2002) *Those Were the Days . . .: British Police Cars*, Poundbury, Dorset: Veloce Publishing Ltd.

Wallot, J. P. and Fortier, N. (1998) Archival science and oral sources. In The Oral History Reader, R. Perks & A. Thomson (eds), 365–378. London: Routledge.

Walters, P. (2009) 'Qualitative Archiving: Engaging with Epistemological Misgivings. Qualitative Archiving: Engaging with Epistemological Misgivings', *Australian Journal of Social Issues*, 44, 3, 309–320.

Watson, K. (2004) *Poisoned Lives. English Poisoners and their Victims*, London: Hambledon and London.

Weaver, J. (1995) *Crimes, Constables and Courts,* Kingston, Ontario: McGill-Queen's University Press.

Wells, H.G. (1896) *The Island of Dr Moreau* (available online at Project Gutenberg: www. gutenberg.org.).

Wells, H.G. (1933) *The Shape of Things to Come* (available online at Project Gutenberg: www. gutenberg.org.).

West, D. (1982) *Delinquency: Its Roots, Careers and Prospects*, London: Heinemann.

Wetzell, R. (2000) *Inventing the Criminal. A History of German Criminology 1880–1945*, Chapel Hill and London: University of North Carolina Press.

Wiener, M. (1990) *Reconstructing the Criminal. Culture, Law, and Policy in England, 1830–1914,* Cambridge: Cambridge University Press.

White, J. (1986) *The Worst Street in North London. Campbell Bunk, Islington, Between the Wars* London: Routledge and Kegan Paul.

Wiener, M. (2004) *Men of Blood. Violence, Manliness, and Criminal Justice in Victorian England*, Cambridge: Cambridge University Press.

Wiggin, M. (1948) *My Court Casebook* London: Sylvan Press.

Wiles, R., Charles, V., Crow, G., & Heath, S. (2006) 'Researching Researchers: Lessons for Research Ethics', *Qualitative Research*, 6, 3, 283–299.

Williams, C. (2000) 'Counting Crimes or Counting people: Some Implications of Mid-Nineteenth Century British Police Returns', *Crime, Histoire et Societies/Crime, History and Societies*, 4, 2, 77–93.

Williams, R. (1961/1965) *The Long Revolution*, London: Chatto and Windus. Reissued with additional footnotes, Harmondsworth: Penguin, 1965. (http://en.wikipedia.org/wiki/ The_Long_Revolution)

Williams, R. (1977) *Marxism and Literature*, Marxist Introductions Series, London: Oxford University Press.

Williams, R. & Orrom, M. (1954) *Preface to Film,* London: Film Drama.

Wilson, D. (2011) *Looking for Laura. Public Criminology and Hot News*, London: Waterside Press.

Windschuttle, K. (2000) The Myths of Frontier Massacre in Australian History, Parts 1, II & III', *Quadrant*, vol. 44, no. 10.

Winlow, S. and Hall, S. (2012) 'What is an 'ethics committee'?: academic governance in an epoch of belief and incredulity', *British Journal of Criminology*, 52 (2), pp. 400–416.

Wright, P. (1985) *On Living in an Old Country*, London: Verso.

Zedner, L. (2006) 'Policing before and after the Police: The Historical Antecedents of Contemporary Crime Control', *British Journal of Criminology*, 46, 1, 78–96.

INDEX